William R. Guilfoyle

Australian Botany

specially designed for the use of schools

William R. Guilfoyle

Australian Botany

specially designed for the use of schools

ISBN/EAN: 9783337311629

Printed in Europe, USA, Canada, Australia, Japan

Cover: Foto ©Paul-Georg Meister /pixelio.de

More available books at **www.hansebooks.com**

AUSTRALIAN BOTANY

SPECIALLY DESIGNED

FOR THE USE OF SCHOOLS

BY

W. R. GUILFOYLE, F.L.S.

C. M. ROYAL BOTANICAL SOCIETY, LONDON; DIRECTOR OF THE
MELBOURNE BOTANIC GARDENS; AUTHOR OF THE 'A B C OF BOTANY,
ETC. ETC.

Second Edition

'Since the days of LINNÆUS, who was the great reformer of this part of Natural History, a host of strange names, inharmonious, sesquipedalian, or barbarous, have found their way into Botany, and by the stern but almost indispensable laws of priority are retained there. It is full time, indeed, that some stop should be put to this torrent of savage sounds, when we find such words as Caluchechinus, Oresigenesa, Finaustrina, Kraschenninikovia, Gravenhorstia, Andrzejofskya, Mielichoferia, Monactineirma, Pleuroschismatypus, and hundreds of others like them, thrust into the records of Botany without even an apology. . . The author has been anxious to do something towards alleviating this grievous evil, which at least need not be permitted to eat into the healthy form of Botany clothed in the English language.'—*The Vegetable Kingdom*, pp. xv.-xvi., by Dr. LINDLEY, F.R.S., F.L.S., etc.

GEORGE ROBERTSON
MELBOURNE, SYDNEY, BRISBANE, AND ADELAIDE
MDCCCLXXXIV.

[The Copyright of this Book throughout Her Majesty's Dominions is secured by Entry at Stationers' Hall, London.]

PREFACE TO THE SECOND EDITION.

—o—

It cannot but be highly gratifying to the author of any work to find that his efforts have been appreciated, and more especially when that appreciation leads to the issue of further editions.

I have therefore much pleasure in saying that, owing to the demand for the first edition having exhausted the issue, and from the flattering notices appearing in nearly all sections of the press, it has become necessary to issue this second edition.

As already stated in the preface to the first edition, the book does not profess to have any special value to the learned in the science, but to be suited to the requirements of beginners. This is all I claim, and if I have succeeded in my intentions, am amply satisfied. While saying so much, attention may be drawn to the fact that the present edition is greatly enlarged, and I venture to hope improved. Alterations in the text and additions such as were deemed advisable have been made, and although the first book was to some extent applicable mainly to

Victoria, the present one has been made, as will be found, to comprehend the requirements of students with regard to Australian botany generally.

The first edition, as will be seen by the notices appended at the end of this work, has not only been favourably and generally commented on by the press, but has received the still higher compliment of having been reprinted by at least two influential newspapers especially interested in botanical, horticultural, and agricultural matters. For some of the blocks used in illustrating Lesson II., I am indebted to Albert Molineaux, Esq., proprietor of *The Garden and Field*, Adelaide. I am also indebted to G. P. O. Tepper, Esq., F.L.S., of Ardrossan, S.A., who in the same magazine (1881) edited the first edition of this work to suit the requirements of South Australian botanical students. I am also indebted to Mr. Tepper for many valuable suggestions of which I have availed myself, and desire to express my obligations. To the editor of *The Town and Country Journal*, Sydney, who published the first edition in 1880, I owe my acknowledgments for allusions to certain New South Wales plants.

WILLIAM R. GUILFOYLE.

BOTANIC GARDENS, MELBOURNE, 1884.

PREFACE TO THE FIRST EDITION.

IN writing this little rudimentary work, which has no higher aim than that of familiarizing the beginner with the principal parts of plants and their manner of growth, the author has endeavoured throughout to keep in view the suggestion of the great botanist whose words are quoted on the title-page. Notwithstanding the importance of Botany in science, art, and commerce, and the great value of at least a general knowledge of its principles in a young country like Australia, its practical alphabet is surrounded by so many difficulties as to remove it from the list of subjects ordinarily taught in our Schools. This unfortunate circumstance is principally attributable to the fact that classical languages have been employed in conferring botanical names. Doubtless this was and is necessary for the higher purposes of the science; since Latin and Greek form a common ground on which botanists of all countries can meet in constructing an universal nomenclature. Very much has been done from time to time by Sir William and Sir Joseph Hooker, Dr. Lindley, Mr. Bentham, and other eminent botanists in bestowing common names. These celebrated scientists, by their labours in this direction, have greatly simplified the study of Botany; and it has been the author's aim to follow in the same track with reference to Australia. At present the beginner is discouraged at finding himself confronted on the threshold of Botany by a bewildering array of long words. He is met by crabbed terms at every point; and discovers that he must combine with his lessons the acquirement of a host of foreign and — as Dr. Lindley calls them—'sesquipedalian' words. Hence one of the most valuable and naturally interesting sciences is greatly neglected. To those who have mastered the Elements of Botany, the scientific phraseology may be comparatively easy of acquisition; but it must be admitted that it is nauseous and overwhelming to a neophyte. It was with the object of divesting the approaches to this science of some of these learned terrors that the subjoined lessons were undertaken. It has been the special study of the author to explain as fully as possible every technical term. He has preferred to err in the direction of profuse description rather than by leaving any matter imperfectly explained. The intention is to place the lessons in such simple form that any Teacher, though previously unacquainted with the principles of Botany, may find no difficulty in comprehending and explaining the lessons; using a black-board in copying the diagrams, and causing the scholars to dissect some of the specimens mentioned as examples. In this manner the class can be prepared for more advanced botanical studies. When this elementary work has been mastered, the student will have acquired much botanical information in a gradual and easy manner. He will have ascended the hill of knowledge by gentle gradations. Looking back, he will be surprised at the progress he has made, and will feel encouraged to press onward.

The primary object of these lessons being to divest the botanical path of stumbling-blocks in the form of 'too much learning,' it will be readily understood that they do not profess to treat exhaustively of the seeds, leaves, flowers, etc., of the different orders. A general knowledge of the construction of plants having been imparted, the road will be clear for studying the Linnæan and Natural Systems of Botany as given in other works. An outline of these Systems will be found, however, towards the end of this book. A Glossary is also appended, giving the botanical term applied to each common name used in the text, accompanied by a short account of every plant so mentioned. If further information respecting any plant be considered desirable, the Glossary will furnish the botanical classification under which it is ranked in more extended works.

With a view to placing the lessons under the crucial test of practical experience, the MS. was submitted to the following, amongst other experienced gentlemen:—Mr. Ellery, F.R.S.; Professors Irving, Pearson, Halford, Strong, and Andrew; Mr. Morris (Church of England Grammar School), Mr. Venables (Education Department), etc. It is satisfactory to the author to remark that the opinion given was in every instance highly favourable as to the merits of the work as an elementary book, particularly adapted for the use of Schools. Many very valuable suggestions made by some of the above-mentioned gentlemen have been adopted; and the author trusts that his little book will achieve its designed purpose.

WILLIAM R. GUILFOYLE.

BOTANIC GARDENS, MELBOURNE,
March 1878.

CONTENTS.

Lesson	PAGE
I.—Seeds,	1
II.—Structure of Plants,	7
III.—Roots,	14
IV.—Stems,	18
V.—Leaves,	25
VI.—Flowers,	33
VII.—Fruits,	49
VIII.—Acotyledons,	56
IX.—Systematic Botany,	60
Simple Directions for the Collection and Preservation of Specimen Plants,	70
Examination or Dissection of Flowers and Fruits,	76
Australian Vegetation,	78
Glossary,	94

Principal Plants of Economic Value—

No. 1. Plants used as Food, yielding Esculent Roots, Leaves, etc.,	182
,, 2. Plants yielding Edible Fruits, Nuts, etc.,	184
,, 3. Spice and Condiment Plants,	187
,, 4. Medicinal Plants,	188
,, 5. Plants yielding Gums, Resins, and Balsams,	190
,, 6. Fibre Plants used in the Manufacture of Clothing, Cordage, and Paper,	191
,, 7. Plants used for Dyeing,	193
,, 8. Principal Timber Trees of Commerce,	194
Wild Plants found around Melbourne, and common in New South Wales, Queensland, South Australia, and Tasmania,	196
Natural Orders of Plants represented in Australia,	210
Botanical Index,	213
Press Notices of Previous Books,	219

AUSTRALIAN BOTANY.

LESSON I.

SEEDS.

In tracing the progress of a plant through all its stages, and pointing out the various organs developed at its different periods of growth and their uses, it is desirable to commence with the *seed*, explaining its organization and gradual change into the young plant; then showing in succeeding lessons the structure of *Root*, *Stem*, *Leaf*, *Flower*, and *Fruit*, the circle will be complete, since the fruit of a plant is the vessel which produces its seed.

Seeds, with few exceptions, are found in vessels which, as just stated, are the fruits of the plants which produce them. Wholesome or poisonous, palatable or tasteless, juicy and melting like the orange and nectarine, or wooden and uneatable like the cone of the sheoak and the seed-vessel of the gum-tree, they are all botanically termed *fruits;* and they are as varied in shape, size, substance, and qualities as the plants from which they spring. A cherry, for instance, is a fruit or seed-vessel, the hard stone containing the seed. A pea-pod is another form of fruit, the peas being the seeds. Subdivision according to the Natural System of Botany—the one now generally adopted—has placed in widely different orders, plants having apparent points of resemblance; but it may be stated that the general principle on which plants are classified in the Natural System is by an examination of their fruits. In a future lesson, however, the qualities and component parts of fruits will be described. Our present business is with the seed.

Generally speaking, seeds have two or more coats or skins, though exceptions exist, as in the naked or skinless seeds of Pines and Cycads.[1] The outer skin of a seed is termed the *testa* (shell); the inner skin is the *tegmen* (covering). The testa may be compared to the shell of an egg; the tegmen, to the thin skin lining that shell. This comparison is frequently made; for as the *albumen*[2] or white of an egg nourishes the *embryo*[3] or future bird while in the shell, so the albumen surrounding many seed-germs nourishes the embryo plant when it commences to grow, supporting it until it is strong enough to shake off the testa or shell, and draw its own nourishment through its roots.

Some kinds of seeds—such as those of the pea, bean, orange, and Eucalyptus or gum-tree—have no albumen surrounding them. Such seeds are termed exalbuminous. Seeds possessing it are albuminous—such as wheat, barley, maize, grasses, and buttercups; in these the albumen is

---

[1] Cycads, which include Zamia, Macrozamia, etc., belong to the order Cycadeæ, and are in close relationship with Conifers (*Pine tribe*). These plants are termed gymnospermous (having naked seeds), because the seeds are not contained in a true ovary.

[2] Albumen, the nutritious matter stored up with the embryo, called also perisperm and endosperm.

[3] Embryo, the young plant contained in the seed.

starchy or farinaceous. The seeds of the castor oil plant are remarkable for their abundant albumen, which is of a fatty nature, and produce the castor oil of commerce.

The *germination* (growth) of a seed is the starting into action of the principle of life which, if sound, it possesses. In other words, it is the commencement of growth in the sleeping *germ* of the future plant.

Heat, moisture, and air are necessary for the proper germination of seeds. Many interesting experiments may be performed to show the effect which the absence of one (or more) of these elements has upon the progress of a germinating seed. When totally deprived of them, seeds have been known to preserve uninjured their power of germination for very many years. Reliance must not, however, be too readily placed on all of the wonderful tales related respecting the germination of seeds after the lapse of centuries. The history of botany contains sufficient wonders to astonish and delight the student, without the introduction of imperfectly authenticated or romantic assertions.

When fully developed, the infant plant consists of—
1. Cotyledon or cotyledons (seed-leaves).
2. Plumule (bud, or first stage of growth).
3. Radicle (starting-point of the root).

Cotyledons are the *seed-leaves or lobes of the young plant.*

Flower-bearing (Phanerogamous) plants are divided into two great classes, according to the number of cotyledons possessed by their seeds. Thus, plants belonging to the monocotyledons have only *one* seed-leaf. Those belonging to the dicotyledons have *two* seed-leaves. By differences in seed, root, leaf, and stem, these two classes can generally be determined. Monocotyledons, for instance, may usually be known by the *venation* or marking of their leaves, which have straight or curved unbranched lines running almost or quite parallel with the midrib, which is a continuation of the leaf-stalk, as a rule running through the middle of the leaf. Monocotyledons include grasses, palms, aloes, rushes, the ordinary garden lilies, and many other species. They are also termed *endogens* or 'inside growers.' Most dicotyledons, on the contrary, have their leaves marked with a network of veins, branching more or less over the leaf. The plants belonging to this class are also termed exogens or 'outside growers.' A further explanation of the terms endogen and exogen will be given in a future lesson.

The PLUMULE is the bud in the embryo or first stage of growth, indicating the future stem. In some seeds, as in the pea, it is plainly perceptible; in others it is very indistinct.

At the summit or apex of some seeds, as of the Orange, Almond, or Pea, a brown spot is observed, formed by the union of certain vessels which proceed from the hilum; this spot is the *chalaza*, and it is connected with the hilum, or *base* of the seed, by a vessel which passes alone the *face* of the seed, and is termed the *raphe*.

The RADICLE (o, fig. D) is situated below the plumule (A, fig. D), and is the germ (starting-point) of the root. It always points to the *micropyle* or foramen (3, fig. A), which is a small hole in the *hilum* (*umbilicus*) or scar through which nourishment is conveyed to the young seed or nucleus[1] by the *funiculus* (cord) attaching it to the *placenta* of the seed-case. The hilum, like the plumule and radicle, is distinct or obscure in different plants. It is plainly marked in the pea and bean; indistinctly in the wattle.

[1] Nucleus, a central mass or kernel.

It should be noticed that while the micropyle constitutes the organic apex of the ovule, the chalaza indicates that of the seed.

In order to examine the mode of germination or growth in seeds belonging to each of the two great classes of flowering plants (monocotyledons and dicotyledons), obtain a common garden pea, as representing the dicotyledons. A reference to diagrams A and D will indicate the principal parts mentioned.

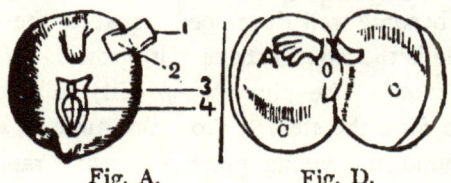

Fig. A.   Fig. D.

FIG. A.—A, a pea, enlarged. 1, the *testa*, torn to show 2, the *tegmen*.[1] 3, the *micropyle* or *foramen*. 4, the *hilum*.

FIG. D.—D, a pea, split in halves. A, the *plumule*. O, *radicle* or *radicula*. CC, *cotyledons* or seed-leaves.

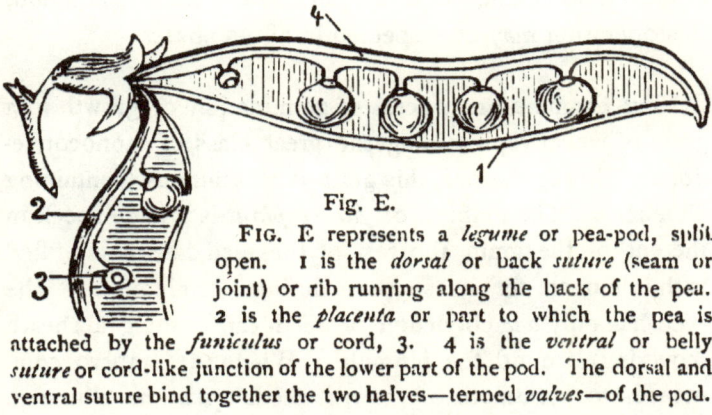

Fig. E.

FIG. E represents a *legume* or pea-pod, split open. 1 is the *dorsal* or back *suture* (seam or joint) or rib running along the back of the pea. 2 is the *placenta* or part to which the pea is attached by the *funiculus* or cord, 3. 4 is the *ventral* or belly *suture* or cord-like junction of the lower part of the pod. The dorsal and ventral suture bind together the two halves—termed *valves*—of the pod.

Having thus acquired a knowledge of the organs of growth, let a practical experiment be tried by soaking a pea

---

[1] Sometimes called Endopleura.

in water for several hours, and then examining it, when it will be found larger and heavier—it has commenced to grow or germinate. If left in water for a still longer period, its outer skin will burst, in consequence of the swelling of the seed-leaves. If sown in the ground after having been well soaked, and carefully taken up for examination after several days have elapsed, the plumule and radicle (starting-points) will have become well developed between the cotyledons. The radicle is the first to strike out, growing downwards to form the root. The plumule speedily follows, springing upwards to form the stem. From this time, if undisturbed in the ground, the young plant will make rapid progress. The cotyledons (seed-leaves) will gradually collapse as the growing plant drains them of their substance, until they are quite dried up in the testa, by which time the plant's roots will be vigorous enough to support it. By sowing a number of peas, and taking them up periodically for examination, this operation may be inspected in all its phases.

Next examine the process of germination or growth in a grain of wheat representing the great class of monocotyledons. Unlike the pea, this grain is albuminous (containing albumen). The embryo or *future plant* is a mere speck in the end of the grain, the rest of the seed-case being filled with albumen for its support during germination. The seed has only *one* cotyledon or seed-leaf, forming a sheath (covering) around the plumule. When the embryo commences to germinate or grow, it feeds upon the albumen. The great difference between this seed and that of the pea is, that instead of the seed-wheat radicle or young root elongating in a downward direction, thus forming the root, it remains stationary, while from its lower end small fibrous (thread-like) rootlets issue, protected by sheaths at the points where they spring from the radicle. A representation of this kind of root will be found in Plate I. fig. 2, p. 15, showing a root of wheat.

These differences in the parts of seeds, manner of growth in the root, and number of seed-leaves, must be remembered as indicative of the two great classes to which the pea and the wheat respectively belong.

The vegetable kingdom, according to the Natural System of Botany, is arranged in two great divisions or Sub-Kingdoms, viz. 1. *Phanerogamous* or '*Flowering* plants,' and 2. *Cryptogamic* or '*Flowerless* plants.' The two classes of division 1—namely, Monocotyledons and Dicotyledons—have been mentioned. The second division or third class —namely, Cryptogams or Acotyledons (without seed-lobes) —comprises flowerless plants. In the plants belonging to this class are included many species of Australian vegetation, amongst which are the extensive families of ferns, mushrooms, and mosses. The acotyledons, however, will form the subject of a separate lesson.

<small>During this and subsequent lessons, occasional recapitulations should be made of the botanical terms used and their signification. Only those words are given which are absolutely indispensable.</small>

LESSON II.

THE STRUCTURE OF PLANTS.

IN germinating,—starting into active life,—the seed, as we saw in the previous lesson, developed two parts, the one pointing upward (plumule), the other downward (radicle).

From this small beginning the most complex and wonderful organism, called a 'plant,' is gradually evolved by continual additions to its substance from without, partly from the soil and partly from the air. These substances are changed within the plant into something totally unlike their former appearance. To understand the mode in which this is carried on, we have to learn what is the structure of the organism.

If a very young part of any plant be viewed under a high-power microscope, minute bladders will be noticed, formed of a very thin skin, filled with a peculiar matter, which in living plants is in continual motion. These minute bladders are called *cells*, and the enclosed matter *protoplasm*, which seems to be the real living matter of the plant, to which all the rest forms either the framework or the food.[1]

The tissues of plants may be simply divided into two kinds—Cellular or Parenchyma, and Woody or Prosenchyma.

The following diagrams, A and B, show parenchyma or thin-walled cells—cellulares or plants multiplied by spores—greatly magnified,—*A* showing spherical loose cells; *B*, cells closely packed (polyhedral).

Plants formed of these alone, like the yeast plant, moulds, mushrooms, mosses, liverworts, etc., are called cellular plants. The spaces between the veins of leaves, the pith of stems, and all the softer portions of the plant, including

[1] Protoplasm, 'first-formative matter,' a general term for the living substance of plants and animals; strictly speaking, 'a clear viscid substance from which tissues are made. It contains nitrogen as an essential ingredient, in addition to the three elements—carbon, oxygen, and hydrogen.'—SNAITH and FIELD.

the pulp of fruits, etc., are termed parenchyma or cellular tissue.

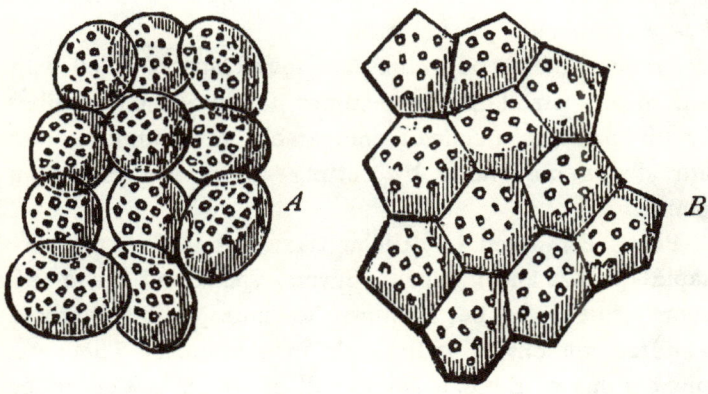

Diagram *C* shows prosenchyma or woody tissue—1, woody fibres; 2, same showing interior.

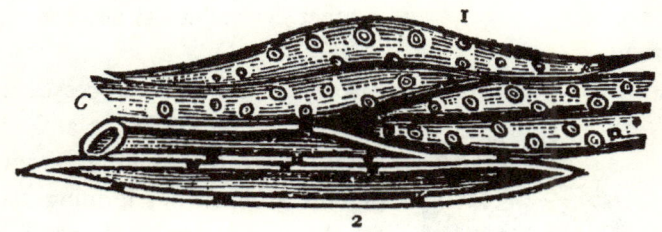

Prosenchyma consists of woody fibres (lignine) closely packed. It is formed by the gradual thickening of the cell-walls, and close union of several into bundles, which are of various lengths, overlapping each other, but always terminating at both ends in a point. These long thick-walled cells are in fact the woody substance of the plant. The inner bark (liber or bast), the nerves and veins of leaves in all ordinary flowering plants (vasculares), are prosenchyma.

Flowering plants are composed of cellular and vascular tissue combined.

Between the woody fibres are found spaces filled with air, mostly small, but sometimes forming regular tubes or air passages (lacunæ) comparable to chimneys, and are always observable by cutting across any part of a plant.

Plants composed of cellular tissue alone increase very rapidly in size and number. Several species of the mushroom tribe have been known to multiply to nearly a hundred millions of individuals in a minute. The yeast plant is one of these, a single cell of which is said to be $\frac{1}{8000}$ part of an inch across.

The cells of some plants contain crystals of lime and other salts called raphides, in which case starch, chlorophyll, oils, sugar, and other granular structures are absent.

Those cells actively assisting in the vital processes are surrounded in higher plants by fibres, winding spirally around definite groups, thus forming *ducts* for the sap to rise or descend in. Each cell is closed all round, and without any opening. Thus the contents can only get through the cell-wall by a mysterious process of oozing through, termed *endosmose* (ingoing) and *exosmose* (outgoing), produced by forces which,

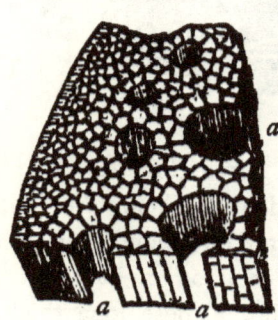

Cellular tissue, showing—*a, a, a,* air passages or lacunæ.

though only acting upon the most minute particles (molecules), are still sufficient to produce the ascent of the sap from the lowest root fibre to the highest twig of the most gigantic tree.

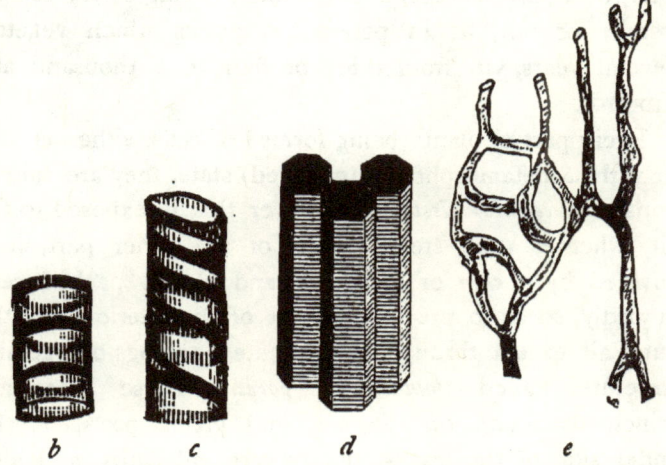

b   c   d   e

The above diagrams illustrate various ducts or vessels —*b*, annular fibres; *c*, spiral fibres; *d*, scalariform vessels; *e*, lactiferous vessels containing a fluid called latex, abundant in the dandelion, thistle, and other composites.

By the increase of cells, in number and size, is produced the *growth* of the plants. The cells, when mature, mysteriously exhibit first a slight contraction in the middle, growing gradually deeper, until at last completely divided into two, in each of which the same process is repeated successively for a certain time, viz. as long as the cell-wall remains thin enough. As the older ones thicken by deposition of lignine, each dies, and only serves afterwards to strengthen and support the organism, while new and active ones continually form at *either* extremity. Upon the uninterrupted continuance of this process depends their vitality. When it ceases, the individual *dies*. This occurs either at definite periods, as in annuals (plants living one year, or a part thereof) and biennials (dying in the second year); or not, as in perennials, plants which vegetate several years, viz. from three or four to a thousand and upwards.

Every part of plants being formed of cells, either as such or with a metamorphosed (changed) state, they are said to consist of *cellular tissue*. Wherever this is exposed to the air, whether root, stem, leaves, or any other part, it is covered by a *skin* or *epidermis*, and closely packed cells inwardly, so as to prevent contact of the interior with the outer air except through very minute openings of peculiar structure, called *stomata* or *pores*. These latter are principally found on the soft and green parts, as the under side of the leaves, the flowers and fruits, and also the stems of herbs, grasses, etc.

According to the locality in which cells are situated, their functions differ in such a way as to ensure the required results. Thus in the leaves they are fitted to absorb carbonic acid with the air and moisture of the atmosphere. The former they decompose under the influence of light. Its carbon is retained and changed into wood substance. The charcoal of the wood is produced almost entirely from this source. The oxygen, so indispensable for animal life, is again exhaled. This accounts for the invigorating effect of a walk in the woods or green fields.

At the tips of root fibres, again, the cells are fitted to

take up substances contained in the soil, in a form *soluble in water*, and in such proportions as are required by each individual species of plant, which differ widely for different orders, and even sometimes for closely-related species. As each plant requires a certain fixed number of mineral ingredients, and also a fixed percentage of each, the absence (or insufficiency of supply) of even a single one of them prevents their blooming or seeding, and causes ultimate death.

Tip of Root, showing uncovered cells and fibrils, which absorb the moisture and salts from the ground.

This explains why, for example, wheat yields less and less seed on fields cultivated for a number of years. Some of the mineral substances of the soil assisting in its structure have become exhausted. Thus we see how important some knowledge of the structure of plants is to every one. Want of information may bring about the ruin of thousands. The only remedy is replenishment of the wanting substances.

The juices or sap collected by the roots *ascend* towards the top; those gathered by the leaves *descend* by means of the forces mentioned above, not in *separate* channels, like arteries and veins, but penetrating each other in every individual live cell, each appropriating its own share of the nutriment passing. This process is most actively carried on by the cells and fibres of the inner white bark next to the wood in dicotyledonous plants and the inner soft layers of monocotyledons, and explains why the former grow gradually thicker and the latter not; layers of cells being continuously formed under the covering of the epidermis around the outside in the first, which increase the diameter successively, while in the latter the increase of cells takes place interiorly, narrowing the hollow of the stem, but not changing the original dimensions laterally. This is the reason why the terms Exogens (outward growers) and Endogens (inward growers) are applied to these two great divisions.

Having now learned something about the internal structure of plants, and thereby gained some insight into their economy, the technical description of the various parts of plants, with their varied modification of external form, will prove more intelligible and interesting, especially if we turn into the fields and examine for ourselves, when we will find that the more we become familiar with the actual appearance of the various forms, the more delight we will find, while the horrors of 'sesquipedalian' terms vanish before we are aware of the fact.

LESSON III.

ROOTS.

THE *Roots* of plants, though not so diversified as the upper growth, have many important differences in shape. The broad signification of the word *Root* is that portion of the plant which grows beneath the ground, holding firmly in the soil, and absorbing or taking up nourishment for its sustenance.

There are exceptions to this, as to many other botanical rules. The ivy, for instance, as shown in Plate I. fig. 3, throws

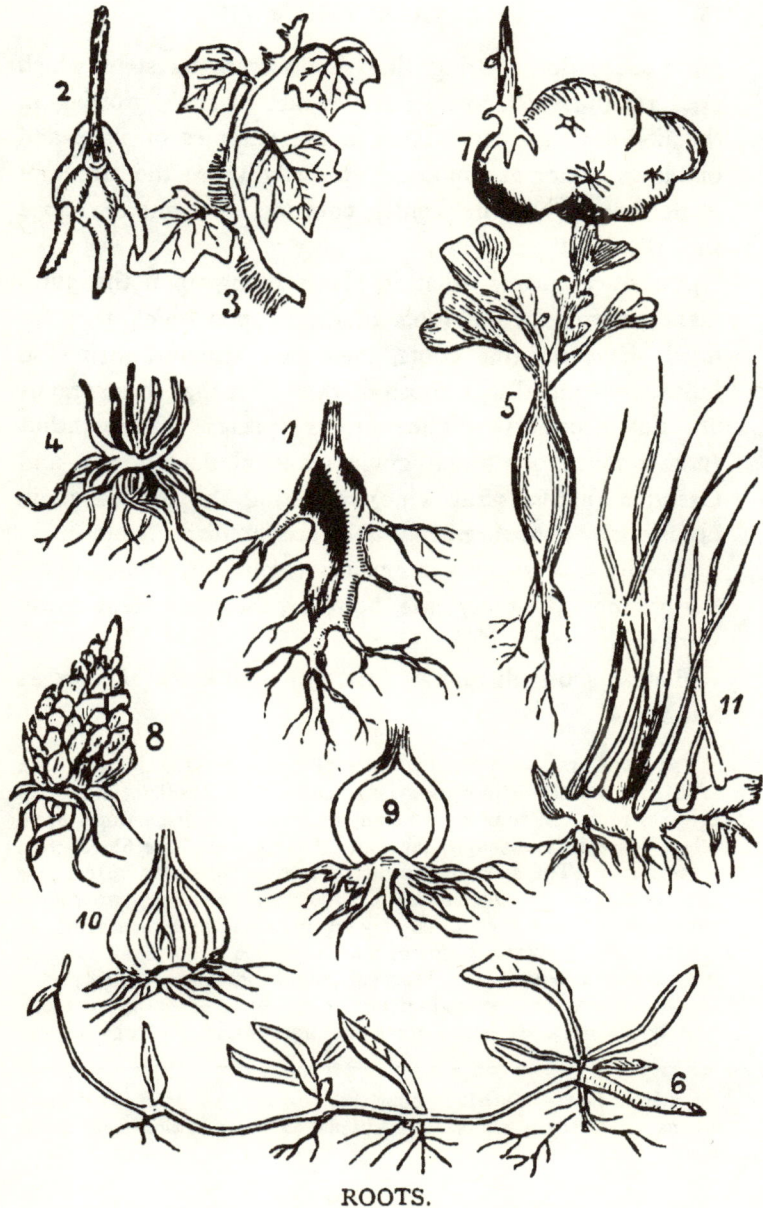

ROOTS.

1. Axial.
2. Adventitious.
3. Aerial.
4. Fibrous.
5. Fusiform.
6. Soboles.
7. Tuberous.
8. Scaly Bulb.
9. Corm.
10. Tunicate Bulb.
11. Rhizome.

out a succession of fringe-like shoots from its stem, which are termed *aerial* roots, from the fact of their growing in the air—in this instance often in the crannies of walls and buildings, acting as supports, especially where the structure is decaying; and frequently covering the whole surface with the plant.

Parasitical plants—that is, plants living upon the nutriment gathered by the roots of those upon which they are fixed—have no true roots, their cell structure being so infinitely blended with those of their host that these organs are not necessary. The various species of Loranthus (native mistletoe) which grace many kinds of trees, and Cassytha (native scrub vine) rendering the Mallee scrub occasionally almost impenetrable, are familiar examples.

The roots of many water plants (aquatics) do not reach the ground. In every case, however, the roots point downward.

Plate I. shows diagrams of the principal kinds of roots, as follow :—

FIG. 1. AXIAL—a *tap* or *true* root of gum-tree (Eucalyptus). An axial root, strictly defined, is a lengthening of the radicle into a tap or main root. In some cases merely delicate fibres issue from it; in others—especially the aged tap-roots of large trees—the fibres attain a great size. The axial or tap-root, however, maintains throughout its character as the chief root. Dicotyledons (producing two cotyledons or seed-lobes), except in a very few instances, have axial roots.

FIG. 2. ADVENTITIOUS root of wheat. When a root is not *axial*, it is said to be *adventitious*.[1] Monocotyledons (producing one cotyledon or seed-lobe), not possessing tap-roots, have adventitious roots. The ivy, though its aerial roots are adventitious, belongs to the

---

[1] Adventitious — differing from the natural state of anything; organs produced in abnormal positions, as roots arising from aerial stems.

dicotyledons from its other characteristics, and is therefore classed with them. In most cases adventitious roots are fibrous, springing from the unelongated radicle (young root). Roots of this kind often become additionally branched by other fibres issuing from them. Grasses in general have adventitious roots.

FIG. 3. AERIAL root of ivy. Other examples of this kind of root are found in the mangrove, screw-pine, Moreton Bay and New South Wales fig-trees.

FIG. 4. FIBROUS root of kangaroo-grass. This description of root is generally stringy or thread-like. Most annuals have fibrous roots.

FIG. 5. FUSIFORM root of radish. A spindle-shaped tap-root, and therefore an axial or true root. The native yam and native parsnip are examples.

FIG. 6. SOBOLES or *creeping stem* of swamp-weed. A name applied to stems which run along the ground, throwing out a succession of fibres below, and stalks above the surface. Examples:—Strawberry, violet, and many grasses.

FIG. 7.[1] TUBEROUS or *lobe* root of potato. A swollen underground stem, with the crown on its surface. Examples:—Native sundews, grass lily, Australian Colchicum, Dahlia, some Oxalis, or Wood-sorrel, and many orchids.

FIG. 8. SCALY BULB of lily. Bulbs are divided into three kinds, as shown in figures 8, 9, and 10. The *scaly bulb* is a thickened root, with the crown on the lower end.

FIG. 9. CORM of Victorian Crocus. Differing from a scaly bulb in having a solid stem, with a very small proportion of broad, thin scales. Examples:—Native snowdrop, Ixia, European Crocus, sword lily.

FIG. 10. TUNICATE BULB of Jonquil. This form of bulb possesses hollow spheres, decreasing in size towards the centre; the outer spheres being of a soft texture, and hardening as they approach the middle. Examples:—Daffodil, Amaryllis, tuberose, tulip, snow-flake, onion, and Hyacinth.

FIG. 11. RHIZOME or *root-stock* of native sheathed-rush. An irregularly-shaped, fleshy stem, growing horizontally below or in some degree above the surface. New stems spring from the upper portion, the lower part becoming rotten and useless. It generally bears marks of former leaves and occasional buds. Examples:—Danubian-reed, butterfly-flag (Iris), and several kinds of fern.

---

[1] Figures 7, 8, 9, and 10 are by some botanists termed 'underground stems.'

LESSON IV.

STEMS.

The *stem* is that part of a plant which bears, or has formerly borne, leaves. Stems do not necessarily grow above the ground, some plants having underground stems. The majority, however, are above the surface. Stems support the foliage and flowers, supplying them with moisture from the roots. The stem springs from the bud or plumule, as shown in Lesson I. Stems may be divided into two kinds, *herbaceous* and *woody*. The word 'herbaceous' is variously applied. It signifies plants producing annual stems from perennial or long-lived roots. It also means thin, green, and cellular (having cells), and is generally used to indicate soft-wooded plants, such as the potato, garden sage, perennial Phlox, Dahlia, etc.

> The following are the principal kinds of stems:—
> ERECT STEMS, such as those of ironbark, messmate, stringy bark, giant-gum, red-gum, blue-gum, or 'fever-tree,' jarrah, myrtle-tree of Victoria, and others, generally termed trunks.
> CLIMBING STEMS, as in the grape vine, pea, etc., have *tendrils*,[1] or fine shoots. In other plants, such as the ivy, trumpet flower (*Tecoma radicans*), they have aerial roots serving the same purpose. In a third class, of which the native virgin's bower (*Clematis aristata*) is an example, the leaf-stalks closely resemble

---

[1] '*Tendrils* (cirrhi) are usually abortive petioles, or abortive peduncles, or sometimes abortive ends of branches.'—BENTHAM.

tendrils, and perform the same duty of enabling the plant, vine or climber, to climb and cling to its support.

TWINING STEMS, as in the French or kidney bean, Convolvulus, European honeysuckle, twist themselves around their supporters without the aid of tendrils, aerial roots, or leaf-stalks. The stem itself grows round the object to which it clings.

CREEPING STEMS, or runners, as in the strawberry, the native scarlet runner (*Kennedya prostrata*), melons, and cucumbers, which trail along the ground, or sometimes even under it. Some produce roots from the underside at certain joints, thus giving rise to a number of young plants, as the strawberry.

Stems are either *hollow*, as in bamboos and grasses;[1] naturally *solid*, as in wattles and most large trees; *spongy* or *pithy*, as in the native paper-grass and sword-rush of the coast; *succulent* or *fleshy*, as in the numerous species of cacti.

Trees have generally hard, woody stems or trunks, varying from 30 to 500 feet in height, and are almost peculiar to dicotyledons. Some large palms and ferns are called trees, from the great size of their stems.

Shrubs, large or small, are plants seldom possessing a distinct central stem. They are inferior in size, but are always woody. Examples:—Fuchsia, Correa or native fuchsia, privet, heath, lantern flower, Epacris or native heath, Diosma, Australian holly, and pouch thorn or native box (*Bursaria spinosa*).—See Glossary.

[1] The stem or stalk of grasses is termed a CULM

PLATE II.

Fig. 1.   Fig. 2.   Fig. 3.

FIG. 1. EXOGENOUS stem (showing cross section).

Dicotyledon—two cotyledons (seed-leaves).—New wood on the outside formed between the old wood and the bark, and producing two seed-leaves (cotyledons) in early growth or germination. Examples:— Eucalyptus (Australian gum-tree), wattle (Acacia), pine, cypress, sheoak, Australian honeysuckle (Banksia), English honeysuckle (Lonicera), Hakea, Australian heath (Epacris), Erica or common heath, Victorian laurel (Pittosporum undulatum), cherry, plum, apple, peach, orange, geranium, rose, Daphne, Camellia, Rhododendron, etc. etc.

FIG. 2. ENDOGENOUS stem (showing cross section).

Monocotyledon—one cotyledon (seed-leaf).—New wood developed towards the centre of the plant and producing one seed-leaf (cotyledon) in early growth (germination). Examples:—Cordylines, palms, lilies, orchids, grasses (including wheat, oat, barley, maize, sugar-cane, etc.), hyacinth, tulip, Aloe, Agave, Yucca, asparagus, snowflake, Crocus, onion, Iris, Gladiolus, ixia, etc. etc.

FIG. 3. ACROGENOUS stem (showing woody cross section).

Acotyledon—without cotyledons (seed-leaves).—Produces new wood at the top only. Examples:—Tree ferns.

This division, which is generally placed under the head of cryptogams (flowerless plants), includes Filices (ferns), Musci (mosses), Lichens, Algæ (seaweeds), Fungi (mushrooms). See chap. 8, p. 56.

The following table shows at a glance the distinguishing characteristics of the three great classes of the vegetable kingdom :—

Exogenous or dicotyledons	Endogenous or monocotyledons	Acrogenous or acotyledons
Flowering plants (phanerogams)	Flowering plants (phanerogams)	No true flowers (cryptogams)
Two or more cotyledons	One cotyledon	No cotyledons
Wood in rings	Wood in isolated bundles	Wood in patterns (not rings)
Net-veined leaves	Parallel-veined leaves	

As mentioned in a previous lesson, the stem—as well as other parts of the plant—presents distinguishing characteristics by which monocotyledonous and dicotyledonous plants can be readily distinguished. It is in relation to the stem that the words *exogen* (outer growth) and *endogen* (inner growth) are applied, as will now be explained.

Exogens or Dicotyledons.
(Producing two seed-leaves in early growth.)

The plants belonging to this class form a large majority of the vegetable kingdom. All the native trees of Great Britain are exogens; while our Australian bottle-trees, gums, wattles, Pittosporums, sheoaks, native tea-trees, and many others, are exogens. The stem of an exogen, in its early period of growth, is a cylinder of *cellular tissue*. This tissue consists of a number of very small cells massed together, and containing a colouring matter called *chlorophyll*, generally green, which will be further mentioned in the lesson on 'Leaves.' Through these cells the matters absorbed by the root pass to nourish the plant. As the exogen becomes older, successive layers of woody tissue are yearly formed in rings round the *pith* or heart of the stem. Each successive ring is formed *outside* the previous one, those nearest the heart of the stem being the earliest formed. Hence the term exogen, signifying 'outside grower.' Examine a cross section of the stem of a gum-tree or wattle as an example. See Plate II. fig. 1, p. 20.

ENDOGENS OR MONOCOTYLEDONS.
(Producing one seed-leaf in early growth.)

Though not so large in number as the exogens, this class includes many beautiful and valuable plants. The graceful tribe of palms, the screw-pines, club-lilies, and other genera found in Australia are monocotyledons. The stems of endogens increase in diameter by *vascular bundles* —fibrous vessels growing *inwards*, towards the stem. (See Plate II. fig. 2, p. 20.) Hence the term endogen or 'inward-grower.' Endogens have no annular rings, heartwood (*duramen*), or true bark. Generally speaking, their leaves are continuous with the stem. The softest part of the stem is the centre, which is sometimes hollow; the hardest part is the outside or rind. In some endogens, such as the Dracæna or Cordyline, the outer skin never hardens, consequently the stem sometimes becomes bulky.

Bark is the outer covering of exogens. It varies greatly

in thickness, shape, and texture. Its thickness is generally in proportion to the age of the plant; though some species, gums for instance, shed their bark yearly. The outer bark is the *epidermis;* the fibrous inner layer is the *liber* or *bast.* Many kinds of bark are of great commercial and medicinal value. That of wattles is very highly esteemed for tanning; that of gums, tea-trees, Pimeleas, and other Australian plants for paper-making, oils, resins, dyes, ropes, etc.

Branches are lateral (*growing from the side*) additions to the principal stem. Generally speaking, they are either *erect, horizontal,* or *pendulous.* In some trees, as in the *Araucarias,*—Norfolk pine, bunya-bunya, and Moreton Bay pine,—they grow in *whorls* or parts arranged at the same level round the stem, in a manner resembling the radiation of the spokes of a wheel. Some trees shed their branches. The principal branches are *limbs,* the smaller ones *branchlets* and *twigs.* Some stems and branches are armed with spines or thorns; others have glandular hairs more or less poisonous. Branches spring from the buds at the *axis* or angle of junction of stem and leaf. These angles are *nodes,* the spaces between are *internodes.* Palms and some other monocotyledons produce no lateral branches, having as a rule only a crown of leaves at the top of the stem, with a terminal leaf-bud in the centre. If this bud be destroyed, the plant can grow no higher, and in some cases it dies. The author, when visiting the South Sea Islands in H.M.S. *Challenger,* in 1868, saw several instances of wanton destruction of noble cocoa-nut palms fringing the coral beach, which had been cut down by traders for the sake of the tender leaf-buds or 'sailors cabbage.' The aborigines of New South Wales and Queensland, and occasionally the settlers, eat the young leaves of the cabbage and bangalo[1] palms.

Note.—The Sydney *Town and Country Journal*, when publishing the first edition of this work in 1880, added the following footnote to the above lesson:—

'We think it advisable here to remark, for the sake of our young friends and others desirous of making themselves familiar with the terms used to designate the various parts, and forms of parts of plants, and which may be termed the A B C of botany, the advisability of copying on paper both the text and the diagrams, as well as copying from nature the corresponding parts of other plants, thus fixing in the mind the matter contained in the lessons, and at the same time acquiring skill in sketching. Each lesson should be thoroughly understood and mastered before passing on to the next, and after this they should be frequently recapitulated until the terms can be used with facility in common conversation. In fact, most of the words are in reality English words, such as should be familiar to every person supposed to be respectably acquainted with his or her mother tongue. They are also such as should be employed by educated persons of every class in familiar conversation on topics suitable for their use, and do not necessarily imply botanical knowledge on the part of those who employ, or of those who hear and understand them.'

[1] Often spelt bangalow.

LESSON V.

LEAVES.

Leaves are organs of (1) *respiration*, (2) *evaporation*, and (3) *assimilation;* for most plants breathe through them, absorbing carbon and other elements of plant food. The general application of the word 'leaf' is well understood; but it must be borne in mind that in a botanical sense the word is not only applied to the *foliage* leaves, which are mostly green, but also to the *flower* leaves or *petals*, which are generally coloured. Leaves greatly vary in size. Some are only a small fraction of an inch long, and no wider than a thread. Others are from thirty to forty feet in length— the latter enormous size having been attained by the leaf of a sago palm in the Royal Gardens at Kew. The magnificent shield-like leaves of the Victoria Regia or Royal water-lily sometimes measure from five to six feet across. A specimen of this plant may be seen in the Melbourne and the Adelaide Botanic Gardens. The leaves of some of the Australian fan palms are sufficiently broad to protect one from a shower of rain.

The leaves of some plants decay and fall in autumn, and are replaced by a fresh crop in the following spring. Such plants are called *deciduous* or 'leaf-shedders.' The British oak, the cherry, pear, apple, ash, elm, and willow, are examples of deciduous trees, their stems and branches being leafless and naked during the winter season. *Evergreens* are plants which continue to bear green leaves all the year round, the leaves sometimes remaining for several years. Such leaves are termed *persistent*. Most of the native Australian plants are evergreens. Gums, Hakeas, wattles, ferns, and Victorian laurel are examples. Leaves differ greatly in their margins, which are of various shapes, as under :—

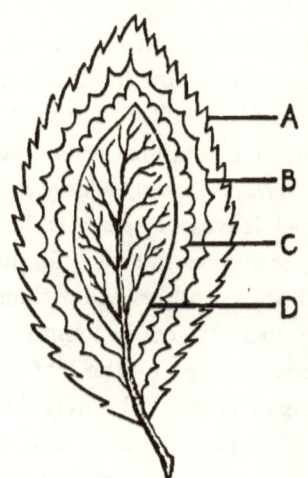

A, *serrate* or saw-edged. B, *dentate* or toothed. C, *crenulate* or having rounded marginal divisions. D, entire, or having an unbroken edge. Another kind of leaf—*retroserrate*—has the teeth placed downwards instead of upwards as in the serrate leaf. By reversing this page, A will represent a retroserrate leaf. The native yam has this kind of leaf.

Cauline leaves are those developed from the stem. *Ramose* leaves grow from the branches. *Radical* leaves spring from so near the root as to have the appearance of coming directly from it. *Sessile* or sitting leaves have no apparent foot-stalk, but appear to sit directly on the branch or stem. A *sheathed* leaf, such as is seen in most grasses, has a prolongation of the leaf-stalk, which surrounds the stem.

Alternate leaves, as in the Rose and Camellia, grow one above the other. *Opposite* leaves coincide or grow directly opposite each other. When more than two leaves are opposite, they are *whorled* (*forming a ring round the stem*). There are other arrangements of the leaf on the stem, not necessary for present mention.

Leaves have cells containing a colouring matter, generally green, termed *chlorophyll*.[1] In many Australian plants the leaves are turned edgeways towards the sun, as, for instance, the *Eucalypti* or gum-trees. *Stipules* are small

---

[1] The colouring matter of flowers is not solid like chlorophyll, but dissolved in the fluids of cells; it is called '*chromule*' or '*chromogen*.'

appendages found in pairs at the base of the leaf-stalk : they are generally absent in monocotyledons.

Vernation, or the manner in which leaves are folded in the bud before they expand, is a subject for the advanced student. A thorough knowledge of leaves is of great importance, since by it botanists are often able to classify a plant when it is inconvenient or impossible to procure other parts of it for examination.

Venation means the distribution of veins in the leaves, as mentioned in Lesson I.

In the wattle and some other plants, the leaf-stalk is sometimes so much flattened and extended as to resemble a leaf. This peculiarity is termed a *phyllode*. In some cases the true leaf is found growing at the end of the phyllode. (See Plate III. figs. 3 and 4, p. 31.) In some Australian wattles no true leaves are produced, the phyllodes alone serving the same purpose. The leaf-stalks of some water plants are filled with air, enabling the plant to float or rise above the surface.

Leaves are of two kinds, *simple* and *compound*. The former vary in shape. They may be very deeply divided towards the midrib; they may have one unbroken leaf; yet they are *simple* leaves. The *compound* leaf has its blade divided into *leaflets*, varying in number. The leaflets are separated from the midrib by stalks. Beginners should be careful not to fall into the error of calling leaflets *leaves*. They are merely *parts* of leaves, as will be seen by the following Diagram I.

Leaves are furnished with *stomata*[1] or breathing apparatus, often on both sides of the surface, but generally under-

[1] From *stoma*, a mouth.

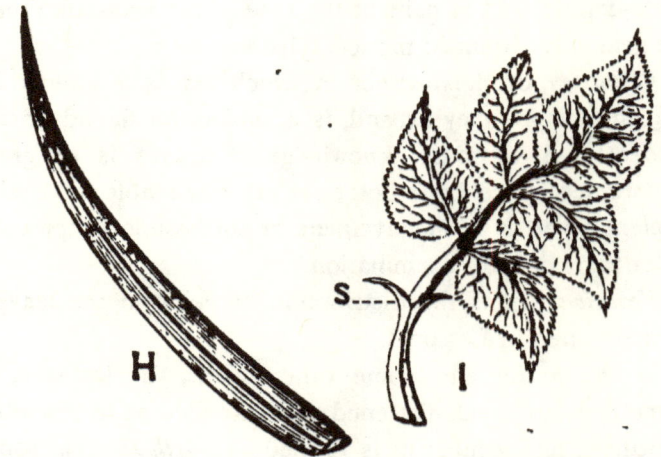

Fig. H.—*Simple* leaf of native flax-lily (monocotyledon).
Fig. I.—*Compound* leaf of rose. S, *stipules* (dicotyledon).

neath. These are minute openings in the skin of the leaf. In water plants, leaves that float have stomata on the upper surface only; leaves entirely under water have none at all.

Opuntias and others of the cactus tribe have stomata on their succulent branches and stems.

Some plants have leaves termed *sensitive* or *irritable*, from the fact of their showing a sense of feeling when touched. The well-known sensitive Mimosa is of this class. The leaves of the native sundews are covered with glandular hairs—that is, hairs tipped by a gland or cell, containing a sticky fluid, strong enough to hold insects settling on them. Many other plants show a most remarkable degree of sensitiveness.

The surfaces of leaves are—

Glabrous or smooth. Examples:—Victorian laurel, New Zealand laurel, Camellia, looking-glass bush, Moreton Bay fig.

Scabrous or rough. Sunflower, Jerusalem artichoke.

Hirsute or hairy. Rock rose, Verbena, Heliotrope, some Pelargoniums and Geraniums, native Fuchsia (*Correa*).

Setose or bristly. Nettles, spotted thistle, borage.

Viscous (*clammy* or *sticky*). Sundews, tobacco, some cypresses (*Cupressus*).

There are subdivisions of these kinds of surfaces.

The subjoined Fig. K shows a leaf of Victorian laurel, with the reticulated or branched veins (venation) peculiar to dicotyledons clearly defined.

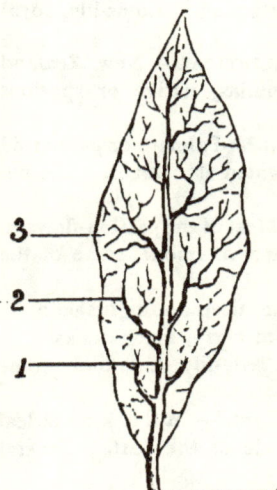

FIGURE K.

1 is the *midrib* (*Costa*[1]), giving off 2, the *primary veins*. The smaller network of veins branching all over the leaf are *secondary* veins (3). 4 is the *petiole* or leaf-stalk.

When the cellular portions of a leaf have decayed, by being steeped in water, the vascular portions — namely, the midrib and primary and secondary veins, together with the petiole — are left, forming what is called a 'skeleton leaf.' The veins of a dicotyledonous leaf appear like network; while in the generality of monocotyledons they are straight or slightly curved.

Plate III. p. 31, shows leaves of the following shapes :—

FIG. 1. PINNATE leaf of elderberry ash.—A compound leaf, having leaflets arranged on each side of a central rib. Examples :—Rose, jasmine, Wonga Wonga vine, Moreton Bay jasmine, English ash, Wistaria.

FIG. 2. PINNATIPARTITE leaf of native celery.—A simple leaf cut

---

[1] Costate, *provided with ribs, as applied to the prominent bundles of vessels in leaves.*

into lateral segments, the divisions extending nearly to the central rib. Other examples: Poppy and celandine.

FIGS. 3 and 4. PHYLLODE.—A leaf-like stalk, enlarged so as to resemble a true leaf. In the diagram, fig. 3 shows the true leaf of a wattle; fig. 4, the phyllode. Many wattles are examples.

FIG. 5. RENIFORM or kidney-shaped leaf of kidney-weed.—The kidney-fern of New Zealand and Pelargoniums are examples.

FIG. 6. CORDATE or heart-shaped leaf of native Fuchsia (*Correa speciosa*). Examples:—Violet, periwinkle.

FIG. 7. ORBICULATE or circular leaf of another kind of native fuchsia—*Correa alba.*—Quince, native mint-bush (round-leaved).[1]

FIG. 8. PELTATE or shield-like leaf of Nasturtium. Lotus-lily, royal water-lily.

FIG. 9. OBLONG, OVATE, OVAL, or ELLIPTICAL.—New Zealand laurel, edging or border box, some Magnolias, native or spurious sarsaparilla, kangaroo grape-vine.

FIG. 10. PALMATE leaf of castor oil plant.[2]—Palmate or palmatifid leaves have radiating venation, and are divided into lobes. Flame-tree, plane, sycamore, rice-paper plant.

FIG. 11. TRILOBED or three-lobed leaf.—Most of the passion-flowers.

FIG. 12. TERNATE.—Strawberry, Japanese Anemone, some of the wood-sorrels.

FIG. 13. SINUATE.—Queensland tulip-tree, firethorn-nightshade.

FIG. 14. HASTATE or halbert-shaped. Sea-berry, many docks.

FIG. 15. SAGITTATE or arrow-shaped. Nile-lily, Caladium, some Arums.

FIG. 16. PERFOLIATE leaf of 'diggers delight.'—In this kind of leaf the stem appears to pass through the blade of the leaf. Several European honeysuckles.

FIG. 17. UNDULATE or waved leaf of Victorian laurel.—The bay-tree is another example.

FIG. 18. RHOMBOID or quadrangular.—Queensland diamond-leaf laurel, native bower spinach, celery-pine.

DIGITATE leaf. Examples:—Horse Chestnut, p. 129.

---

[1] In the first edition of this book, p. 19, the word *globular* was improperly mentioned in the description of orbiculate leaf. The former term is sometimes applied to fruits and roots.

[2] *The leaf of the castor oil plant is, properly speaking, a peltate-palmatifid leaf, because it is fixed to the stalk within the margin.* If the two edges nearest the petiole of most pelargoniums were joined, the result would be a peltate leaf.

PLATE III.

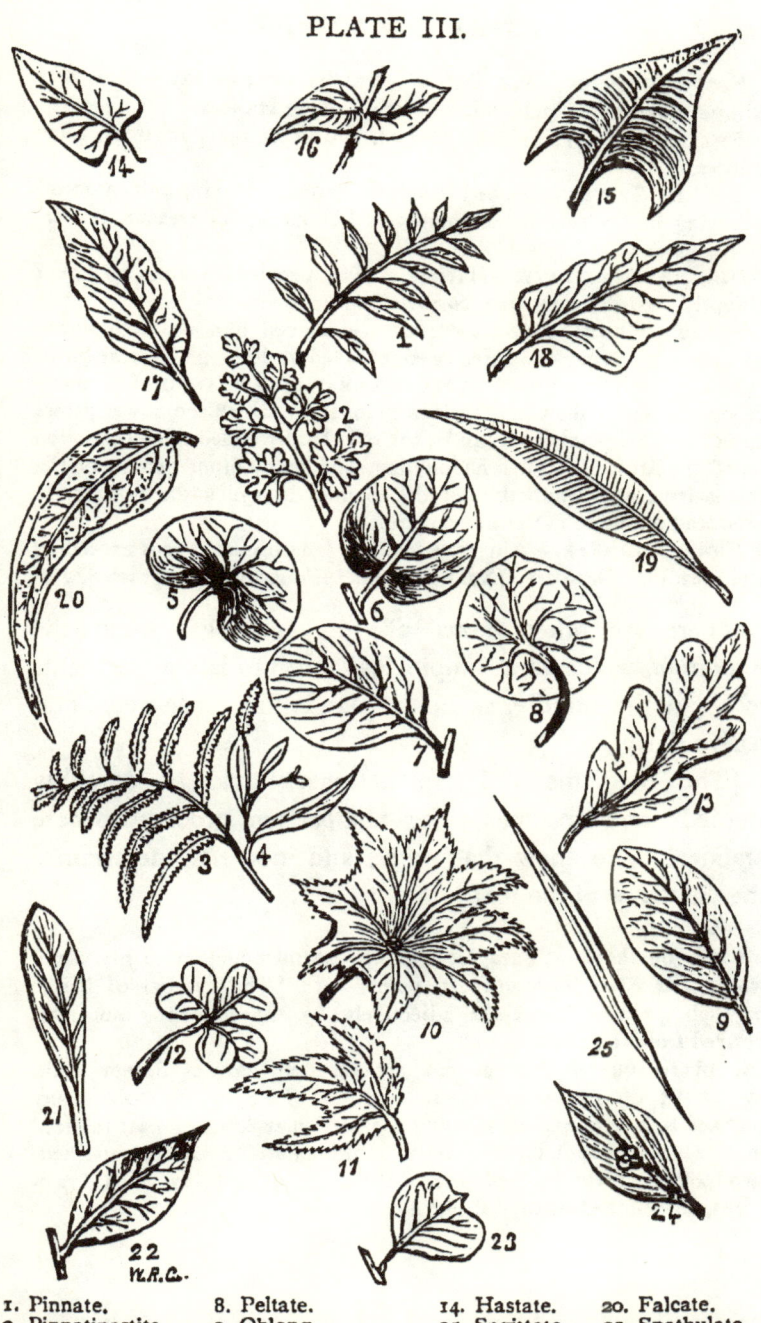

1. Pinnate.
2. Pinnatipartite.
3 & 4. Phyllode (4).
5. Reniform.
6. Cordate.
7. Orbiculate.
8. Peltate.
9. Oblong.
10. Peltate-palmatifid.
11. Trilobed.
12. Ternate.
13. Sinuate.
14. Hastate.
15. Sagittate.
16. Perfoliate.
17. Undulate.
18. Rhomboid.
19. Lanceolate.
20. Falcate.
21. Spathulate.
22. Apiculate.
23. Cuneate.
24. Butcher's broom.
25. Linear.

Fig. 19. LANCEOLATE leaf of oleander or rose-bay.—Narrowly elliptic, tapering to each end. Valerian, some Hakeas.

Fig. 20. FALCATE or sickle-shaped.—Most of the gum-trees, some wattles.

Fig. 21. SPATHULATE or battledore-shaped.—Having a linear form, enlarging into a rounded extremity. Pot marigold, treasure-flower, native sundew.

Fig. 22. APICULATE.—Having a soft terminal point, springing abruptly. Alpine gum-tree, corn-leaf.

Fig. 23. CUNEATE or CUNEIFORM.—Shaped like a wedge placed on its point. Native hop-tree (wedge-leaved variety), native scar-bush.

Fig. 24. APICULATE. FLATTENED LEAF-LIKE BRANCH of butcher's broom, given to show the curious manner in which the flower grows upon it. This plant is said to be the only hard-wooded monocotyledon found in Great Britain. Epiphyllum and many other genera of the cactus tribe are remarkable for the manner in which the flowers are produced upon the flattened branches.

Fig. 25. LINEAR.—A narrow leaf, the length many times exceeding the breadth. Grass tree (Xanthorrhæa). Found in most grasses.[1]

There are other forms of leaf; amongst them the *pinnatifid*, which is a simple leaf cut into lateral segments to about the middle, as in the dandelion, Cape-weed, and native daisy.

[The diagrams and explanations should be carefully studied; and specimens for comparison procured where practicable, to show that *shape*, and not *size*, determines the character of the leaf.]

---

[1] Mr. Bentham, at paragraph 44 in the introduction to his useful work, *The Flora Australiensis*, points out: 'The number of leaves or their parts is expressed adjectively by the following numerals derived from the Latin:—
uni bi tri quadri quinque sex septem octo novem decem multi
 1   2 3   4   5   6   7   8   9   10   many
prefixed to a termination, showing the particular kind of part referred to. Thus—unidentate, bidentate, multidentate, mean one-toothed, two-toothed, many-toothed, etc. Bifid, trifid, multifid, mean two-lobed, three-lobed, many-lobed,' etc.

LESSON VI.

FLOWERS.

Having examined the general characteristics of Seeds, Roots, Stems, and Leaves, we come to the Flowers. Inflorescence, or the manner in which flowers are arranged on their stalks, is the first matter requiring explanation.

The regular kinds of inflorescence may be divided into two classes—*definite* and *indefinite*. *Definite inflorescence* is when the primary or central axis terminates at an early period in a flower, and is thus limited in its upward growth; it is also called *centrifugal*, because the central flower expands first, and those on the branches afterwards. Examples :—Lily, carnation, laurustinus, hawthorn, Helichrysum, Ranunculus, Pimelia. *Indefinite inflorescence* is when the central axis gives off flowers and continues to grow in an upward direction or spreading horizontally; and as the flowers farthest from the centre—that is, from the base of the axis—open earliest, it is called *centripetal*. All the flowers of such inflorescence are axillary. Examples: —Foxglove, wallflower, mignonette, Gladiolus, Dianella, Comesperma, Lythrum salicarium, etc.

Examine a stalk bearing a bunch of flowers, as the Verbena. It will be seen that each of the florets or little flowers which make up the bunch has a small stalk, by which it is joined to the main stalk. This small stalk is a pedicel (*supporting a single flower*). Sometimes the pedicels are surrounded at the base by bracts,[1] which are termed collectively an involucre. The main stalk to which all the pedicels are joined is the peduncle. The peduncle is also called the primary axis.

Divisions of the peduncle are also termed axes; a single division is an axis. *Bracts* are leaf-like developments attached to the flower-stalk, or connected with the flower. The green floral leaves of many flowers are bracts. The manner in which flowers are borne on the stalk is distinguished by a variety of names. The principal ones are subjoined, with examples. Other divisions of less importance exist.

Capitulum or head (of which there are many modifications).—A number of florets without flower-stalks, that is, *sessile*, packed on the top of the peduncle *or main stalk*, and expanding from the outside towards the centre. Examples:—Marigold, treasure-flower, daisy, dandelion, and Cape-weed (all of which are composites or compound flowers). Genera belonging to various other orders also have *capitules* or flower-heads.

Spike.—An unbranched peduncle bearing a number of flowers, either without flower-stalks, or having them so short as to be scarcely perceptible. The flowers may be spirally (*twisted like a screw*) or otherwise arranged. Examples:—Lavender, vervain, plantain or rib-grass, native grass-tree, native foxtail, Cape-wattle, Veronica, and Calistemon. The wheat is a compound spike, very dense.

Spikelet.—A small spike. Examples:—Rye, and the oat which is a panicle of *spikelets*.

Panicle.—A collection of spikelets on long peduncles.

---

[1] *Bract*, a hood.

Examples :—Olive, lilac, privet, native sarsaparilla,[1] fringe-lily, and most grasses.

Raceme.—A cluster of flowers resembling a spike, but having distinct foot-stalks (pedicellate). Examples :—Golden wattle, Berberis, Cape-broom, Deutzia, wallflower, stock, mignonette, Aloe, cabbage and most *cruciferæ* (erect racemes), and Wistaria (pendulous raceme).

A raceme is sometimes compound. Example :—Privet (*Ligustrum vulgare*), flowers pedicellate.

A scapose raceme has a long peduncle or naked flower-stalk (scape) with one or more flowers terminating in a tuft of bracts, and often with radical leaves at its base.

Corymb (sometimes compound).—A kind of raceme or cluster in which the outer or lower stalks or peduncles are longest, thus making the top of the flowers nearly or quite level. Examples :—Cauliflower, native star of Bethlehem, Victorian laurel, sweet-william, and hawthorn. An inflorescence which sometimes grows into a raceme is often corymbose in its early state, the *wallflower* for instance.

Spadix.—A succulent or fleshy spike of incomplete flowers, and contained within a sheathed spathe or bract. Flowers unisexual or bisexual but on the same spadix. Examples :—Nile or trumpet-lily, Caladium, Arum. Palms generally have a *branched* spadix and spathe.

Umbel.—Numerous stalked flowers issuing from one

---

[1] The true Australian sarsaparilla is *Smilax glycyphylla*, not Hardenbergia monophylla, which is properly called *spurious* or Victorian *sarsaparilla*. The root of the latter is reputed to possess properties similar to those of the *Smilax*, but the idea is erroneous. The Victorian sarsaparilla belongs to the order Leguminosæ. The one is a monocotyledon, the other a dicotyledon.

PLATE IV.

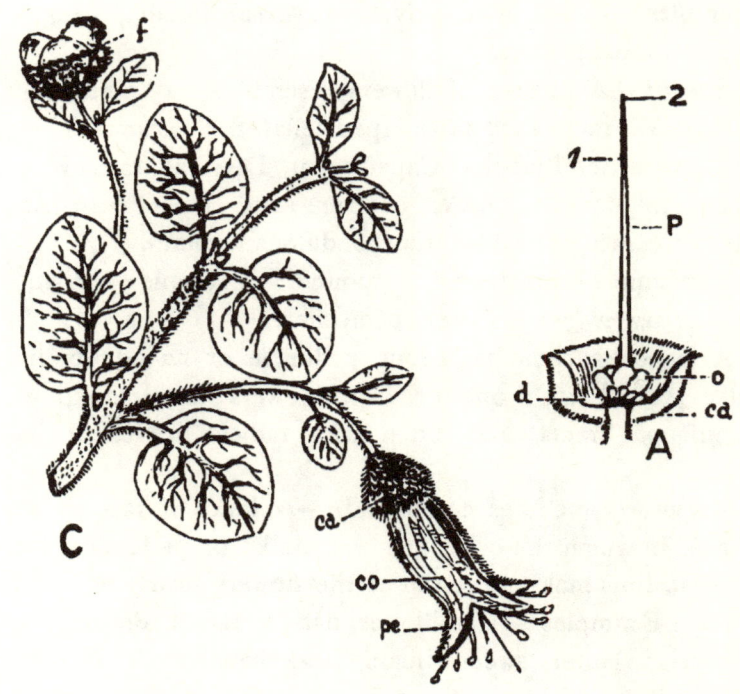

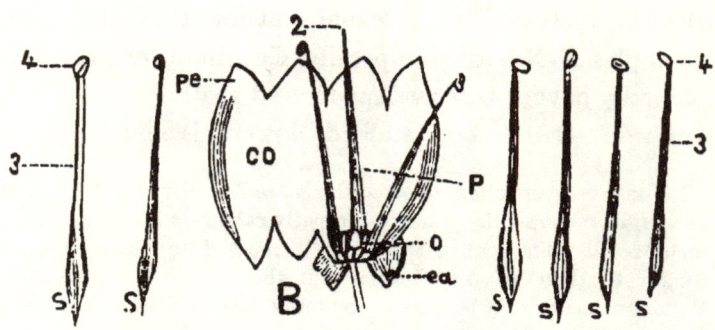

NATIVE FUCHSIA.—(CORREA SPECIOSA.)

PLATE V.

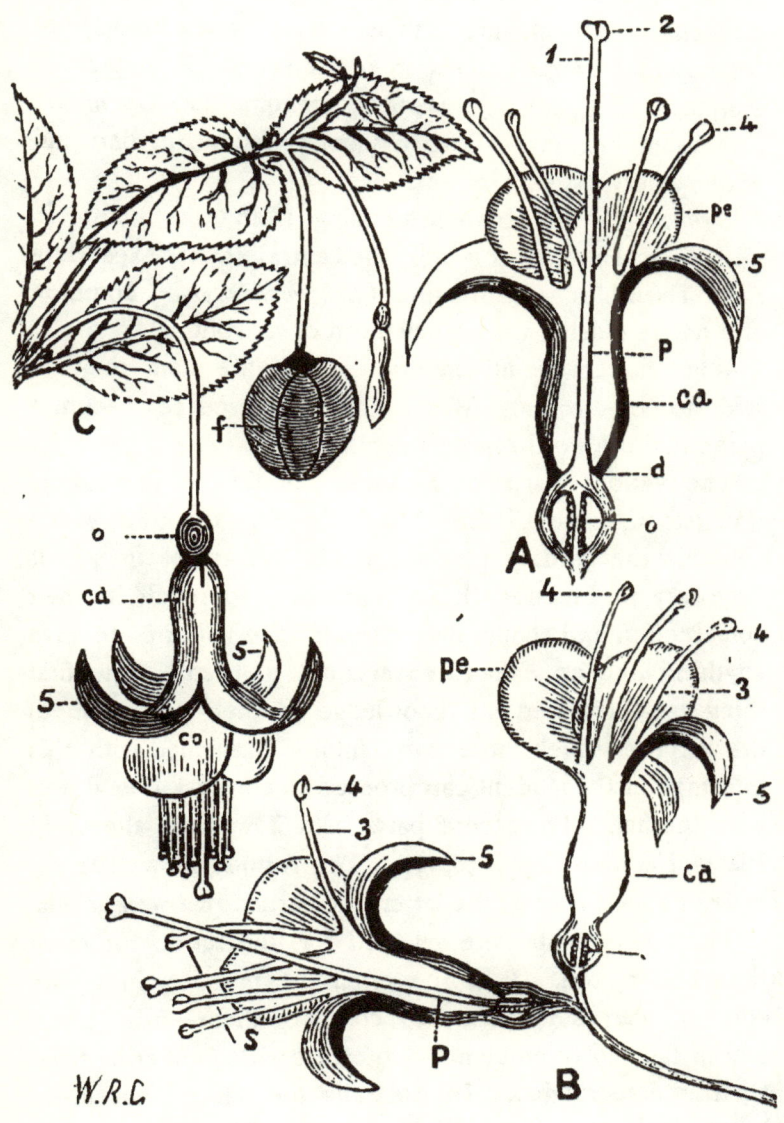

TRUE or GARDEN FUCHSIA.

point, the stalks resembling the wires of a partly opened umbrella. Umbels are either simple (one umbel) or compound (several umbels in one flower). Examples:—Simple umbels, cherry, scarlet geranium (*Pelargonium*). Compound umbels:—Garden parsley, fennel, garden and native celery, parsnip, carrot.

Cyme. — Several branches rising from one point, in umbels, racemes, or corymbs, the central flowers expanding first. Examples:—Laurustinus (*dichotomous cymes*), common and native elder, Chinese hawthorn or maybud.

When flowers are all on one side of the stem they are said to be *secund*. When the inflorescence becomes pyramidal the word *thyrse* is applied.

The various parts of a flower should be thoroughly understood, since it is from the flower that the fruit, which contains the seed, is produced. At the same time, it is necessary to mention that flowers vary so much in their construction and shape, that it would take volumes to give anything like an exhaustive account of them. The first thing to be acquired is a knowledge of their parts, and of the purposes which those parts fulfil. Furnished with this information the student can proceed to contrast one flower with another. The several parts of a flower are shown in Plates IV. and V. pp. 36, 37. The former shows the so-called native Fuchsia; the latter, the garden or *true* Fuchsia.

These two plants were selected for illustration for more than one reason. It is too often the practice, in giving common names to plants, to compare them—from some real or fancied resemblance—to others widely differing from them in construction. In Australia the names thus given by the early settlers still cling to many plants, though they are in some cases ridiculously misapplied. Hence it has been said of this country that its pears are wooden; its grapes disagreeable in taste and growing on weeds; its currant bushes prickly, and its gooseberry bushes without thorns; while its cherries have their seeds on the outside. The 'native Fuchsia' is one of these very inaptly applied names, as will be seen when the parts of each flower shown in Plates IV. and V. are contrasted.

A complete flower usually consists of four parts—CALYX,[1] COROLLA,[2] STAMENS, and PISTIL. These are also termed the four *floral whorls*.[3] A flower containing less than four whorls is *incomplete*. The calyx is the outside whorl. Next comes the corolla. The stamens and pistil are the inner whorls, called *andrœcium* (stamens) and *gynœcium* (pistils), and are the reproductive organs of the plant. Most people know the difference between *double* and *single* flowers of the same species, as in the wallflower, pink, Rose, Pelargonium,—commonly called geranium,—and many other well-known plants. But though the double flowers are popularly

---

[1] *Calyx*, a cup.

[2] *Corolla*, a wreath or garland.

[3] Mr. Bentham, in his *Flora Australiensis* (a work with which every student of Australian botany should endeavour to make himself familiar), says, in paragraphs 92 and 93, xiii., introduction :—'The number of parts in each whorl of a flower is expressed adjectively by the following numerals derived from the Greek :—

Mono di tri tetra penta hexa hepta octo ennea deca, etc., poly
 1   2   3   4   5   6   7   8   9   10   many

Thus, a flower is disepalous, trisepalous, tetrasepalous, polysepalous, etc., according as there are 2, 3, or many sepals.

Diandrous, triandrous, polyandrous, etc., according as there are 2, 3, or many stamens.

Digynous, trigynous, polygynous, etc., according as there are 2, 3, or many *carpels* (modified leaves, of which the pistil is composed, whether combined or distinct).

considered superior in point of beauty to single flowers of the same kind, they are inferior to them from a botanist's point of view, since they are in reality deformities. A double flower is produced by the conversion of the inner whorls—the stamens and pistil—into parts resembling the outer ones. The more completely this is effected by crossing, the more double the flower becomes, but the less capable of producing seed, from the fact that the nature of its fertilizing organs has been completely changed. Hence double flowers, termed 'sports' by gardeners, are considered unnatural by botanists. Double flowers, however, are sometimes reproduced from seeds, but this cannot be accomplished unless some of the fertilizing organs are perfect.

The following are the parts of a perfect flower :—

The calyx or *flower-cup* (Plates IV. and V. *ca*) is the outer floral envelope. It is usually, though not always, green. In some flowers it is small, in others large; and in some—as in the *true* Fuchsia—coloured. In the native Fuchsia it is green. A perfect calyx consists of one or more pieces called *sepals*. In Plate IV. the calyx is in one piece, therefore it has but one sepal, and is termed *monosepalous*. In Plate V. the calyx is divided into four sepals, hence it is *polysepalous* or 'many-sepaled.' The margin of a calyx may be altogether or nearly entire, as in Plate IV., or deeply divided, as in Plate V. A divided calyx may be *notched*, *toothed*, or *cleft*. In some plants the calyx falls off soon after the flower opens. In others it remains, becoming inflated (as in the skin of the currant) or else fleshy. In gum-trees (*Eucalypti*) the calyx opens by the upper part falling off in the shape of a cap or lid, called an *operculum*.

It is important to notice whether the calyx is entire or cleft (divided). When the calyx is partly separated, it is called dentate (toothed). When separated half way down, it is cleft; and when all the way down, it is termed *partite.*

The corolla is the second or inner floral envelope. It is composed of those coloured leaves which generally form the most attractive portion of the flower, being very seldom green. It has one or more pieces called *petals*, and is either *monopetalous* (*one petal*) or *polypetalous* (*many petals*). In Plate IV. the corolla (*co*) is entire for the greater portion of its length, in the shape of a tube, having four short petals at the end. This is termed a *tubular corolla.* In Plate V. the corolla (*co*) is very distinctly divided into separate parts, as will be found on examining the figure. Petals are of different shapes and sizes. The principal distinctions are:—

1. *Papilionaceous corolla*, meaning 'like a butterfly,' so named from the resemblance of the petals to the wings of that insect. The flower of the pea is a good example.

2. *Cruciform corolla.*—Four petals arranged in the shape of a cross. The cabbage and wallflower are of this kind.

3. *Rosaceous corolla.* — Having five similarly shaped petals, spread open like a rose; as the apple and quince blossoms, rock-rose (Cistus).

Corollas, like leaves, are of all sizes, from the tiny chickweed to the giant Victoria Regia and the extraordinary Rafflesia Arnoldi. (See Glossary, heading 'Rafflesia.')

In the *gamopetalous* or *monopetalous* corolla, the leaves cohere more or less, so as to form a corolla of a single piece.

In a *gamosepalous* or *monosepalous* flower, the parts of the *calyx* cohere more or less, so as to *form* a single piece. Of course, as with the *corolla*, the *margin* may be dentated or serrated or divided, for some little distance, but it is *gamosepalous* on account of the length of the tube.

Some plants—such as the gums, Hakeas, Grevilleas, Banksias[1] (*Australian honeysuckles*), docks, and nettles—have no corolla; they are therefore *apetalous* (without petals). Others, like the willow, have neither calyx nor corolla. This is called a *catkin mode of inflorescence.* Grasses and cereals have also substitutes, called glumes (husks). It is incorrect to use the word calyx in reference to grasses.

A catkin or amentum bears scaly bracts. The willow, osier, hazel, poplar, birch, and walnut are examples. The catkin differs from a true spike in being deciduous, and bearing unisexual (one sex) flowers, which are not contained in true floral envelopes.

Stamens (Plates IV. and V., S) are composed of two parts — the *filament* or stalk, and the *anther* or pollen-bag (4). In some plants there are no filaments, the anthers are then *sessile* (without a foot-stalk). Filaments may be in *tubes*, *bundles*, or *loose;* so may the anthers.

Anthers are composed of two halves or lobes, fixed at the top of the filament where such exists, and have in the interior of each lobe a cell or cells containing the pollen or fertilizing dust.

The manner or position in which the stamens are attached to parts of the flower is termed *insertion ;* they may be under, around, or upon the ovary. See figs. 8, 9, 10.

1. Below the base of the *ovary* — *hypogynous*—(Plate

---

[1] See illustration on cover.

IV. *o*, p. 36, and Fig. 10), as in the native Fuchsia, Lily, and Primrose, poppy, cabbage, wallflower.

2. On the upper portion of the calyx, so as to appear to grow on it, but free from the ovary (*perigynous*),[1] as in the Rose, almond, apricot, hawthorn, apple, and cherry.

3. When seated on the ovary itself, or adhering more or less to it (*epigynous*). Examples:—Ivy, gourds, carrot, or any of the *Umbelliferæ* order.

When the stamens are below the base of the ovary, as in the native Fuchsia (Plate IV., S, p. 36), they are termed inferior (*hypogynous*), the ovary superior. When the stamens are above the ovary, as in the true Fuchsia (Plate V., S, p. 37), they are superior, the ovary inferior. The pollen contained in the anthers is like a very fine powder, in most cases of a yellow colour, presenting beneath the microscope very beautiful forms.

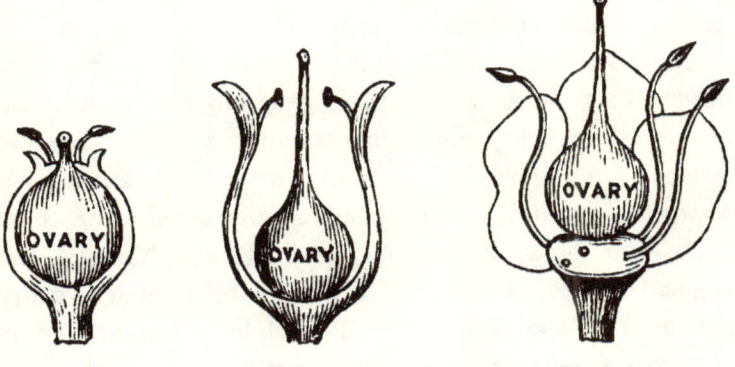

Fig. 8.　　　Fig. 9.　　　Fig. 10.

The stamens, then, are either hypogynous, fig. 10, peri-

---

[1] The term *epipetalous* is applied when the stamens are attached to the *corolla*, as in the Primrose and Convolvulus, and this is usually the case with *monopetalous* flowers.

gynous, fig. 9; or epigynous, fig. 8; or they are gynandrous, adhering with the pistil into a column, as in the Orchis.

Cohesion, adhesion, and suppression of the whorls are conditions of the flower which should be well studied.

Cohesion and adhesion mean growing together—that is, cohesion, a union of like parts, as stamens with stamens, or petals with petals; adhesion, union of stamens to corolla, of ovary to calyx, corolla to stamens, etc. The term suppression implies that an organ has been arrested in its growth, or has never been fully developed. In some flowers, as stated p. 42, the corolla is absent, in others the stamens as well as the corolla, or the corolla and pistil. A single series of organs therefore very often constitutes the flower, as the pistil by itself, or the stamens, minus all other parts. For illustrations in the above, see *Linnæan System*, p. 62.

Æstivation of a flower, means the arrangement of its petals, or parts of them, in the bud.

The *pistil*[1] (Plates IV. and V., P) or pistils—for some flowers have more than one—is generally a tube fixed on the top of the ovary, and communicating with it inside the stamens. Sometimes it is seated on a disk (*between the stamens and ovary*).[2] The pistil usually consists of three parts—the thread-like *style*[3] (Plates IV. and V., A 1), the stigma[4] (Plates IV. and V., A 2), and the germen or ovary (Plates IV. and V., A o). The style is not absolutely necessary for the perfection of the pistil.

---

[1] *Pistil*, a seed-bearer.
[2] *In the first edition of this work, p. 34, a clerical error occurs regarding the parts of the pistil. The stigma and ovary are necessarily the essential parts of the pistil.*
[3] *Style*, a rod.   [4] *Stigma*, a point or apex.

The *disk* (Plates IV. and V., *d*) is absent in some flowers. It is commonly a fleshy or glandular body of a yellow or greenish colour; sometimes inserted round the base of the ovary, as in Plate IV.; sometimes in adhesion to and above it, as in Plate V.; and occasionally under the ovary.

'The perigynous and epigynous insertions of the stamens being easily confounded, the term calycifloral has been given to all plants whose corolla (whether mono- or polypetalous) and stamens are inserted ON THE CALYX, and this whether the calyx be below the ovary, as in the apricot, or *above* it, as in the Campanula, coriander, and madder. The term thalamifloral has been given to plants whose POLYPETALOUS corolla and stamens are inserted *below the pistil*, or hypogynous; and corollifloral, to plants with a MONOPETALOUS staminiferous corolla inserted BELOW THE PISTIL, or hypogynous, as in the primroses.'

—*Le Maout and Decaisne.*

The *ovary* contains the ovules[1] or seed-germs. It is formed either of one bladder-shaped piece, or of several pieces joined at the edges, the junction being the suture (shown in fig. E in Lesson on 'Seeds,' p. 5). Each piece is a *valve*. The ovary has one or more cells, each containing one or more seed-germs, fixed to the placenta or inner part of the ovary by the funiculus (cord) in the manner described in Lesson I. The placenta has a direct communication with the tube of the pistil for the purpose of fertilizing the seed-germs, without which process they could not become perfect seeds. Some flowers are without a pistil.

The *perianth* is the envelope which surrounds the flower; but this term is more frequently used when the calyx is

[1] *Ovule*, a little egg.

hardly distinguishable from the corolla, as in the lilies, etc. etc. Calyx and corolla alike, or of the same colour.

The term *monochlamydeæ* (single or simple) is employed to describe those plants which have but one floral envelope or calyx. The Grevilleas, Hakeas, and Banksias furnish examples. They have no petals (Apetalæ).

A *dichlamydeous* flower has two whorls, *calyx* and *corolla*. Examples :—Wallflower, lily, Amaryllis, Narcissus, dock (Rumex), tobacco (Nicotiana).

An *achlamydeous* (naked) flower has no floral envelope or perianth, that is, neither calyx nor corolla. Examples :— Ash (Fraxinus), Willow (Salix), Birch (Betula). It may, however, be protected by one or more bracts, as, for instance, in the *Carex* and others of the Cyperaceæ, which are common throughout Australia.

Flowers are—

(1) *Monœcious* (*unisexual*), when the male and female flowers are distinct, but on the same plant.[1]

(2) *Diœcious*, when the male and female flowers are on distinct plants.[1]

(3) *Polygamous*, when there are male, female, and hermaphrodite (*bisexual*) flowers on the same plant.[1]

Occasionally *neuter* flowers, or such as have no sexual organs, occur, as in the blossoms of some Hydrangeas,

---

The flowers of a plant or species may be said collectively to be diclinous (a general term often used, meaning unisexual), whether Monœcious, Diœcious, or Polygamous, and monoclinous (hermaphrodite) when stamens and pistils are in the same flower.

[1] See examples, p. 64.

Viburnum opulus, and in the outer whorls or Capitula (heads) of some of the order Compositæ.

The mode of *Fertilization*, by which the flower becomes a fruit or seed-vessel, must now engage our attention.

Whatever may be the construction of flowers, they are all perfected in one way, namely, by one or more grains of pollen finding their way to the stigma or top of the pistil. This necessary operation is brought about in different ways. Insects and birds sometimes carry the pollen-dust from one plant to another. Some plants discharge their pollen in the air, and the wind conveys a portion of the powder to the stigmas of similar plants ready for fertilization. In one way or another the pollen is thus carried from the anther of one plant to the stigma of another plant of its own species, and the process of fertilization commences. Pollen is produced very plentifully; only a small proportion, in comparison with the amount wasted, accomplishing its mission. It is also a curious fact that in plants which have both stamens and pistil, the pollen of the stamen is frequently produced at a time when the stigma is not ready for its reception. In such cases the pollen cannot fertilize flowers of the plant producing it, because before the pistil is perfect the pollen is shed. As a general rule, no perfect seed can be produced without the help of pollen; though one or two instances to the contrary have been pointed out, as in the case of a Queensland plant belonging to the spurge family (*Cœlebogyne Ilicifolia*) or *Queensland spurge holly*. A plant of this species, without stamens, having a pistil only, it is said produced perfect seed (?) in the Royal Gardens at Kew. ' *There was no possibility of pollen reaching the pistil to fertilize it; for at that time no pollen-*

producing plant of its species existed in Europe.' To explain the last sentence, it may again be stated that though the native and true Fuchsias, shown in Plates IV. and V., pp. 36, 37, have both stamens and pistil, many plants have tamens without pistil, or *vice versa*. It is therefore necessary for the pollen from the stamen-bearing plant to find its way to a kindred plant bearing a pistil, and lodge on the stigma of that pistil, before fertilization can take place. In this manner gardeners produce *hybrids* or *varieties*, by fertilizing the pistil of one plant with the pollen of another. It must be clearly understood, however, that plants will only fertilize others of their own kind. The pollen from one variety of Fuchsia will fertilize another kind of Fuchsia; but the pollen from a Geranium will not fertilize a Fuchsia, nor *vice versa*. Neither will the pollen of a Correa (*Australian* or *native Fuchsia*) fertilize a true Fuchsia, since they belong to distinct orders.

When the pollen reaches the stigma of a similar plant it begins to develop a minute fibre, which gradually makes its way down the tube of the pistil into the ovary, where the ovules or future seeds are deposited. Coming in contact with an ovule or ovules, this fibre enters the micropyle (fig. A, p. 5) and fertilizes the ovule. Then the ovule swells until it becomes a perfect seed. As the fruit approaches maturity the funiculus or cord becomes plainer, showing the mode by which the seed is connected with the placenta.

Thus the flower accomplishes its mission changing into a seed-vessel or *fruit*. Generally speaking, soon after the stigma is fertilized, the calyx, corolla, and stamens drop off. Their work is done; and the *flower* dies, giving place to the seed-vessel. In some plants the calyx or the corolla may remain for a time. It is then termed *persistent*. The gum-trees in general have a persistent calyx (*flower-cup*).

Compare the various parts of the native Fuchsia or Correa with those of the true Fuchsia:—

NATIVE FUCHSIA (CORREA). (PLATE IV. p. 36.)	TRUE FUCHSIA. (PLATE V. p. 37.)
Calyx (*ca*).—Cup-shaped, entire, monosepalous, green.	Calyx (*ca*).—Cleft, polysepalous (*many sepals*), coloured.
Corolla (*co*).—Four short petals, united into a tube for nearly all its length.	Corolla (*co*).—Four long petals, distinctly divided.
Stamens (S).—Eight, free at the bottom of the corolla.	Stamens (S).—Eight, inserted in the neck of the calyx (*flower-cup*).
Pistil (*P*).—Stigma very finely pointed, scarcely perceptible.	Pistil (*P*).—Stigma broad-shaped, very perceptible.
Disk (*d*).—Below the ovary.	Disk (*d*).—Above the ovary.
Ovary (*o*).—Superior (*above*).	Ovary (*o*).—Inferior (*below*).
Leaf.—Cordate, margin entire.	Leaf.—Dentate, margin slightly toothed.
Stem.—Rough.	Stem.—Smooth.

These botanical comparisons will serve to show the inaccuracy with which common names are sometimes given to plants.

Further examples of superior and inferior flowers and fruits will be found on contrasting the order Amaryllideæ—jonquil, snowflake, daffodil, etc.—with the order Liliaceæ, such as fringe-lily, tulip, true lilies (Lilium). The former have an inferior calyx, the latter the reverse.

LESSON VII.

FRUITS.

A fruit, botanically speaking, generally consists of two parts, the pericarp or seed-vessel (*covering of the fruit*), and the seed or matured ovule or ovules contained in the pericarp. In point of fact, the fruit is the ovary arrived at its mature stage. The word fruit is often misunderstood; thus a pine cóne is as much a fruit as a peach, orange, or apple.

Fruits are of many shapes, sizes, and substances. They may be flat, globular, angular, cylindrical, conical, etc. They are either smooth, rough, prickly, or warty. They are divided into two classes, *dehiscent* (*opening or discharging seeds*) and *indehiscent* (*not opening*). Dehiscent fruits are those which discharge their seeds by the bursting of the pericarp. The separating parts of such seed-coverings are termed valves, as in the shells of a pea, which is a dehiscent fruit. Indehiscent fruits, such as the apple, cherry, and loquat, set their seeds free by the decay of the fleshy matter surrounding them; fruit-eating birds often free this kind of seed. Fruits have one or more cells. The pea, for instance, has several seeds in one compartment. It is therefore *unilocular* or one-celled. An apple has five cells, each containing a seed; it is therefore *multilocular* or many-celled.[1]

All fruits are either simple (*apocarpous*) or compound (*syncarpous*).

Apocarpous.[2]—Having the carpels[3] quite distinct from each other, one *series* only formed from each flower.

---

[1] In descriptive botany a fruit is always supposed to result from a single flower, unless the contrary be stated. It may, like the pistil, be syncarpous or apocarpous; and as in many cases carpels united in the flower may become separate as they ripen, an apocarpous fruit may result from a syncarpous pistil.—BENTHAM.

[2] *Apocarpous* (*disunited*).

[3] *Carpel* or *carpidium*, literally a fruit.

Examples:—1. When each carpel is considered to be a separate fruit — Columbine, Ranunculus, raspberry, strawberry, bramble. 2. When the pistil is formed of a single carpel — Pea, bean, apricot, nectarine, cherry, wheat, oat, maize, etc.

Syncarpous.[1]—Carpels united so as to form one ovary or pistil. Examples:—Heart's-ease, violet, Iris, lily, tulip, Campanula, poppy, foxglove, Datura, Syncarpia albens, (*Australian turpentine tree*), primrose, snap-dragon, etc.

The pericarp may be the ripened ovary by itself, or the calyx-tube and ovary united. In some fruits one or more of the seeds contained in the ovary may prove abortive or barren before the fruit is perfected. An acorn, for example, has but one cell and one seed when ripe; yet in its early stage the ovary has three cells, with two ovules in each cell.

The pericarp is divided into three parts—

1. The epicarp (or exocarp)—outer covering or coat.
2. The sarcocarp (mesocarp)—fleshy or middle coat.
3. The endocarp—inner coat.

In the hazel-nut and walnut these parts are united into one substance.

The hard covering called the stone of a peach, apricot, almond, or plum, which encloses the kernel, is termed the endocarp; see Drupe, p. 53. On examination of these indehiscent or succulent fruits, the parts mentioned can be plainly observed. The pod of the pea (p. 5, Lesson I., 'Seeds') contains an epicarp, a sarcocarp, and an endocarp. The inner covering of the valves of the pea-pod is the endocarp.

The term succulent as applied to fruits means those in

[1] *Syncarpous (consolidated).*

which the pericarp gradually becomes soft and juicy. The apple, pear, orange, and gooseberry are also good examples of succulent fruits.

When a fruit is ripe, its sound seeds are perfect, and the plant is ready to deliver them. In dehiscent fruits (*discharging seeds*) the process is a simple one. Most people have noticed the common garden or scarlet geranium (*Pelargonium*), when its flowers have, as it is termed, 'run to seed.' The seed-vessel bursts and curls up, ejecting the seeds. In the wallflower another modification of this process is found, and in the gum or Eucalyptus yet another. As the great purpose of the fruit is the production and protection of the seed for the reproduction of its species, examination will show that it is dehiscent or indehiscent, according as best suits the nature of the seed which it contains.

Fruits generally dehisce or scatter their seeds in one of three ways :—

1. By *valves*, opening along the lines of the *sutures* (*joints*), as in the pod of a pea (see fig. E, p. 5). Such dehiscence is termed *valvular*.

2. By an *operculum* (lid or cap) which falls off and leaves the lower part covered, as in the fruit of the 'common purslane' (Portulaca oleracea), pimpernel, henbane, plantain, and some mosses (Musci). *Circumcissile* is the word used to indicate this mode of dehiscence.

3. By *pores*, as in the poppy, termed *porous* dehiscence.

A number of sub-divisions of the above also exist.

Subjoined is a list of the principal kinds of fruits, which should be procured when possible for examination and comparison :—

Pome. — A fleshy or succulent fruit, indehiscent, with many cells, few seeds :—Apple, quince, pear, loquat.

Drupe.—A pulpy, indehiscent stone fruit :—Cherry, plum, peach, olive, apricot, nectarine, English laurel, almond.

In these, beside the epicarp, sarcocarp, and endocarp (see previous remarks), there is the inner dry and often hard endocarp, called the putamen of the kernel.

The putamen may consist of several nuts or stones, each enclosing a seed, in which case they are called pyrenes.

Bacca. — A berry, the seeds becoming loose from the placenta—*part to which the seeds are attached by the funiculus (cord)*—as the fruit ripens :—Currant, grape, gooseberry, tomato, barberry, potato, chilli, kangaroo apple, native gooseberry, Cactus, English holly, English myrtle, Fuchsia.

Pepo.—Which, strictly speaking, is also a berry, is generally a large pulpy fruit with hard or thickened rind, one-celled, many-seeded :—Gourd, melon, cucumber, pumpkin, vegetable marrow.

Follicle.—A pod-like fruit, formed by a single carpel (*leaf forming the pistil or part of which the fruit is formed*) dehiscing by one side only (*ventral suture*) :—Larkspur, columbine, flame tree, Australian bottle tree, Pæony, silky oak (Grevillea).

Capsule.—A dry fruit, variously opening by valves, lid, teeth, or pores : — Aloe, Victorian laurel, poppy, thorn apple, violet, native tea tree, Eucalyptus.

Glans or *Nut.* — A dry, single-seeded, one-celled fruit, generally contained in a cup :—Acorn, hazel.

Samara or *Winged Seed.*—A sort of nut, having two or

more seeds, each in the middle of a thin membrane:—Elm, ash, sycamore, maple.

Achene. — A dry, not fleshy, one-seeded indehiscent carpel:—Native and English buttercup, thistle, rose (achenes in a hollow receptacle), dandelion, Australian virgin's bower, artichoke, and strawberry, containing many one-seeded carpels.[1] In the last mentioned the receptacle forms itself into a fleshy body, and the minute achenes spread over the surface.

Legume.—A two-valved pod, both valves opening to discharge the seeds:—Pea, native scarlet-runner, bean, spurious or Victorian sarsaparilla, black, silver, and golden wattles.

Siliqua[2] and *Silicula.*—A kind of pod composed of two carpels:—Wallflower, radish, stock, cabbage, turnip, watercress, and all Cruciferæ.

Lomentum.—A legume with cross divisions, having a seed in each division. Some Acacias and Cassias. The Queensland cigar Cassia is a good example.

Caryopsis.—A dry indehiscent fruit, closely united to the

---

[1] It must be borne in mind by the student that a carpel is a modified leaf, of which there may be several composing the pistil; also one of the small parts of which compound fruits are composed. Therefore the fruit as well as the pistil may be said to be composed of one or more carpels.

The carpels or ovaries on the outside of the strawberry are the produce of a single flower, and the fleshy portion on which they rest is called a *torus*. The numerous carpels of the mulberry and the pine apple are the produce of not *one*, but of as many distinct flowers. The small nut-like bodies in the inside of a fig are *fruits*, each having a distinct ovary and flower of its own.

[2] The siliqua is elongated, and differs from the legume in the valves dehiscing from a frame-work to which seeds are attached. The silicula is much shorter, or broader than long, and contains fewer seeds. The latter has sometimes a double placenta or part to which the seeds are attached by the funiculus (cord).

pericarp or covering :—Maize, oat, kangaroo grass, wheat, barley. (Allied to the achene.)

Cone.—Having woody scales or bracts, covering seed or seeds :— Murray pine, cypress, sheoak, stone pine, and nearly the whole of the pine tribe (Coniferæ), as well as the Cycadeæ, Zamia, etc.

Strobilus.—A sort of cone with membranous scales and seeds in carpels (the small parts of which form compound fruits):—Brewer's hop.

Hesperidium.—A modification of the berry. 'An aromatic glandular epicarp, a dry and spongy mesocarp, an endocarp covered with watery cells, which spring from the walls of the cavities and extend to the seeds :—Orange, lemon, citron, shaddock.'—*Le Maout and Decaisne.*

There are less important sub-divisions of some of the above.

Contrast the fruit of the native fuchsia or correa with that of the *true* fuchsia :—

FIG. F.—FRUIT OF NATIVE FUCHSIA (CORREA SPECIOSA).

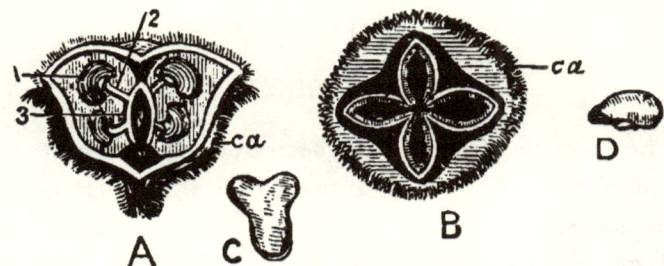

A, longitudinal section of fruit magnified, showing four seeds; 1, attached by the funiculus; 2, to the placenta; 3, persistent calyx, *ca*; B, cross section of fruit; C, follicle or fruitlet or carpel, containing two seeds; D, seed magnified.

Fruit composed of four carpels (see cross section B).

Fig. G.—FRUIT OF TRUE FUCHSIA.

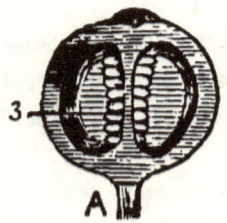
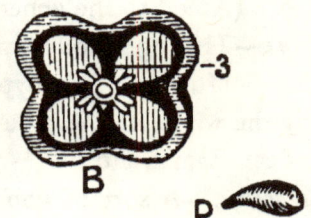

A, longitudinal section of fruit magnified, showing seeds attached to placenta; 3, funiculus minute; B, cross section of fruit; D, seed magnified.

The classification of fruits is a matter upon which botanists often differ. Desvaux described 45, Dr. Lindley 36, Dumortier 33, Richard 24, Mirbel 21, Geartner 13, and Linnæus 5 kinds. It will, however, only be necessary for the student to study those mentioned in the above lesson to enable him to gain a fair knowledge of the principal forms of fruits.

LESSON VIII.

ACOTYLEDONS.

The preceding lessons have been devoted to the consideration of plants belonging to two of the three great classes or divisions.

Acotyledons—signifying without cotyledons—form the remaining division.

Plants belonging to this class are so different from those of the other two divisions as really to form a distinct branch of botanical study. It was therefore considered advisable to make them the subject of a separate lesson.

Acotyledons include cryptogams or flowerless plants; acrogens, having stems which increase in growth by the summit, and having a peculiar construction; ferns (*Filices*); Algæ or seaweeds; Fungi, mosses, and lichens (see Plate II. fig. 3, p. 20, showing stem of a tree fern).

As the name of the class implies, the plants belonging to it are without cotyledons or seed-leaves. Some of them are even destitute of stem, branch, or leaf; for the acotyledons include the lowest forms of vegetation, down to the mildew seen in stale bread, cheese, fruit, etc. Nevertheless they are all, in their several ways, developed specimens of plant life, no matter how mean or minute their appearance. Many noble and beautiful plants belong to this class. Foremost amongst them are those graceful species of vegetation—the ferns.

Ferns[1] are generally perennial (*lasting year after year*) plants. Some kinds, natives of warm climates, grow to a considerable height (often 40 or 50 feet), and are termed arborescent or tree ferns. In many parts of Australasia fern gullies exist, and are the favourite haunts of these plants, which love shade and moisture. In such spots they are found of all shapes and sizes; from the tall tree fern, expanding its crown of cool green fronds or leaves under the shelter of the huge trees overshadowing them, down to the tiny yet equally beautiful specimens of the tribe; some of them so small that they may be crushed underfoot

---

[1] With regard to the number of species in this family there is great diversity of opinion. Sir William Hooker, in his *Synopsis Filicum*, has described 2300 species; but since the publication of that valuable work many new kinds have been discovered, and the approximate number may now be safely given at over 3000 distinct species, not including varieties.

without being noticed. Very often a trickling stream of water from some adjacent spring winds through the gully; while overhead the dense foliage of the large trees is interlaced with innumerable bright-flowering creepers, forming a canopy of vegetation.

Collecting fern specimens has long been a favourite pursuit with people of all classes. By a simple process, described in p. 70, they can be made to retain their beauty of shape when dried. A fernery, or collection of living ferns, is considered almost indispensable in a public or private garden of any pretensions. From the facility with which fern leaves can be obtained in nearly all parts of Australia, there should be no difficulty in procuring them for the purpose of examination.

Fern leaves are called *fronds*. When young, before they spread, they are rolled up on the stem in a crozier-shaped bud. On the leaves are generally found the peculiar organs, termed *spores*, contained within a *sorus*,[1] which supply the place of seed-vessels, and which are arranged irregularly along the leaf; either on the margin along its venation (*system of veins*) at the back, or along its lower surface. Fern stems are of different kinds, underground or aerial, rhizomes (*creeping stems growing partly underground*) being common in some species. When matured, the stems of many large tree ferns are hollow (see Plate II. fig. 3, p. 20), and their broad green fronds often cap the stem at a height of forty feet and upwards. On these stems—naturally naked, and often having a blackened, charred appearance—epiphytal ferns frequently flourish. *Epiphytal* signifies 'growing upon another plant.' It is distinguished

[1] *Sorus* (plural *sori*), seed patch or cluster of sporangia, thecæ, etc.

from *parasitical by the fact that an epiphyte, though it grows upon another plant, does not injure it by absorbing its sap or otherwise destroying it*, as is the case with parasites like the mistletoes. The staghorn and elkhorn ferns of New South Wales and Queensland—so named from the shape of their fronds—are epiphytes; and their handsome green leaves agreeably relieve the dull hue of the stems on which they are frequently found growing. The bird's-nest fern (*Asplenium nidus*) is often found growing as an epiphyte. Epiphytal ferns are not peculiar to the stems of tree ferns; they grow freely on other large trunks, deriving their nourishment from the humidity of the atmosphere. Ferns are *acrogenous*— that is, they increase their stems by the summit, the trunk sometimes having the shape of a cylinder. Acrogens have another very curious characteristic, a description of which can only be understood after the student is thoroughly grounded in that part of botany relating to the reproduction of plants.

Algæ, the seaweeds, need not be described at length. Many of the species are utilised for food and other useful purposes; and the same may be said of the mosses.

Lichens include some of the lowest forms of vegetation; the variously coloured stains seen on rocks and buildings are masses of lichens. Others hang like tufts or beards from the branches of trees.

Fungi are cellular plants, of peculiar construction. Mushrooms belong to this sub-division; so do most of those destructive agents which attack grain crops and fruit trees. *Oidium tuckerii* or vine disease, rust in wheat, and ergot of rye are examples. Mould on cheese and bread also belong to the fungi.

LESSON IX.

SYSTEMATIC BOTANY.

An explanation of the different parts of plants having been given in the preceding lessons, the student, on reaching this point, should have acquired sufficient information to warrant him in proceeding to the study of more advanced botanical works. At this stage, therefore, it is advisable to give in plain language an outline of the two great systems of botany. When the principles of these divisions are mastered, the road to a thorough knowledge of the science will be fairly open, the rate of progress depending on the industry of the student.

One of the questions frequently asked on botanical subjects is, 'How many plants are there in the world?' Systematic Botany, by classifying all known plants, has brought us to an approximate result; but though round numbers give certain figures, it must be remembered that new plants are continually being discovered; and when Australia,[1] New Guinea, Borneo, Sumatra, Celebes, and other parts of the Malayan Archipelago are exhaustively explored, doubtless a very great addition will be made to the list. A few remarks on the discovery and classification of plants may fittingly precede an outline of Systematic Botany.

Previous to the seventeenth century the general know-

---

[1] Baron von Mueller, who is undoubtedly one of our greatest authorities on Australian Botany, estimates that the total number of vascular plants indigenous to Australia is 8800, of which number he says 1250 are found also in other countries, leaving 7550, or rather more than six-sevenths, as purely Australian.

ledge of plants was meagre, though the ancients made some progress in the science. In 1694, Tournefort published a work in which he indicated 10,146 kinds of plants; and it was this botanist who first made an attempt at division, by arranging the number mentioned into nearly 700 genera. The great Linnæus, however, in the eighteenth century, first collated and divided the vegetable kingdom into defined classes. He was the author of scientific nomenclature; and though in the course of time his system has been superseded by another arrangement, to him belongs the undisputed honour of originating a method by which the study of botany was facilitated and rendered positive. Nor is his renown lessened by his frank admission that the system was merely an artificial and temporary one, pending the time when deeper investigation and riper knowledge would lead to a more natural and perfect system. Though that time has long since passed, the claims of Linnæus as the greatest botanist of all time, will mainly rest on his successful creation of a botanical classification, replacing the confusion in which he found the science.

The last arrangement made by Linnæus gave the following number of known plants:—5790 dicotyledons, 881 monocotyledons, and 623 acotyledons (cryptogams); total, 7294 plants, divided into 1239 genera. Passing over Willdenow, Aiton, and other progressive botanists, we find that in 1819 De Candolle defined the number of scientifically known species as 30,000, about a third of which were in cultivation. Louden, in 1839, enumerated 31,731 species, distributed amongst 3732 genera. In 1853, Dr. Lindley gave the number of known plants as 66,432 dicotyledons, 14,000 monocotyledons, and 12,480 cryptogams. Bentley, in 1863, estimated the number at 100,000 flowering plants, and 25,000 cryptogams. In round numbers, the known plants of the world amount to 90,000 dicotyledons, 20,000 monocotyledons, and 40,000 acotyledons; total, 150,000: out of which the number of plants actually in cultivation may be set down as 40,000 species, not counting races or varieties.

THE LINNÆAN SYSTEM.

This system is based on the organs of fertilization—the stamens and pistils—of plants.

There are twenty-four classes, the following being representatives of those classes:—

CLASS I. **Monandria** (one stamen).—Starwort, Canna (Indian shot), Centranthus (valerian).

CLASS II. **Diandria** (two stamens).—Olea (olive), Ligustrum (privet), Veronica (speedwell).

CLASS III. **Triandria** (three stamens).—Wheat, Gladiolus (corn flag), Iris, couch and most grasses.

CLASS IV. **Tetrandria** (four stamens).—Holly, Persoonia (geebong), Grevillea, Telopia (native tulip or waratah), Banksia (native honeysuckle), Plantago (rib grass).

CLASS V. **Pentandria** (five stamens).—Drosera (sundew), Daucus (carrot), Solanum (potato), Viburnum (laurustinus), Nicotiana (tobacco).

CLASS VI. **Hexandria** (six stamens).—Daffodil, lily, Amaryllis, Doryanthes, Aloe.

CLASS VII. **Heptandria** (seven stamens).—Æsculus (horse-chestnut), Calla (Æthiopian lily).

CLASS VIII. **Octandria** (eight stamens).—True Fuchsia, Tropæolum (nasturtium), Boronia (native rose).

CLASS IX. **Enneandria** (nine stamens).—Laurel, Rheum (rhubarb).

CLASS X. **Decandria** (ten stamens). — Rhododendron, Dianthus (pink), Ruta (rue), Cercis (Judas tree), Hydrangea, Ceratopetalum (Christmas bush).

CLASS XI. **Dodecandria** (eleven to nineteen stamens).— Reseda (mignonette), Sempervivum (house leek), Callicoma (black wattle of New South Wales).

CLASS XII. **Icosandria** (twenty or more stamens on the calyx).—Rose, Cactus, Persica (peach), Eucalyptus (gum-tree), Pyrus (apple).

CLASS XIII. **Polyandria** (twenty stamens or more on the receptacle). — Ranunculus (buttercup), Delphinium (larkspur), Papaver (poppy), Magnolia.

CLASS XIV. **Didynamia** (four stamens—two long and two short). — Verbena, Thymus (thyme), Digitalis (foxglove), Lavandula (lavender), Antirrhinum (snap-dragon).

CLASS XV. **Tetradynamia** (six stamens—four long and two short).—Cheiranthus (wallflower), Brassica (cabbage), Sinapis (turnip), Mathiola (stock), Raphanus (radish), Iberis (candytuft).

CLASS XVI. **Monadelphia** (stamens united at the base into one bundle).—Passiflora (passion flower), Patersonia, Malva (mallow), Hibiscus, Pelargonium.

CLASS XVII. **Diadelphia** (stamens united into two bundles).—Pisum (pea), Erythrina (coral-tree), Medicago (lucerne), Trifolium (trefoil).

CLASS XVIII. **Polyadelphia** (stamens united in many bundles.—Citrus (orange and lemon), Tristania, Melaleuca (paper-bark tree), Hypericum.

CLASS XIX. **Syngenesia** (stamens united into a tube, and

the flowers into heads).—Bellis (daisy), Calendula (marigold), Lactuca (lettuce), thistle, Dahlia, Helianthus (sunflower).

CLASS XX. **Gynandria** (stamens and pistils united into one column).—Orchis, including Diuris and Dendrobium (rock lily), Stylidium.

CLASS XXI. **Monœcia** (stamens in one flower, pistils in another on the same plant).—Cucumis (cucumber), Ricinus (castor oil plant), Casuarina—Australian oak—sometimes Diœcious, Morus (mulberry), native Mulberry (Hedycarya), Victorian Sassafras (Atherosperma), some Carex.

CLASS XXII. **Diœcia** (flowers bearing pistils only, and flowers bearing stamens only on different plants).—Salix (willow), Smilax (sarsaparilla), Aucuba Japonica, Phœnix (date palm), Poplar, Vallisneria spiralis, native Snowdrop (Anguillaria [1]).

CLASS XXIII. **Polygamia** (in some flowers, stamens only; in others, pistils only; in others, both pistils and stamens on the same plant).—Rhagodia, Celtis, Trema, some palms.

CLASS XXIV. **Cryptogamia** (flowers concealed).—Lichens, mosses, mushrooms, ferns, seaweeds.

These Classes take their names from Greek words, descriptive of their construction. Thus, Class 1 is termed *monandria*, signifying 'one stamen.' Class 2 has *two* stamens; Class 3, *three* stamens; and so on, up to Class 10 (*decandria*), which has *ten* stamens. Class 5, possessing five stamens, includes one-tenth of the whole vegetable kingdom. Class 11 comprises all those plants having from

---

[1] Pistillate, stamenate, and bisexual plants of Anguillaria are often found growing together.

twelve to nineteen stamens fixed to the bottom of the receptacle. Class 12 has twenty or more stamens fixed to the inside of the calyx. Class 13 has more than twenty stamens attached to the receptacle. Class 14 has *four* stamens, two of which are longer than the others. In Class 16 the stamens are united into one set by their filaments, forming a case surrounding the lower part of the pistils, but separated at the top. In Class 17 the stamens are also united by filaments, but are in two bundles, the thicker one forming a case which surrounds the pistil, the smaller one leaning towards the pistil. In Class 18 the stamens are bound by filaments into more than two sets. No. 19 consists of a number of small florets attached to one receptacle, and in one calyx. In Class 20 the stamens are attached to the pistil. The 21st Class has flowers of different kinds on the same plant, some having pistils, others stamens. No. 22 consists of plants having stamens only on one plant, and pistils on another. Class 23 has two, and occasionally three, sorts of flowers on one plant— the first kind have stamens and pistils on the same flower; the second kind stamens only; the third kind pistils only. The 24th Class comprises plants with invisible flowers (cryptogams),—to this class belong ferns, mushrooms, seaweed, mosses, lichens, etc. These classes are further subdivided into orders, distinguished by the number of pistils, the first ten orders ranging from one to ten pistils. The eleventh order has either eleven or twelve pistils; the twelfth order has *over* twelve pistils.

Within these classes and orders Linnæus placed all plants, the number of orders varying in the different classes.

THE NATURAL SYSTEM.

This is the system now generally adopted. Ray, a celebrated botanist, made the first attempt at an arrangement of plants according to a Natural System; but Bernard de Jussieu was the first to practically demonstrate the system, by arranging a royal garden in France in accordance with its principles. He was, however, of an extremely reticent disposition; and it was reserved for his nephew, Laurent de Jussieu, to develop and make public the new mode of arrangement. After thirty years' continuous labour, his *Genera Plantarum*, published in 1789, was accepted as the long sought substitute for the artificial system of Linnæus. With the Jussieus—as with the Darwins, De Candolles, Herschels, and Hookers—talent in a peculiar walk of science appears to have been hereditary. Adrien, the son of Laurent de Jussieu, also became a distinguished botanist. He was the author of several very valuable botanical works.

According to the Natural System now in general use, the vegetable kingdom is divided into *Sub-Kingdoms*, *Classes*, *Sub-Classes*, *Orders* or *Families*, *Genera*, *Species*, *Varieties*, and *Races*.

A *Class* is an union of many orders or families having one or more main similar characters. Example:—Dicotyledons.

A *Sub-Class* contains those plants which have, in addition to the former, other characteristics.

A *Natural Order* or *Family* is a collection of genera, resembling each other in a botanical sense. Example:— Rosaceæ.

A *Genus* (plural genera) comprises a number of species having points of resemblance. Example :—Rosa.

A *Species* is a plant belonging to a genus resembling the plants that produced it, and bearing seed from which similar plants spring. Example :—Burnet rose (*Rosa spinosissima*). The apple and pear are separate species of the genus Pyrus; the plum and apricot of the genus Prunus.

A *Variety* is a plant which by the influence of soil, climate, or cultivation changes in shape, colour, taste of fruit, or otherwise. Varieties (or *hybrids*) cannot be depended on to reproduce similar plants from seed, as they have a tendency in successive generations to return to the original stock. Some, however, are consistent, producing seed from which spring plants resembling the original. These are termed *Races*. Wheat and other cereals are races.

Thus, we should say :—Scotch roses are *varieties* of the Burnet rose, which is a *species* of the *genus* Rosa, belonging to the *order* or *family* of Rosaceæ, in the *class* of Dicotyledons.

Under the Natural System plants are arranged according to the relative and subordinate importance of their different organs; whereas the Linnæan System is based upon an examination of the flowers only. The three great divisions already explained are further subdivided according to the disposition of these organs. Hence while the student, from the instruction already given, should be able to discriminate between dicotyledons, monocotyledons, and acotyledons, he must search under those several heads for the family to which a specimen belongs. It would be impossible in a work like the present to attempt even an outline of these subdivisions. The works of Sir Joseph Hooker, Professors Oliver and Balfour, Dr. Lindley, Mr. Bentham, and other eminent botanists are open to the advanced student; and in their pages can be found at length the great mass of information respecting the various orders of plants, their subdivisions and characteristics.

The great advantage of the Natural System, as compared with that of Linnæus, is that while by the latter system it is necessary to examine the flower of a specimen before a decision can be made respecting its classification; by the Natural System similarities in plants, though they may not happen to be in flower, are taken into account, and go far in determining the orders to which they belong. Expert botanists can often readily classify a plant under the Natural System by an examination of a single leaf, stem, or fruit. The primary object, in fact, is to place together those plants allied in structure, by comparing their different organs of growth, and arranging them according to their several affinities. Various families have points of resemblance which make them form, as it were, the links in a chain; and the history of botany goes to prove the theory correct, by the periodical discovery of plants supplying the missing links in that chain. It is, however, to be regretted that this otherwise excellent arrangement has been disfigured and rendered difficult by the introduction of a crowd of synonyms. In none of the sciences can greater difference of opinion be found amongst accepted authorities than in botany. Hence arises confusion of names, and invention of fresh terms, very distracting to a beginner.

From the previous Lessons a general idea will have been gathered of the Natural System. The three great classes of which it is composed, namely, monocotyledons, dicotyledons, and acotyledons, are again subdivided according to their natural characteristics, and placed in families. It must be remembered that exceptions exist to most rules. Thus it may happen that the parallel veins of a leaf apparently indicate that it belongs to the monocotyledons, yet its other characteristics may class it with the dicotyledons. The comparison of all points, where possible, is the best mode of proceeding in such cases. The majority of those characteristics determine the nature of the plant, though one or more of them may occasionally be wanting. Procure specimens of seeds, leaves, stems, etc., and test them by this method. The student can then proceed to acquire a knowledge of the Natural System in its entirety. As the construction of the principal groups is studied, inspection of living specimens will assist the memory. By such practical work it is quite possible to become a fair botanist, without the fatigue of acquiring a host of terms serviceable only to the professional botanist or scientist.

If the student requires further information respecting any of the plants to which common names are given in this book, a reference to the Glossary will in most cases give its botanical name, for facility of reference to more exhaustive works on the orders of plants. In searching for such information, the Glossary must be referred to according to the first initial letter in the common name. Thus, native cherry will be found under the letter N ; the *true* cherry under C.

SIMPLE DIRECTIONS FOR THE COLLECTION AND PRESERVATION OF SPECIMEN PLANTS.

WITHOUT entering upon such elaborate details as might be necessary for the instruction of an advanced student desirous of undertaking a botanical excursion, it may not be out of place to append a few plain directions, by which the beginner can collect ordinary specimens of plants for examination and preservation.

A taste for plant-collecting, once formed, grows insensibly; and those who commence by selecting a few desultory specimens, are very likely to end by possessing a fair collection. Nothing more advantageous to the dissemination of botanical principles could be devised, than such a method of rendering the study of the science an object of active enterprise. Interest is at once enlisted; the preparation and drying of specimens attract the attention of the family circle; a healthy spirit of emulation is often aroused in the acquirement of rival collections; and thus the circle of information becomes widened.

The subjoined directions are intended for those who, having studied the foregoing lessons, may feel desirous of examining such plants therein mentioned as may be procurable.

Collecting.—First, as to collecting. It would of course be easy to point out the most suitable paraphernalia for a botanizing excursion; but the object is to obtain specimens with as little apparatus as possible. A good stout pocket-knife, having a broad strong blade, and a small sharp one, will be found very serviceable. The large blade will be useful for digging up small specimens, removing mosses and lichens, etc.; while the sharp blade must be employed in cutting off sprays or branchlets from large plants. Two pieces of thick pasteboard, say a foot long by ten inches broad, and a few dozen pieces of paper of the same size, will be necessary. The experience of the author in plant-collecting (sometimes under very unfavourable circumstances for the purpose) points to the fact that, as a matter of expediency, old newspapers will be found very serviceable for placing the specimens between. They must, however, be thoroughly dry. Two straps (with buckles) long enough to admit of being drawn tightly round the pasteboard covers with their contents, will complete the inexpensive equipment of the collector.

If the desired specimen happens to be a small, slender plant, a few inches only in length, it may be preserved entire. In such a case, the broad blade of the pocket-knife should be used to dig it up by the roots, working round the latter in such a manner as to avoid injuring them. The roots should be well shaken, and carefully washed as soon as possible. Grasses and similar slender plants may be folded as many times as may be necessary; a stitch in the paper, loosely made with coarse thread, will temporarily hold the folds in their places. In the case of ferns, two fronds at least should be obtained. Some orchids and most succulent plants are difficult to preserve—such plants should be dipped in boiling water (excepting the flowers) as speedily as possible, to destroy their vitality, which is so intense in some kinds that they will continue to grow even after being placed under a heavy pressure.

In selecting specimens of large shrubs, trees, etc., take if practicable a branchlet having young shoots besides matured leaves. If flowers and fruit can be obtained on the same spray, so much the better. In every instance be careful to choose healthy specimens, thoroughly representative of the plants from which they spring; and on the margin of the paper on which they are placed note at once the name, when and where gathered, height of plant, and all other remarks calculated to aid future reference.

As the specimens are obtained, they should be carefully laid in their natural positions on sheets of dry paper. When enough have been obtained, the papers and their contents must be placed between the pasteboard covers, and tightly strapped; one strap being buckled across the length and the other across the breadth of the boards. In this manner they can be conveyed home for drying.

Drying.—The same operation of packing may be repeated for drying specimens, increasing the quantity of paper between each layer. Place a board or any level substance upon the top piece of pasteboard, and a weight of say 30 or 40 pounds upon that. Change the paper daily for a week, drying it as changed to avoid waste. Delicate plants should be placed between very thin paper. Thick stems may be split, to flatten them. Care must be taken to give plants their natural shape. When quite dry, the specimens may be gummed or glued to sheets of dried paper, but for botanical reference it would be better to leave them loose.

To examine a dried plant, moisten it well with warm water, if expedition is necessary. Tuberous or bulbous roots should have a piece cut off the side on which they are to be fastened to the paper. A journal of remarks, and a progressive number given to each specimen, recorded on the paper on which it is preserved, and under which number full particulars respecting it are entered in the journal, will render matters methodical and easy from the start. There are not wanting in Australia lovers of botany, who, if the suggestion were made, would think it worth while to offer prizes to scholars for the best collection of dried plants within a given time, accompanied by an intelligent explanation of them. Nor need this incentive be offered only to the young. If it be a healthy sign to find all classes of the community taking an interest in flower and fruit shows, and competing for prizes at them, it will be conceded that a pursuit which must necessarily cause the mind to retain the knowledge of a number of plants, is certainly not inferior in usefulness. The man who cultivates beautiful flowers has provided himself with an intellectual, healthful, and pleasurable occupation; but he who commences the formation of a herbarium must employ comparison, observation, and reflection; and if he enters upon the undertaking heartily, he cannot fail to acquire knowledge which—especially in a young country like Australia—may prove of infinite use to himself or his family in a realistic point of view.

'Small beginnings have often great endings,' and the most abstruse science may be presented in such a manner as to prove attractive to the student. If, as the author hopes, his suggestions are adopted by school teachers generally, botany will take its proper place as a necessary branch of education. No geographical lesson will then be complete without a glance at the vegetation of the locality or country under description. The pointing out of the Australian Alps will be accompanied by a verbal sketch of their vegetation, and an interest thus be infused into the bare description of places, heights, and distances. The truth of the doctrine that nature created nothing in vain will be made manifest, and the reproach removed, that in a land remarkable for its botanical wonders, nine-tenths of the rising generation are practically ignorant of the vegetation of the country in which they were born.

Examination or Dissection.—Before attempting to ascertain the family and genus of a plant, a knowledge of the Natural System must be acquired. It will, however, be found most useful (even with the knowledge the student has acquired from the preceding pages) to undertake a classification of specimens. The following rules must be observed :—First, determine the division or class. Next, the family or order. Then the genus. Next the species, and perhaps the variety. With the aid of the Lessons and Glossary material progress should be made.

Ferns.—In the lesson on acotyledons, allusion was made to the fact that the collection of ferns is a favourite pursuit. A few lines of practical direction as to their preservation may therefore be interesting. In order to dry ferns, put them carefully between pieces of stout, dry blotting-paper; being particular to place them flat, and in their natural positions. When the whole number of specimens have been thus disposed of, cover them with a board at least one inch longer and wider than the paper, and place on the board a weight of about 60 pounds, so arranged as to give an equal pressure. For the first three or four days change the paper daily, replacing it with dry sheets; straighten any leaves which may be out of their natural position; and correct any other faults, before the specimens stiffen. After that period change the paper twice, on alternate days. After a week's pressure, remove the specimens and place them between clean sheets of paper, where they may be allowed to get finally dry. Carefully followed, these instructions will enable any person to form a collection of these graceful plants. After any specimens are thoroughly dried, all that is necessary to preserve them is to keep them in a portfolio with covers heavy enough to give a moderate degree of pressure.

Mounting.—This must be done according to taste. The plants may either be stitched, gummed, or glued to stiff paper. Camphor will be found useful in preventing the attacks of ants and other insects.

EXAMINATION OR DISSECTION OF FLOWERS AND FRUITS.

The following notes from Bentham's 'Flora Australiensis' will be of value to the Botanical Student.

'To examine or dissect flowers or fruits in dried specimens, it is necessary to soften them. If the parts are very delicate, this is best done by gradually moistening them in cold water; in most cases, steeping them in boiling water or in steam is much quicker. Very hard fruits and seeds will require boiling to be able to dissect them easily.

'For dissecting and examining flowers in the field, all that is necessary is a penknife and a pocket lens or simple microscope, with a stage holding a glass plate, upon which the flowers may be laid; and a pair of dissectors, one of which should be narrow and pointed, or a mere point, like a needle, in a handle; the other should have a pointed blade, with a sharp edge, to make clean sections across the ovary. A compound microscope is rarely necessary, except in cryptogamic botany and vegetable anatomy. For the simple microscope, lenses of $\frac{1}{4}$, $\frac{1}{2}$, 1, and $1\frac{1}{2}$ inches focus are sufficient.

'To assist the student in determining or ascertaining the name of a plant belonging to a flora, analytical tables should be prefixed to the orders, genera, and species. These tables should be so constructed as to contain, under each bracket, or equally indented, two (rarely three or more) alternatives as nearly as possible contradictory or incompatible with each other. Each alternative referring to another bracket, or having under it another pair of alternatives further indented.

'The student having a plant to determine, will first take the general table of natural orders, and examining his plant at each step to see which alternative agrees with it, will be led on to the order to which it belongs; he will then compare it with the detailed character of the order given in the text. If it agrees, he will follow the same course with the table of the genera of that order, and again with the table of species of the genus. But in each case, if he finds that his plant does not agree with the detailed description of the genus or species to which he has thus been referred, he must revert to the beginning and carefully go through every step of the investigation before he can be satisfied. A fresh examination of his specimen, or of others of the same plant, a critical consideration of the meaning of every expression of the characters given, may lead him to detect some minute point overlooked or mistaken, and put him into the right way. Species vary within limits which it is often very difficult to express in words, and it proves often impossible in framing these analytical tables so to divide the genera and species, that those which come under one alternative should absolutely exclude the others. In such doubtful cases both alternatives must be tried before the student can come to the conclusion that his plant is not contained in the Flora, or that it is erroneously described.

'In those Floras where analytical tables are not given, the student is usually guided to the most important or prominent characters of each genus or species, either by a general summary prefixed to the genera of an order or to the species of the genus, for all such genera or species; or by a special summary immediately preceding the detailed description of each genus or species. In the latter case this summary is called a *diagnosis*. Or sometimes the important characters are only indicated by italicizing them in the detailed description.

'It may also happen that the specimen gathered may present some occasional or accidental anomalies peculiar to that single one, or to a very few individuals, which may prevent the species from being at once recognised by its technical characters.'

AUSTRALIAN VEGETATION.[1]

It has often been remarked by travellers and tourists that there is great monotony in the scenery of Australia. Those, however, who have explored our fern gullies, or climbed our mountains, will not deny the fact that Australia possesses greatly varied and much beautiful landscape scenery. Even along the coast-line the lover of the picturesque will often be fascinated with the spacious bays and well-wooded successions of beach bordering them, and the bold bluffs, headlands, and long stretches of rock-bound shore.

To the enthusiastic collector of botanical specimens, every yard of progress made through the inland districts reveals fresh objects of interest. Fatigue is disregarded, as one plant after another is added to the portfolio; and when, at the end of the day, the botanical treasures gleaned are surveyed, the collector will feel well repaid for the toil and trouble he has undergone in collecting them. Perhaps some rare or curious plant—a great prize in the lottery of search—will have rewarded his exertions; but no day can pass without numbers of specimens having been found

[1] This chapter has been written with the object of pointing out to students of botany and others availing themselves of holidays and visiting different parts of the colonies, some of the characteristics and beauties of Australian vegetation.

worthy of a place in the herbarium of a botanical student. At the present time, when a network of railways is rapidly covering Australia, the facilities for botanical excursions are exceptionally great. Yet we find even those charming spots contiguous to our own metropolis comparatively unvisited. Mount Macedon, Fernshaw, and Dandenong, for instance, though so near to Melbourne, are little known to its citizens. The lover of nature would feel delighted with a visit to these localities. If he wander through their thickly-wooded glens and rich fern gullies, where streamlets of pure spring water gently trickle, and on the banks of which the 'woolly tree-fern' (*Dicksonia antarctica*), overshadowed by lofty gum-trees, often grows to more than thirty feet in height, he will be filled with wonder and admiration. Striking out from the beaten tracks, the visitor can plunge at once into the primeval forest, forcing his way through the most impenetrable thickets of 'dogwood' (*Prostanthera lasianthos*), native hazel (*Pomaderris apetala*), musk (*Olearia argophylla*), cotton-wood (*Senecio Bedfordii*), Pimelea, and pepper-tree (*Drimys aromatica*); occasionally encountering a gigantic 'stringy-bark' (*Eucalyptus machorrhyncha*) or 'messmate' (*Eucalyptus obliqua*) towering majestically above or lying prone among the underwood, its mighty stem—often as much as fifteen feet in diameter—completely blocking the way. Clear spaces of grass-land may sometimes be met with, margined with jungles of 'Tasmanian tea-bush' (*Leptospermum scoparium*), 'native furze' (*Hakea ulicina*), 'native hop' (*Daviesia*), etc., whilst the brilliant inflorescence of the native heath (*Epacris*), which is plentifully sprinkled over the landscape, lends to it an additional charm. On entering those sylvan wilds, one is struck with the tranquillity of the scene. Silence reigns, and is seldom broken except by the cry of a lyre bird (native pheasant), or perhaps the 'whish' of a startled wallaby.

The tree-ferns vie with each other in the magnificence of their frondage.[1] No matter how grand the scenery may be in other respects, no matter how majestic the trees, the graceful forms and bright green of the ferns will always arrest the attention. At almost every step, one crushes underfoot the 'native mint' (*Mentha Australis, M. laxiflora,* etc.) and other herbs which emit a fragrant perfume. In the steep gullies and ravines, where there is moisture, scores of beautiful dwarf ferns occur, such as *Aspidium, Doodia,* maiden-hair ferns (*Adiantum assimile* and *A. Æthiopicum*), *Blechnum, Gleichenia, Pteris, Lindsaya, Lomaria,* etc. These catch the eye at every step, and the real lover of plants will often pause during his ramble to admire their singular beauty. That most remarkable of all ferns, *Todea barbara* (*Syn. T. Africana*), found generally in the beds of creeks, though seldom attaining a height of more than four or five feet, has a bulky trunk, almost as broad as the plant is high. It frequently weighs as much as 14 to 15 cwt. From the tallest trees droop festoons of the 'native supple-jack' (*Clematis aristata*), binding their limbs together, or interlacing them, with their rope-like stems, covered with moss, and often forming, at considerable height, a canopy

---

[1] Forests of these *Dicksonia antarctica* and *Alsophila Australis* (the 'mountain tree-fern'), many acres in extent, are of frequent occurrence in Victoria, New South Wales, Queensland, and Tasmania. The dark stems of the former fern in Victoria are often clothed with epiphytes and climbers, such as *Fieldia Australis, Polypodium scandens, Lyonsia straminea, Hymenophyllum Tunbridgense,* etc.

of foliage too dense for the ardent rays of the sun to pierce. The mountain slopes are sometimes clad with 'native mulberry' (*Hedycarya angustifolia*), *Cassinia*, 'prickly wattle' (*Acacia juniperina*), 'elderberry ash' (*Panax sambucifolia*), and many other species of underwood, in the midst of which rise lofty gums; whilst in the open spaces the 'hill tree-fern' (*Alsophila Australis*) flourishes, occasionally standing out, sentinel-like, on the ridges, exposed to the sun. In well-shaded situations the fronds of this fern are very luxuriant, and measure fully fifteen feet in length. Upon some of the spurs small forests of the grass-tree (*Xanthorrhœa arborea*) occur, forming a novel and effective contrast to the other vegetation. Leaving a romantic fern gully, with its wealth of foliage, the tourist may probably come abruptly upon a host of these singular plants with stems scarred and blackened by the bush fires that have swept over them. The change is often so sudden as to greatly heighten the contrast between them and the scene of beauty quitted but a moment previously. The Upper Yarra, Fernshaw, Dandenong districts, and the shores of the Gippsland Lakes, furnish splendid examples of Victorian forest grandeur.

The native nettle (*Urtica incisa*) grows to a considerable height amongst the brushwood, often making its presence realized before being observed, by the virulence of its sting. The *Eucalyptus amygdalina*[1] sometimes rears its proud

---

[1] It has been frequently stated that specimens of *Eucalyptus amygdalina*, variety *regnans*, have been found more than 500 feet in height, but the assertion has never been thoroughly proved to be correct. Trees, however, of 396 feet in height can be pointed out by the settlers at Fernshaw and Dandenong. The late director of the Melbourne Botanic Gardens (Baron von Mueller), in one

head to an altitude of nearly four hundred feet, towering far above the native beech (*Fagus Cunninghami*),[1] whose dense, dark foliage, in contrast with the bright green of the fronds of the tree-ferns, presents a charming picture. Conspicuous during a ramble in such places are the sassafras (*Atherosperma moschata*), cheesewood (*Pittosporum bicolor*), Victorian plumwood (*Notelæa ligustrina*), native holly (*Lomatia Fraseri*), silver wattle (*Acacia dealbata*), native cherry (*Exocarpus cupressiformis*), smooth holly (*Myrsine variabilis*), Victorian laurel (*Pittosporum undulatum*), hazel

of his interesting lectures,—'The application of Phytology to the Industrial Purposes of Life,'—delivered on the 3rd November 1870, says: 'An idea of forest value may be formed when we enter on some calculation of the supply of timber or other products available from one of our largest Eucalyptus trees. Suppose one of the colossal *Eucalyptus amygdalina* at the Black Spur was felled, and its total height ascertained to be 480 feet, its circumference towards the base of the stem 81 feet, its lower diameter 26 feet, and at the height of 300 feet its diameter 6 feet. Suppose only half the available wood was cut into planks twelve inches in width, we would get, in the terms of the timber trade, 426,720 superficial feet, at one inch thickness, sufficient to cover $9\frac{3}{4}$ acres. The same bulk of wood cut into railway sleepers 6 feet × 6 inches × 8 inches, would yield in number 17,780. Not less than a length of twenty-three miles of three-rail fencing, including the necessary posts, could be constructed. It would require a ship of about 1000 tonnage to convey the timber and additional firewood of half the tree; and 666 drayloads, at $1\frac{1}{2}$ tons, would thus be formed to remove half the wood. The essential oil obtainable from the foliage of the whole tree may be estimated at 31 lbs.; the charcoal, suppose there was loss of wood, 17,950 bushels; the crude vinegar, 227,269 gallons; the potash, 2 tons 11 cwt. But how many centuries elapsed before undisturbed nature could build up, by the subtle processes of vitality, these huge and wondrous structures?'

[1] This tree is often called by the settlers 'myrtle,' though it belongs to the order *Cupuliferæ*. In New South Wales and Queensland the *Eugenia Smithii* and *Eugenia myrtifolia* are called myrtle, lillypillies, and native rose apple.

(Pomaderris), and numerous other species. Amongst the shrubs, the native musk, native mulberry, Pimeleas, native snow-bush (*Olearia Stellulata* variety), native woodbine or coffee-bush (*Coprosma hirtella*), native mint-bush (*Prostanthera*), scrub-box, and native currant (*Coprosma Billardieri*), are perhaps the most frequently met with. But of all the gigantic trees [1] found in Victoria, none can surpass the grandeur of *Eucalyptus amygdalina*, var. *regnans*.

[1] As regards gigantic trees, it is generally supposed that the largest trees in the world have been found in California and the West Indies. In Rhind's *Vegetable Kingdom*, we read at pp. 701, 702, speaking of *Sequoia* (*Wellingtonia*) *gigantea*, or 'Mammoth tree'—'There are specimens of this tree which, if not the most ancient, are unquestionably the largest vegetable forms ever discovered, and, in all probability, the most stupendous creations in the world, fossil or recent. The tree was first found at a spot called Calaveros Grove, near the head waters of the Stanislaus and San Antonio Rivers, in long. 120° 10′ W., lat. 38° N., and about 4590 feet above the sea-level. The age of some of the Californian trees is estimated at 3000 years, and for others a still higher antiquity is claimed. Lord Richard Grosvenor, in 1860, confirmed a statement which had often been repeated, that one specimen was 450 feet in height, and 116 in circumference. Most of the specimens now standing in the Mammoth-tree Grove, according to a statement by the proprietor of the *Kew Miscellany*, are of the average height of 300 feet; one of them, known as the "Mother of the Forest," measured 327 feet in height, and 90 feet in circumference. Another tree, the "Father of the Forest," has long since bowed his lofty head, and lies prone on the earth. He still measures 112 feet in circumference at the base, and in length can be traced 300 feet to where the trunk was broken by falling against another tree; at this point it measures 18 feet in diameter, and according to the average taper of the trees, this giant must have reached a height of 450 feet. A hollow tunnel has been burned through the trunk for 200 feet, capacious enough for a person to ride into it on horseback. Some of the trees have been destroyed from mere wantonness, others from cupidity. In the progress of this execrable vandalism, the felling of one tree, we are boastingly told, employed five men for twenty-two days, not in chopping it down, but in boring it off with pump augers. It was then only displaced by means of wedges, driven with butts of trees, like

A glance at any map [1] of Victoria will show that the 145° of longitude passes near Lake Moira, on the Murray, at the northern boundary of Victoria, and cuts through Melbourne on the south, dividing the colony as it were into halves. If, therefore, we call that portion on the right hand side of 145° eastern, and that on the left, western Victoria, the process of description will be rendered much more easy. To make this still more simple and capable of being understood, if we cut out the northern portion of eastern Victoria,

battering-rams. This noble tree was 302 feet high, and 96 feet in circumference at the ground. Upon the stump, "on the 4th July," thirty-two persons were engaged in dancing four sets of cotillons at one time, and besides these, adds the account, there were musicians and onlookers.' Again, in Dr. Lindley's *Vegetable Kingdom*, p. 551, it is stated—'The locust trees of the West Indies (*Hymenæa Courbaril*) have long been celebrated for their gigantic stature; and other species are the *Colossi*, of South American forests.' Martius represents a scene in Brazil, where some trees of this kind occurred, of such enormous dimensions, that fifteen Indians, with outstretched arms, could only embrace one of them. At the bottom they were 84 feet in circumference, and 60 feet where the boles became cylindrical. By counting the concentric rings of such parts as were accessible, he arrived at the conclusion that they were of the age of Homer, and 332 years old in the days of Pythagoras; one estimate, indeed, reduced their antiquity to 2052 years, while another carried it up to 4104, from which he argued that the trees cannot but date far beyond the time of our Saviour. Other famous trees have been known of enormous bulk and great antiquity, one of which (*Dracæna Draco*) has been described in the Glossary.

[1] For some of the information contained in this chapter as regards the Eucalypti and Acacias in Victoria, I am indebted to a map, showing the distribution of forest trees, compiled for the State Forest Board by Mr. A. Everett, from the record maps in the office of the Surveyor-General, A. J. Skene, Esq., and other authentic sources, under the direction of R. Brough Smyth, Esq., late of the Mining Department. The notes by Baron von Mueller are interesting, and the map would be of great use to tourists who take an interest in the vegetation of Victoria.

W. R. G.

which has for its western boundary the north-eastern telegraph line, extending from Seymour to Wahgunyah, a rough idea will be given of the vast territory in which the stringy-bark is found, spreading over large tracts, and forming dense forests. This is particularly to be observed in the districts extending southward from Chiltern and Beechworth, following the Yarra track, and occupying the mountain ranges in the centre of the colony. In higher elevations it often forms nearly the whole of the arboreal vegetation, while, in lower situations, its forests are frequently interspersed with the messmate. The stringy-bark is found in many other parts of Victoria, but the territory indicated shows the localities where it occurs in the greatest profusion. Where the stringy-bark becomes less dense in eastern Victoria, it is compensated for by other indigenous trees, the box-gum (*Eucalyptus melliodora*), for example, and by, occasionally, the lightwood, or more properly speaking, blackwood (*Acacia melanoxylon*).

On the Mitchell, Tambo, Latrobe, and Macalister Rivers in Gippsland, Eucalyptus trees are very plentiful. The species called 'box' is found in the vicinity of most rivers, usually on knolls and in undulating country with a clayey soil. On the Avon and at Cape Liptrap, wattles (Acacias) abound. Along the Goulburn, and in the district which that river waters, towards the north of eastern Victoria, the box, and red and white gums (*Eucalypti melliodora, rostrata, and leucoxylon*), are found in patches, but the 'stringy-bark' is most plentiful, and forms the principal timber. There are occasional groups of sheoak (*Casuarina stricta* and *C. suberosa*) and Murray pine (*Frenela rhomboidea*) in the district; the former are common near the coast. Again, east of Melbourne, near the 'Yan Yean,' in the north, to Cranbourne in the south, red and white gums prevail. Throughout eastern Victoria, 'ironbark' (*Eucalyptus leucoxylon*—rough-barked variety), 'lightwood,' and native honeysuckle (*Banksia*) are found in various localities. In western Victoria, save in the central range, the country is less mountainous, and in the northern parts large treeless plains are of frequent occurrence. The 'stringy-bark' holds its own in the mountain ranges, and is abundant near some parts of the coast. The 'lightwood' is found in large patches on the range stretching from Mount Ida (Heathcote) to Lake Cooper (Corop), and also in the localities of Campbellfield, Rodney, Kilmore, and in the south-west near Branxholme, Hamilton, and towards Portland Bay. Ironbarks are found on many ranges, in the vicinity of various gold-fields. They are plentiful around Dunolly, Tarnagulla, Whroo, Redcastle, and Talbot; in fact, they are met with in patches throughout Victoria generally. Sheoaks are largely distributed over many portions of the colony; they are numerous in the Port Philip district, especially at Geelong and also at Western Port. Along the banks of the river Loddon, and the left bank of the Murray for nearly its whole length, gum-trees of various kinds, particularly the 'box-gum,' so often mentioned, and the myall Acacia (*A. homalophylla*) are abundant, stretching out into the plains in belts or in clumps. In a vast portion of north-western Victoria, which may be roughly marked on the map by drawing a line from the extreme east of Dimboola, north to Lake Victoria, and again obliquely north from Dimboola to the Murray at Swan Hill, immense tracts of waste land occur, principally covered by the well-known 'mallee-scrub,' which is composed of nine or ten species of dwarf Eucalypti, but especially *Eucalyptus dumosa*, combined with the myall, desert pine, and other trees. In the open parts of these scrubs, particularly near the large lakes and watercourses, the desert pine (*Frenela* or *Callitris*) sometimes occupies considerable areas, whilst as the scrub becomes more open towards the south, in the neighbourhood of Horsham, sheoaks are prominent. From the foregoing brief outline, it will be seen that the 'stringy-bark' is by far the most numerous of the indigenous Victorian Eucalypts.[1] Next come the 'box,' 'messmate,' and ironbark gums; then the sheoaks, 'lightwood,' wattles, Murray pine, and native honeysuckle, in order. Many species of Eucalyptus, besides those specially mentioned, are found in the districts between the extreme north and the extreme south of the colony. The species called 'box' is represented all over Victoria, patches of it being found even in the heart of the mallee scrub-country. The mallee occupies a territory, almost to the exclusion of the other

[1] Of this genus, foremost in point of beauty for floral effect, is the *Eucalyptus ficifolia*, which bears large bunches of bright scarlet flowers. It is a native of Brokes Inlet, Western Australia. This magnificent plant, when in full bloom, is one of the most gorgeous objects possible to conceive. Seen in the distance, it appears like masses of fire. A red flowering variety of *E. calophylla*, red gum of Port Gregory, is also very beautiful. The same might be said, however, of the 'flame tree' (*Sterculia acerifolia*) of Queensland and New South Wales, which, in many parts of those colonies, but especially of the latter, the Illawarra district, for instance, is very plentiful. When met with in the brush-lands, a single specimen presents an almost dazzling effect; but when seen '*en masse*' at a distance, from the mountain slopes, it is indeed a glorious sight. Its splendid display of colour is often enhanced by the refreshing green of the foliage of other trees, and perhaps by a background of far distant mountains suffused with that bluish vapour which renders the scenery peculiarly charming.

trees previously mentioned, where it exists in dense scrubs, covering enormous tracts of country, almost impenetrable except by the aid of the bushman's brush-hook. The messmate is principally found in large quantities in eastern Victoria, in company with the stringy-bark (hence its common name); but it is also scattered over various districts in western Victoria. The sheoaks are most common in the latter, near the coast-line, but are also found in other localities. The ironbarks are found in patches in certain parts of the colony, especially in elevated situations, near auriferous districts. The wattles and the native honeysuckle are found both in high and in low regions, being well distributed; the latter is numerously represented near Portland. The lightwood and Murray pine are more locally confined, but sometimes occupy large areas of country. Two other species of Eucalyptus, not previously mentioned,—*Eucalyptus Stuartiana*, the apple tree; and *Eucalyptus viminalis*, the manna gum,—are also very plentiful on light, moist, sandy soils, usually near the coast. The latter species, often locally known as the peppermint, frequently forms an intermediate link, as it were, between the soil on which the gums—red and white—are found, and the scrubland. A good illustration of this may be seen by striking across from Dandenong, Cranbourne, or Berwick, towards the coast, in the direction of Western Port, Frankston, or Schnapper Point. The Tasmanian blue-gum (*Eucalyptus globulus*) is plentiful in the Otway and Bass ranges, where it attains great perfection; it is found also, in a stunted form, in the Western Port district.

In Tasmania much magnificent scenery occurs; but there is, perhaps, no vegetation in Australia to surpass in richness and picturesque effect that of the brush-lands of northern New South Wales and Queensland. Where it is found in its pristine grandeur it would delight the most unimpressive; and as it approaches the mountains its magnificence increases. No lover of nature, however unacquainted with botany he may be, can fail to admire the effect produced by a gigantic Moreton Bay fig,[1] with its huge winding spurs standing out from it on every side. In some of the spaces between the buttresses, a score or more of persons might find concealment. A Moreton Bay, chestnut (*Castanospermum australe*), a Jambosa a Flindersia, or perhaps a native plum (*Achras*), is often almost absorbed within its trunk. *Nelitris ingens*, the 'scarlet scrub myrtle,' whose branches sometimes bend with the weight of brilliant fruits, clustered among oblong, vividly-green leaves, presents a glorious contrast with the golden-yellow blooms of the Queensland cigar Cassia (*C. Brewsteri*), having flowers quite as bright as those of the Laburnum, which it somewhat resembles. Specimens of the Bangalo palm (*Ptychosperma (Seaforthia) elegans*),

---

[1] The frontispiece of this work is from a sketch by the author, and was published some years ago in the *Sydney Mail*. It represents a specimen of the Moreton Bay fig (*Ficus macrophylla*), as seen at Cudgen, Tweed River, which is between fifty and sixty miles from Brisbane. The extent of the growth of this remarkable tree may be inferred from the relative size of the men at its base. The tropical character of the surrounding vegetation, consisting principally of cabbage palms, Cycas, Zamias, tree-ferns, cedar trees, etc., clothed with Dendrobium, Cymbidium, and other orchids, together with epiphytal ferns, the whole interlaced with climbers, amidst a rank undergrowth of pretty dwarf shrubs, will convey, by the sketch, some idea of the luxuriance of the natural scenery in parts of northern New South Wales and Queensland.

cabbage palm (*Livistona* (*Corypha*) *Australis*),[1] and walking-stick palm (*Areca monostachya*), together with tall tree-ferns of great beauty, covered with orchids, shade with their fronds the shining Laurus, the richly-scented Eupomatia, the waxy-flowered Hoya, and native Convolvulus.

Epiphytal ferns, the 'stag-horn,' 'elk-horn' (*Platyceriums*), and 'bird's nest' (*Asplenium*), grow upon the stems of the tallest trees, and are suggestive of the capitals on a colonnade. These stems are sometimes clad with *Pothos longipes*, or festooned with lawyer palm (*Calamus Australis*). The tall cane called *Flagellaria indica* is frequently drawn up to a height of more than 100 feet, embellishing and diversifying the scenery. Huge climbers, such as *Wistaria megasperma, Lonchocarpus, Derris, Ripogonum, Tecoma, and Passiflora Banksii*, like mighty cables, bind one tree to another, and help to form with their foliage, at more than 150 feet overhead, a screen through which sunbeams rarely pierce.

In the summer season, richly coloured beetles and butter-

---

[1] The geographical limits of this magnificent palm in Victoria have hitherto been but imperfectly known; but while the first edition of this work was going through the press, I received a communication from the renowned explorer, A. W. Howitt, Esq., of Bairnsdale, Gippsland, who, in a letter dated 27th May 1878, says: 'I am not aware that the cabbage palm occurs in any other part of Gippsland than at Mount Raymond, that is, at Cabbage-tree Creek, the source of which rises in that mount. I have not met with any elsewhere in the country, east of the Snowy River, nor have I heard of any other place in Victoria where it is to be found.'

Another authority, Mr. Vavaseur, of Rigby Island, Gippsland Lakes, has also since informed me that at the place indicated by Mr. Howitt, he has frequently seen this noble palm growing to a height of from 100 to 150 feet, and towering majestically above the myrtle and other indigenous trees surrounding it.   W. R. G.

flies may be seen upon the undergrowth, apparently enjoying the pleasant perfume of musk, emitted from a species of *Cucumis*, while the region bird, rifle bird, and green pigeon sometimes paint the scene with their gorgeous plumage. At night, myriads of fireflies flit to and fro, and with the phosphorescent fungi upon decaying wood, impart to those sylvan wilds a brilliancy and splendour which it is impossible to describe. Among the more showy of the flowering and fruiting trees and shrubs which grace the brush-lands of New South Wales and Queensland, a beautiful tree of the myrtle family (*Syzygium Moorei*), and a few others, deserve special mention. The Syzygium (which is a useful wood) is called by the natives 'durabbe.' When in full bloom, its effect in the scrubs is truly charming; portions of the stem, together with the whole of the upper branches, are literally clad with deep crimson flowers, which, viewed from the ground, have the appearance of rich velvet. *Pithecolobium grandiflorum* is often a grand sight when decorated with its scarlet blossoms, as from the length of their stamens they are suggestive of scarlet fringe.

The large vermilion fruits of *Lactaria calocarpa*, and those of *Elæocarpus grandis*, which are blue, seen in the foliage above, or profusely scattered under foot, always attract the attention and please the eye as it roams through those wildernesses of beauty. There is a bouquet-like display of colour even in the fruits themselves. The fruits of *Acronychia Baueri* are white and berry-like, and hang in ponderous masses from the branches; those of the 'bat-and-ball tree' (*Endiandra*), which sometimes grows to more than 100 feet in height, are bright scarlet, and resemble cricket balls; whilst those of the native plum (*Achras*), which are dark purple, vie with the others in richness of tint. The contrast thus afforded often calls forth the admiration of the spectator. These, among many other trees, the red and white cedars, rosewood, etc., profusely ornamented with parasites and epiphytes, grow to a great height, and support the heavy veil of climbers, which defies the sun's rays. There are bits of primeval forest scenery in Australia which, perhaps, could rival that of some of the Brazilian forests in richness. The traveller along a mountain track in parts of New South Wales and Queensland may sometimes stand on the crest of a commanding hill and witness a valley beneath him having the appearance of a picturesque lawn, firm, and inviting to the foot, dotted with a profusion of flowers, and studded with trees, whose apparently short stems are nearly hidden by the lavish verdure around them. A breeze will sometimes sweep down this smiling valley, and the waving sea of vegetation be ruffled under its influence. Bold, rugged, precipitous ridges upon either side frequently rise, tier above tier, and present truly magnificent pictures. As one descends the rocky declivities, clothed with trees and shrubs, the foliage of which is of almost every shade of green, he discovers that the seemingly compact lawn, seen from the uppermost craggy spurs, is simply a canopy spreading over many acres, and composed of trumpet jasmine (*Tecoma jasminoides*), Wonga Wonga vine (*Tecoma Australis*), *Derris scandens*, and other climbers of similar habit and equally robust growth. These climbers are supported by lofty Eucalypti, Ficus, sassafras (*Doryphora*), and 'beefwood' (*Stenocarpus*) trees, which tower up from the vale beneath. But farther down the ledges, past groups of Panax, Achras, Angophora, bangalo, and cabbage palms, forming a second terrace; down past the tree-ferns—*Dicksonia* and *Alsophila*, which often exceed thirty feet in height, their cool green fronds afford yet another canopy in these tortuous ravines, which are strewn with boulders of all sizes, either glassy from the constant dripping of the abundant moisture, or covered with mosses and lichens. Dwarf ferns and kindred plants luxuriating in the richest soil, and enjoying shade and humidity, nestle in a dense undergrowth, amidst decayed trunks of huge trees, either prostrate in picturesque confusion, or clasped by the interminable coils of climbers, often thicker than a man's body, which lend their beautiful blossoms to deck the emerald carpet hundreds of feet above. Such are examples of the primeval grandeur of the vegetation in some parts of Australia, and could anything of the kind be more delightful? Of the beauties of Australian vegetation no more need be said to induce students of botany, or lovers of the picturesque, to make tours during their holidays through the uncultivated parts of this interesting continent. There can be no doubt that as the facility of communication with Europe and America increases year by year, the vast botanical resources of the Australian colonies generally, must keep pace in development, and the beneficence of nature in this favoured land, already so rich in wool and gold, will be shown as much in the commercially valuable productions of its vegetable kingdom.

GLOSSARY.

APPENDED is a short account of every plant mentioned in the foregoing lessons, alphabetically arranged according to their common names. It was no part of the design of this elementary work that a botanical description of the plants enumerated should be included. By giving, as is done, the botanical name and the name of the natural order to which each plant belongs, the teacher or student is readily enabled to refer to more extended works on descriptive botany, in order to obtain that technical information which could not possibly be compressed within the limits of this book. The main object of the glossary is to give a short description of each plant alluded to in the *lessons*: preference in point of length being conceded to those indigenous to Victoria or Australia generally. Many of the plants mentioned in lists—'Principal plants of economic value,' 'Wild plants around Melbourne,' and 'Chapter on Australian Vegetation'—are not described in this glossary. It is hoped, however, that the manner in which the facts are collated will render it a comparatively easy task for the teacher to select therefrom plenty of materials for object lessons.

A

Acacia.—Pp. 20, 54, 190. See also WATTLE, BLACK WATTLE, GOLDEN WATTLE, SILVER WATTLE, and BLACKWOOD or LIGHTWOOD (*Acacia melanoxylon*). The genus Acacia comprises some 300 species. The flowers appear in dense, mostly yellow, clusters or racemes, loading the air with a most delicious perfume. The seeds of most of the Acacias require soaking in hot water for some time before sowing, to assist early germination. The tallest growing Australian Acacia is the 'Blackwood' or 'Lightwood,' which often attains a height of sixty or seventy feet. Besides being a highly ornamental tree, the timber is useful for furniture and implements requiring toughness. Many of our Australian species yield a valuable gum almost equal to Gum Arabic.

Achras.—See chapter 'Australian Vegetation,' pp. 89, 91.

Acorn.—GLANS or NUT of OAK (*Quercus*). (Natural Order, CUPULIFERÆ.) Pp. 25, 51, 195. The Oak is not indigenous to Australia, but has been extensively planted in the different colonies, and may therefore be considered a common tree, though the warmth of the climate prevents the British species from attaining the majestic proportions to which it reaches in its native country. The commercial value of the Oak, and the conspicuous part which it has borne in the history of Britain, render it an object of national interest. The Oaks constitute a numerous family, distributed over a wide geographical range. The Northern hemisphere has a liberal share of different kinds. Other species are found in Java, the uplands of Mexico, South America, and Southern Europe. In cool climates—that of Great Britain, for example—the Oak grows to a great size, and is highly esteemed for its valuable timber and astringent bark, the latter being used by tanners, and for medicinal purposes. In Victoria, however, the scorching heat and hot winds stunt the growth and cut off the leaders, where the trees are in exposed situations. The Oak loves a loamy soil, with a fair proportion of chalk. It sends its gigantic roots deeper in search of nourishment than other trees; hence in England a towering, umbrageous Oak may often be seen side by side with a withered-looking Ash or Elm. Oaks are either deciduous or evergreen; and of varying heights, thickness of stem, and hardness of timber. It may here be remarked that the term 'Oak' has been very inaptly—in fact ridiculously—applied by the early Australian settlers; notably in the case of the various species of *Casuarina*, which are commonly called 'sheoaks.' The Cork Oak (*Quercus suber*), a native of Southern Europe, produces the well-known cork of commerce. The Valonia Oak (*Quercus Ægilops*) is very extensively cultivated along the shores of the Mediterranean. The acorn-cups of this tree produce tannin in large quantities, and of a superior quality. Oak galls, principally obtained from *Quercus infectoria*, a native of the Levant, are used in the manufacture of ink. They are excrescences caused by the punctures of an insect. Such exudations, often of a large size, may frequently be seen on the Victorian Black Wattle. In Japan the leaves of the Silkworm Oak (*Quercus serrata*) support a coarse silkworm (*Bombyx Yamanai*). Many of the North American Oaks are highly prized, not only for their commercial value, but also for the picturesque variety of tint given to the landscape in autumn by their changing foliage. At Fernshaw, and in the

Dandenong ranges, there are some fine specimens of the only indigenous Victorian representative of the *Cupuliferæ* (the order to which the Oak belongs), namely, the Native Beech or Myrtle (*Fagus Cunninghamii*). The spot is a favourite one with visitors, from the imposing appearance of these trees. Some of them exceed sixty feet in height; they are thickly clothed with foliage; their trunks, covered with epiphytal ferns, affording coolness and shade to the vividly green fronds of the tree-ferns flourishing beneath. Some fair specimens of the Oak family are to be seen in many of our public gardens.

African Corn Lily.—IXIA. (Natural Order, IRIDEÆ.) P. 17.—A beautiful genus of bulbous plants, bearing spikes of delicate, various-coloured flowers. A large number of garden varieties are in cultivation.

Amaryllis.—(Natural Order, AMARYLLIDEÆ.) Pp. 17, 46. —A genus of pretty bulbous plants, bearing brilliant trumpet-shaped flowers. The Belladonna Lily (*Amaryllis belladonna*), with pink and white blossoms, is a common and favourite representative of the order. The general idea that the last-mentioned plant is exceedingly poisonous is an erroneous one, arising from the similarity of its specific name to that of the Deadly Nightshade (*Atropa bella-donna*).

Apple.— PYRUS MALUS. (Natural Order, ROSACEÆ.) Pp. 43, 50, 184.—The Crab Apple represents this fruit in its wild, uncultivated state. The numerous varieties produced by assiduous care and cultivation are known throughout the world. The Apple is a very hardy tree, growing nearly as far north as latitude 62°. It thrives best, however, in temperate climates. The wood is highly valued, for its close grain and great hardness, by turners, cabinetmakers, and wheelwrights. The tree grows freely in temperate Australia, particularly in the cooler districts.

Apricot.—PRUNUS ARMENIACA. (Natural Order, ROSACEÆ.) Pp. 43, 51, 53, 184.—Some doubt exists as to the native place of this luscious fruit. Its excellent qualities, however, have caused its general cultivation; and it is a common article in Australian markets.

Araucaria.—(Natural Order, CONIFERÆ.) P. 23.—A handsome genus of coniferous, evergreen trees, widely distributed. The magnificent Norfolk Island pine (specimens of which are so common in Australian gardens) belongs to this genus. The Bunya Bunya (*Araucaria Bidwilli*) of Queensland is another species. The timber of the last-mentioned tree is of great commercial value; its seeds form a staple article of food with the aborigines. *Araucaria Cunninghamii* is commonly known as the Moreton Bay Hoop Pine. The timber is largely exported for flooring-boards. Unlike most of the true Pines, which seem able to adapt themselves to almost any climate, the Araucarias thrive only within certain degrees of temperature. For instance, *Araucaria imbricata* will not grow to any great size in the vicinity of Melbourne, while at Ballarat and in the upland districts of Victoria it succeeds remarkably well. *Araucaria Brasiliensis* (the Brazilian Monkey Puzzle) is rarely seen in cultivation in Australia. It is a magnificent tree in the forests of tropical Brazil. *Araucaria Cooki* (Captain Cook's Pine), and *Araucaria Rulei*, both handsome trees, are natives of New Caledonia.

Artichoke.—CYNARA SCOLYMUS. (Natural Order, COMPOSITÆ.) Pp. 54, 182.—A hardy perennial, naturalized and readily cultivated in Victoria.

Arum.—SNAKE LILY. (Natural Order, AROIDEÆ.) Pp. 30, 35, 188.—An ornamental plant with very acrid leaves and roots.

Ash.—FRAXINUS. (Natural Order, JASMINEÆ.) Pp. 25, 29, 54, 194.—A deciduous tree, with very tough and elastic wood, which is largely used for hoops, oars, coach-building, tool handles, agricultural implements, etc. *Fraxinus Ornus* (Manna ash) yields the Manna sold by druggists. Some of the Australian Gum-trees, particularly *Eucalyptus viminalis*, emit from their leaves a sweet and palatable substance called Manna (*Melitose*), said to be exuded by small insects which feed upon the juices of the leaves.

Australian Bottle-Tree. — STERCULIA (BRACHYCHITON). (Natural Order, STERCULIACEÆ.) Pp. 53, 193. —The generic name of this tree is less known than its common name of Bottle-tree, given to *Sterculia diversifolia* and *Sterculia rupestris* on account of the peculiar shape of their swollen trunks. The bark, when macerated in water, produces a lace-like bast, which has been converted into ropes, cordage, and coarse paper. The Victorian Bottle-tree (*Sterculia diversifolia*) is well known by the aboriginal name of 'Kurrajong' in East Gippsland. The natives manufacture fishing lines and nets from the bark. A sweet, gummy, edible substance exists between the inner bark and the wood. In New South Wales it is generally known as the 'Kurrajong tree,' where it is often felled for stock when pastures fail, and is therefore valuable as a fodder plant. At the Kurrajong Mountains in New South Wales it is called the 'Rattle-trap tree,' on account of the loud rattling noise made by the long racemes of hard woody seeds, capsules, or pods being brought into contact when shaken by the winds. The roots, bark, young shoots, and foliage are readily eaten by stock of all kinds, and their mucilaginous contents are no doubt nutritious. The blacks also make use of the pith and roots of this tree as food.

Australian Colchicum. — BURCHARDIA UMBELLATA. (Natural Order, LILIACEÆ.) Pp. 17, 207.—A common and attractive bulbous plant, bearing umbels of white, star-shaped blossoms. It may be found in profusion in our meadows during early spring.

Australian Virgin's Bower. — CLEMATIS. (Natural Order, RANUNCULACEÆ.) Pp. 18, 196.—The Native Supplejack or Virgin's Bower (*Clematis aristata*) is the species most frequently met with in Victoria. It grows along the coast line on rocky declivities, and reaches to sub-alpine heights. In the moist ravines and fern gullies of Victoria it is found in the greatest perfection, making its way to the tops of the tallest trees, clothing them with a dense canopy of foliage, and drooping in graceful festoons from the branches. The small-leaved Virgin's Bower (*Clematis microphylla*), called in South Australia 'Old man's beard,' is an attractive, soft-wooded climber, chiefly found on the banks of creeks and rivers, and along the coast line, where it grows with such luxuriance as occasionally to completely cover the other vegetation. This species is common to all Australia and Tasmania.

B

Bamboo.—BAMBUSA. (Natural Order, GRAMINEÆ.) P. 19.—This genus of gigantic grasses thrives tolerably in Victoria, but not so well as in New South Wales, Queensland, and South Australia. In their multifarious uses, they supply to the people of the countries in which they are indigenous, the place of the Cocoa-nut with the South Sea Islanders, and the Date Palm with the Arabs. The plant commonly cultivated in Victorian gardens under the name of Bamboo is of the genus *Arundo ;* it belongs to the Reed family, and is not therefore a true bamboo. Its proper name is the Danubian Reed (*Arundo donax*). In New South Wales it is thoroughly naturalized, and is known as 'Spanish Reed.' It is useful as a 'breakwind,' and its rapid growth renders it effective in a very short time after planting. An established plantation of this reed could be burned off easily when cattle were starving for green food, and in a very few weeks it would furnish an enormous amount of succulent shoots per acre.

Bangalo Palm.[1] — SEAFORTHIA. (Natural Order, PALMÆ.) Pp. 24, 92.—The generic name now most in use is PTYCHOSPERMA. This noble plant is unquestionably one of the grandest and most graceful of the Palm tribe. In tropical Australia the indigenous species may be found towering to a height of 100 feet. Their feathered fronds, waving in the breeze, have a magnificent appearance. *Seaforthia elegans* is perhaps the most beautiful of all. *Seaforthia robusta* is found at Illawarra, New South Wales, where it grows to a height of 150 feet. These tall Palms are of great value in landscape gardening where the climate admits of their growth, as by judicious grouping they impart a charming effect to the scenery.

Banksia.—NATIVE HONEYSUCKLE. Pp. 42, 204.

Barley. — HORDEUM. (Natural Order, GRAMINEÆ.) Pp. 3, 182.— From the facility with which this useful

[1] Sometimes written Bangalow.

grain adapts itself to the vicissitudes of clime and temperature, it can be cultivated over a wider geographical range than any other cereal, reaching its greatest perfection, however, in the temperate zone. Many valuable varieties have been produced by careful cultivation. The barley grass (*Hordeum murinum*), which is a fair fodder plant as long as not in seed, is said to be the principal foster plant of the dreaded 'red rust.'

Bat and Ball Tree.—ENDIANDRA VIRENS. (Natural Order, LAURINEÆ.) See chapter 'Australian Vegetation,' p. 91.

Bay Tree.— LAURUS NOBILIS. (Natural Order, LAURINEÆ.) P. 30.—This beautiful evergreen shrub is a native of Southern Europe, where it ranges from 20 to 60 feet in height, but persistently retains its shrubby habit; a fact accounted for by its very free production of suckers. The leaves have a peculiar but agreeable aromatic taste, and are largely used for culinary purposes. An oil is obtained from the berries, both by boiling and expression. It must not be confused with the plant generally grown in Australian gardens as the Laurel. The latter belongs to quite a different order—Rosaceæ. See Laurel.

Bean. — FABA VULGARIS. (Natural Order, LEGUMINOSÆ.) Pp. 2, 51, 54, 182.---This very common and useful vegetable belongs to the sub-order Papilionaceæ (butterfly-flowered), so named from the shape of its flowers. It is an annual, growing to a height of between 3 and 4 feet.

Beet.—BETA VULGARIS and B. CICLA. (Natural Order, CHENEPODIACEÆ.)

Bird's Nest Fern.—ASPLENIUM NIDUS. (Natural Order, FILICES.) See chapter 'Australian Vegetation,' p. 90.

Black Wattle,[1] p. 198.—(Natural Order, LEGUMINOSÆ.) —(The 'Green Wattle' of New South Wales.) ACACIA DECURRENS. P. 54.

Blackwood, p. 194 **(Lightwood).**—ACACIA MELANOXYLON. See chapter 'Australian Vegetation,' p. 85.

Blechnum.—(Natural Order, FILICES.) See chapter 'Australian Vegetation,' p. 80.

Borage.—BORAGO OFFICINALIS. (Natural Order, BORAGINEÆ.) P. 29.—A rough-leaved, hardy annual, bearing pretty cerulean-blue flowers. The leaves possess great refrigerent properties. The well-known 'Forget-me-not' and the prickly Comfrey—*Symphytum asperrimum*—are each of this order, and closely related to the Borage.

Box Gum.—EUCALYPTUS MELLIODORA. (Natural Order, MYRTACEÆ.) See chap. 'Australian Vegetation,' p. 85.

Brewer's Hop.—HUMULUS LUPULUS. (Natural Order, URTICEÆ.) Pp. 55, 182.—A hardy, twining perennial, affecting the banks of rivers and watercourses, and partial to rich alluvial soils. The plant has been in cultivation for centuries for the sake of its *strobile* or cone (composed of a number of scales), which is the Hop of commerce. The plant thrives well in many parts of Victoria, particularly in Gippsland and on the Upper Yarra, where it is extensively cultivated at the aboriginal mission stations and other places. The Hop is a staple product of Tasmania, where it is grown in quantities, and to great perfection.

Bunya Bunya.—ARAUCARIA BIDWILLII. (Natural Order, CONIFERÆ.) P. 23.—A splendid timber tree of South Queensland, where it forms dense forests. It is generally found on the banks of rivers and on mountain

---

[1] The Black Wattle of New South Wales is *Callicoma serratifolia*.

slopes near the coast. It is considered one of the finest of the Araucaria tribe, and in its native regions attains an approximate height of 200 feet. The wood is utilised for furniture and planking. The Bunya Bunya withstands drought better than most of the genus, and flourishes luxuriantly in and around Melbourne, Sydney, and Adelaide. Many very fine specimens exist in the public and private gardens. See also Araucaria.

Burnet Rose.—ROSA SPINOSISSIMA. P. 67.

Butcher's Broom.—RUSCUS ACULEATUS. (Natural Order, LILIACEÆ.) Pp. 31, 32.—This curious plant belongs to the Asparagus tribe (*Asparagæ*), a sub-order of the Liliaceæ. It is a great favourite in shrubberies, from its compact habit, pretty angular foliage, and bright red berries. It is also called the Knee Holly.

Buttercup.—RANUNCULUS. (Natural Order, RANUNCULACEÆ.) Pp. 3, 54, 196.—A large family of herbaceous plants, principally noted for extreme acridity of root and leaves, and beauty of flower in some species. They are widely distributed. Some of them are aquatic plants, such as the Water Celery (*Ranunculus sceleratus*) and Water Crowsfoot (*Ranunculus aquatilis*), both natives of Britain. The beautiful Ranunculi of the florists are varieties of *Ranunculus Asiaticus*. The order is very common in Australia. See Native Buttercup.

Butterfly Flag.—DIETES (IRIS) BICOLOR. (Natural Order, IRIDEÆ.) P. 17.—This beautiful perennial bears large sulphur-hued flowers, the petals having a singular dark-brown circular spot, such as may often be noticed on the wings of a moth or butterfly. It is common in Australian gardens, and is a native of the Cape of Good Hope.

C

Cabbage.—BRASSICA OLERACEA. (Natural Order, CRUCIFERÆ.) Pp. 41, 54, 182.—This common and useful vegetable has by cultivation been increased to numerous varieties. Kale, Broccoli, Brussels Sprouts, Cauliflowers, etc., have sprung from this species.

Cabbage Palm.—LIVISTONA (CORYPHA) AUSTRALIS. (Natural Order, PALMÆ.) Pp. 24, 90.—This magnificent Palm has been found on the borders of Gippsland, and is therefore the only Victorian representative of its tribe. It is principally met with in the valleys and deep ravines of tropical Australia, where it occasionally attains a height of 120 feet. In Illawarra, also at the Bellenger, Clarence, Richmond, Brunswick, and Tweed Rivers, New South Wales, it is very common. The young, undeveloped leaves are eaten by the Queensland natives, who term the plant 'Konda.' When fully grown, the leaves resemble large fans; they are very tough, easily split, and are worked into baskets, hats, and similar articles.

Cactus.—(Natural Order, CACTACEÆ.) P. 19.—A large family, comprising some very grand and strange specimens. Some varieties are common in Australian gardens. The common Prickly Pear (*Opuntia vulgaris*), which grows freely here, belongs to this tribe. Several species of Opuntia have become naturalized in New South Wales and Queensland, and are fast becoming a widely-spread nuisance in some districts. Birds diffuse the seeds, and they soon spread so as to render rich pasture areas impassable and useless. To prevent great loss or expense, proprietors should destroy the evil in the bud, by digging up the young plants, and burying them in deep pits or water holes, as the succulent stems and branches, if merely cut down, will retain life, and make roots and fresh growth.

Caladium.—(Natural Order, AROIDEÆ.) Pp. 30, 35.—This beautiful genus is largely cultivated in gardens and hothouses, principally for the rich colouring of the leafage, which is of a heart-shaped or arrow-headed form. The Caladiums are natives of most warm countries, and notwithstanding their acrid and poisonous qualities, some kinds are used as food by the Polynesians and other islanders. Taro, a principal article of food amongst the natives of the South Sea Islands, is made from the root-stocks (*rhizomes*) of Caladium (*Colocasia*) esculentum, and *Caladium macrorhizum*. Both of these plants are semi-aquatic, and are largely cultivated by the natives, who plant the roots on the banks of running streams, where they are generally left for a period ranging from nine to fifteen months, until the root-stocks have become large. The process of cooking removes their pungent acridity, and renders them as agreeable to the accustomed palate as good bread. They are then baked in native ovens by the islanders, in the same manner as the bread-fruit, and beaten into a doughy mass called 'Poe,' of which the natives consume enormous quantities. The missionaries generally boil the roots for their own use.

Camellia.—(Natural Order, TERNSTRŒMIACEÆ). P. 28.—These exquisitely beautiful plants, indigenous to China, Japan, Borneo, and the Himalayas, are now almost universally cultivated. The Tea plant (*Camellia Bohea*, synonym *Thea chinensis*) belongs to this genus. Numerous double-flowered varieties have been, and are, continually being produced by hybridization. At the present day their name is legion. The Camellia thrives exceedingly well in Australia, and is common in gardens of any pretensions. The leaves of several kinds are largely used in the adulteration of tea.

Cane. — CALAMUS. (Natural Order, PALMÆ.) See chapter 'Australian Vegetation,' p. 90.—A very numerous tribe of climbing Palms. Two or three species occur in Australia. Some species of the Cane are of infinite use for constructing articles of domestic utility, and supply the place of rope to junks or sailing vessels of some countries.

Cape Broom.—GENISTA CANARIENSIS. (Natural Order, LEGUMINOSÆ.) P. 35. — A pretty, free-flowering shrub, indigenous to the Canary Islands, and chiefly grown as a hedge plant.

Cape Wattle.—ALBIZZIA LOPHANTHA. (Natural Order, LEGUMINOSÆ.) P. 34. — A handsome pinnate-leaved shrub or small tree, generally cultivated as a shelter plant. It is of rapid growth, and suited to dry and exposed situations. It is better known as Acacia lophantha, and is often called the Crested Wattle, from the shape of its flowers. It is indigenous to Western Australia, and is principally found near the coast. Probably the name 'Cape Wattle' arose through the plant having been first brought to New South Wales half a century ago from the Cape of Good Hope, having been previously introduced there from Swan River, and become naturalized.

Cape Weed.—CRYPTOSTEMMA CALENDULACEA. (Natural Order, COMPOSITÆ.) Pp. 32, 34, 201. — This weed, which has proved such a pest in many parts of Victoria, was, a few years ago, introduced from the Cape of Good Hope as a fodder plant. It is an annual, flowering in the spring, and giving at that season a bright golden hue to the fields. Wherever it has obtained a footing it has proved destructive to other herbs and grasses, and though, before the flowering season, it affords a nutritious food for stock, it dies off in the middle of summer, after ripening its seeds, leaving the fields quite bare. It is believed to be a good fertilizer when buried.

Carrot.—DAUCUS CAROTA. (Natural Order, UMBELLIFERÆ.) Pp. 38, 43, 182.—This very common vegetable needs no description. Its juice is sometimes used to colour cheese, like the extract of Arnatto.

Cassia.—(Natural Order, LEGUMINOSÆ.) P. 54.—A numerous tribe of trees and shrubs, with handsome pinnate foliage and fragrant yellow flowers. In some species the blossoms are white, or of a purple tint. A few kinds are annuals. Nearly thirty species are found in Australia, including the Queensland Cigar Cassia (*Cathartocarpus Brewsteri*), which is perhaps the most attractive of the genus. In South Australia the commonest species are *C. eremophila* and *C. heterolobia*.

Cassinia.—(Natural Order, COMPOSITÆ.) See chapter 'Australian Vegetation,' p. 81.

Castor Oil Plant or '**Palma Christi.**'—RICINUS COMMUNIS. (Natural Order, EUPHORBIACEÆ.) Pp. 3, 30, 188.— A native of India, but flourishing in most warm countries where it has been introduced. Though only an annual or biennial in England, where it is cultivated for its beautiful foliage, in more suitable climates it becomes arborescent, lasting for a number of years, and attaining from 15 to 20 feet in height. The Australian climate is very favourable to its growth. Castor Oil is obtained from the seeds. A good sample of this oil was prepared for the Paris Exhibition from seeds of plants grown in the Melbourne Botanic Gardens. In New South Wales the Castor Oil plant has long since become so thoroughly naturalized, that in some districts, especially on the alluvial soils of some of the northern and eastern rivers and creeks, it has obtained possession, and monopolizes, as a weed, rich land that has been neglected for years. It is easily cultivated, and requires but moderate skill and capital to establish a plantation. As a crop it would certainly prove more profitable than Maize. The plant was known to, and its medicinal properties valued by, the people of ancient Egypt 4000 years ago, and is mentioned by Herodotus and other Greek as well as Roman writers of classic eras. The plant is more widely known under the old name of 'Palma Christi' than by any other.

Cauliflower.—See Cabbage. Pp. 35, 182.—BRASSICA OLERACEA. (Natural Order, CRUCIFERÆ.)—This common and useful vegetable has by cultivation been increased to numerous varieties. Kale, Broccoli, Brussels Sprouts, Savoy, Red Cabbage, etc. etc., have all sprung from this species.

Celandine. — CHELIDONIUM MAJUS. (Natural Order, PAPAVERACEÆ.) P. 30.—A small British plant, the leaves and stem of which yield a yellow, acrid juice, sometimes used by oculists, and said to have the power of removing warts. It has become naturalized in some parts of New South Wales.

Celery Pine. — PHYLLOCLADUS. (Natural Order, CONIFERÆ.) P. 30. — A fine timber tree, of slender habit, ranging from 60 to 70 feet in height, and chiefly found near rivers and in dense forests. The Tasmanian species (*Phyllocladus rhomboidalis*) furnishes good masts and spars. The New Zealand species, known as the Pitch Pine (*Phyllocladus trichomanoides*), is similarly utilised.

Cheesewood, p. 194.—See Pittosporum; also chapter 'Australian Vegetation,' p. 82.

Cherry.—PRUNUS CERASUS. (Natural Order, ROSACEÆ.) Pp. 25, 38, 43, 51, 53, 184.—A native of Britain. The present numerous varieties are supposed to have sprung from two species only. The value of this fruit is too well known to need comment. The hard and tough wood is largely used for cabinet-work, walking-sticks, pipe-stems, etc. Many varieties of this tree flourish in Australia.

Chilli. — CAPSICUM ANNUUM. (Natural Order, SOLANEÆ.) P. 53.—A well-known annual, bearing red or yellow pods, from which, when dried, Cayenne pepper is prepared.

Chinese Hawthorn. — PHOTINIA SERRULATA. (Natural Order, ROSACEÆ.) P. 38.—Also known as the Chinese Maybud—a beautiful shrub, bearing a profusion of white blossoms. Common in our plantations.

Cinnamon. — CINNAMOMUM ZEYLANICUM. (Natural Order, LAURINEÆ.) P. 187.—This species, from which the supply of Cinnamon bark is chiefly obtained, is a small tree, with bright, glossy leaves. It grows very abundantly in Ceylon. India possesses several species of Cinnamomum, one of which (*Cinnamomum tamala*) also grows in Queensland. *Cinnamomums zeylanicum* and *laurifolium* succeed very well in parts of Queensland and New South Wales, and fairly in the neighbourhood of

Melbourne. The Camphor-tree (*Laurus camphora*) belongs to this order.

Climbing Polypody. — POLYPODIUM SCANDENS. (Natural Order, FILICES.) See chapter 'Australian Vegetation,' p. 80.

Club Lilies. — CORDYLINE AND DRACÆNA. (Natural Order, LILIACEÆ.) Pp. 22, 191.—An extensive genus of palm-like plants, having generally clean erect stems, and round tufted heads of sword-shaped leaves. They produce a profusion of odoriferous flowers, variously white, blue, purple, and lilac, and globular berries of various colours. Many varieties are found in Australia and New Zealand, and, in fact, in most warm countries. In the latter country they are very plentiful, some of them attaining a height of 40 feet. The Maoris manufacture a kind of cloth from the fibre of the leaves. The nearest relation in South Australia to these Club Lilies is *Dianella revoluta*, with narrow very tough leaves, two to three feet long, having blue flowers and blue berries. It is found very frequently about the base of trees and shrubs from the coast to moderate elevations. The South Sea Island varieties of Cordyline are famous for the brilliant colouring of their foliage. The green kinds are largely employed in Australian ornamental gardening for producing a tropical effect. The roots of some species are roasted for food by the natives. They are frequently termed Palm Lilies—a very appropriate name. Mountain slopes, deep gorges or ravines, and the banks of rivulets, are the favourite localities of these plants. The coloured-leaved varieties of our greenhouses and conservatories are among the most beautiful of the tribe.

Cocoa-nut Palm. — COCOS NUCIFERA. (Natural Order, PALMÆ.) Pp. 23, 184.—This magnificent palm, the fruit of which has rendered it known throughout the world, is found fringing the coral beaches of the South Pacific Islands, often in barren, sandy places, washed by the spray of the ocean, in spots where scarcely any other vegetation will grow. It is cultivated in most tropical countries. Every part of this noble tree is of use in one way or another. In advantageous situations it grows to a height of over 100 feet, with a girth of from 3 to 6 feet. Its tender leaf-buds are often eaten by sailors, hence the name Sailors' Cabbage.

Columbine.—AQUILEGIA. (Natural Order, RANUNCULACEÆ.) P. 53.—A tribe of hardy herbaceous, perennial plants, principally found in cool climates, bearing singular, yet beautiful flowers.

Convolvulus.—(Natural Order, CONVOLVULACEÆ.) Pp. 19, 203.—A well-known and extensive family of climbing or trailing plants, variously annual or biennial, and remarkable for their beautiful trumpet-shaped flowers. 'Morning Glory' is another common name. *Convolvulus erubescens* is common in Victoria, New South Wales, and South Australia, and is easily distinguished by its small pink flowers and very changeable leaves.

Corn Leaf.—COTYLEDON ORBICULATA. (Natural Order, CRASSULACEÆ.) P. 32.—A succulent shrub, indigenous to the Cape of Good Hope. The leaves are reputed to possess the virtue of removing corns.

Correa.—NATIVE FUCHSIA. Pp. 19, 29, 30, 37, 49, 55, 197.

Cotton Wood.—SENECIO BEDFORDI. (Natural Order, COMPOSITÆ.)—See chapter 'Australian Vegetation.'

Crocus.—(Natural Order, IRIDEÆ.) P. 17.—A large family of bulbs, flowering in early spring. Cultivation has produced countless kinds, of great beauty and wide diversity of hue.

Cucumber.—CUCUMIS SATIVUS. (Natural Order, CUCURBITACEÆ.) Pp. 53, 185.—A common plant, the qualities of which are well known. Several ornamental species are found in the brush lands of New South Wales and Queensland. In South Australia a species (*Cucumis microcarpa*) overruns fields and gardens, and dry beds of watercourses; and is a very noxious weed. Its fruits and leaves have such an unpleasant and very strong scent, that animals will not touch them.

Currant.—RIBES. (Natural Order, SAXIFRAGEÆ.) Pp. 53, 185.—The black, white, and red varieties of this pleasant fruit are largely cultivated in Tasmania, the gullies of the Mount Lofty Ranges near Adelaide, and Victoria. The plant grows freely from cuttings of the ripened wood. It is a native of Britain and other cold countries.

Cycad.—Embracing the genera CYCAS. Pp. 2, 55. ZAMIA, MACROZAMIA, etc. (Natural Order, CYCADEÆ.) —The genus Cycas, pp. 2, 55, better known as 'Fern Palm' or 'Sago Palm,' comprises the most noble specimens of the order. There are about 50 species, indigenous to the tropical and sub-tropical regions. In Japan a very ornamental variety (*Cycas revoluta*) is used for the sake of its pith, which yields a kind of sago. *Cycas circinalis*, in its native localities, grows to a height of 20 feet. A similar kind of sago is obtained from its stem. Many fine specimens are found in New South Wales, Queensland, and Western Australia, where they grow to 30 or 40 feet in height, presenting a most imposing appearance. *Macrozamia Denisonii* is one of the best known, and the finest of the Australian species. The Queensland Nut Palm (*Cycas media*)—the Baven of the aborigines—ranges in height from 10 to 20 feet; it is generally found near the coast. The nuts of this plant are often macerated by the natives in a running stream, and subsequently in stagnant water. The produce is then converted into a paste, which, when baked, is highly relished by them. The Cycads are very closely allied to the Conifers.

Cypress.—CUPRESSUS. (Natural Order, CONIFERÆ.) Pp. 29, 55, 194.—An extensive genus of handsome evergreen trees and shrubs, highly esteemed for ornamental planting, and also for the excellent timber they furnish. They are of very rapid growth in Australia. Some of the Californian species have been known to make leading shoots of 4 or 5 feet in a year, notably the Monterey or Citron Cypress (*Cupressus macrocarpa*).

D

Daffodil. — NARCISSUS PSEUDO-NARCISSUS. (Natural Order, AMARYLLIDEÆ.) Pp. 17, 49.—A tribe of pretty flowering bulbs, in general cultivation.

Dahlia.—(Natural Order, COMPOSITÆ.) P. 17.—A very handsome genus of bright flowering plants, brought by careful cultivation to great perfection. Some magnificent species of Tree Dahlias have lately been discovered. These throw up stems to a height exceeding 12 feet, lasting for several seasons. Unlike the common Dahlia, which dies down every year, the flowers of the tree Dahlia are single, generally white, and somewhat funnel-shaped.

Daisy.—BELLIS. (Natural Order, COMPOSITÆ.) P. 34. —This favourite perennial is well known. The cultivated kinds produce double flowers.

Dandelion.—TARAXACUM. (Natural Order, COMPOSITÆ.) Pp. 32, 34, 54, 188.—A very common weed, naturalized in almost every civilised country, and very abundant in Australia. The root is used medicinally. The Cape Weed (*Cryptostemma*) is very often mistaken in Victoria for the Dandelion.

Danubian Reed.—See pp. 17, 101, 191, and Glossary, 'Bamboo.'

Date-palm.—PHŒNIX DACTYLIFERA. (Natural Order, PALMÆ.) Pp. 64, 185.

Derris. — (Natural Order, LEGUMINOSÆ.) See chapter 'Australian Vegetation,' p. 90.

Desert Pine.—See chapter 'Australian Vegetation,' p. 85; also Glossary, 'Murray Pine.'

Digger's Delight. — VERONICA PERFOLIATA. (Natural Order, SCROPHULARINEÆ.) P. 30. — A pretty, blue-flowering shrub, with smooth stem-clasping leaves; found in the mountainous districts of Victoria and New South Wales, and deriving its common name from a supposition that its presence indicated auriferous country. It is plentiful in the elevated gold regions of Australia. A beautiful white-flowering species, with bright green serrated leaves (*Veronica Derwentiæ*), occurs in Fern gullies in Victoria and on moist hillsides in the Mount Lofty Ranges, Adelaide, notably along the banks of the Onkaparinga. It deserves cultivation for its really ornamental appearance. There are between seventy and eighty species and varieties indigenous to New Zealand.

Dock. — RUMEX. (Natural Order, POLYGONACEÆ.) Pp. 30, 42, 204. — A numerous genus, extensively dispersed, particularly in cool climates. There are about eight known kinds in Australia, some of which have been introduced. The roots of some species are used in medicine, the leaves of others as a vegetable; an excellent dentifrice is prepared from the powdered roots. It is sometimes inaptly called '*Wild Rhubarb.*'

Dogwood. — PROSTANTHERA LASIANTHOS. (Natural Order, LABIATÆ.) See chapter 'Australian Vegetation,' p. 79.

Doodia. — (Natural Order, FILICES.) See chapter 'Australian Vegetation,' p. 80.

Dragon's Blood Tree. — DRACÆNA DRACO. (Natural Order, LILIACEÆ.) P. 191.—An account of a most remarkable specimen of this plant — the famous Dragon Tree of Teneriffe, believed to be the oldest tree in the world, and destroyed during a storm in 1867 — may be found in any standard work on descriptive botany. Red gum, called 'Dragon's Blood,' is obtained from this Dracæna. The plant thrives remarkably well in the Melbourne Botanic Gardens, which contain some young but healthy specimens. The Dracæna Draco is not to be confused with the Dragon's Blood Palm (*Calamus Draco*), which also produces a red gum, used as a varnish by artists. The latter plant is now included in the genus Dæmonorops, and the gum is obtained from its ripe fruit. Many species of dwarf Dracænas or Cordylines, with variegated and coloured foliage, are cultivated in conservatories; and there are several tall-growing species common in Australian gardens, such as Dracæna or Cordyline Australis, C. Forsteri, and

C. nutans, etc. The roots of most of these contain starch, and are edible. The general name of this genus is '*Palm Lily*,' but in the South Sea Islands it is known as the 'Ti-tree,' the ti being pronounced tea or tee, hence the mistake often noticed in various Australian publications of writing ti-tree for tea-tree, the latter name having been first given to a species of Melaleuca or Leptospernum (*Myrtaceæ*), by Captain Cook, on one of his first voyages of discovery, his crew having employed its leaves as a substitute for tea. It may be remarked that the natives of Sumatra and other islands of the Malayan Archipelago also use as a substitute for tea, the leaves of an allied plant—*Glaphyria nitida*— 'Tree of long life,' which they also call tea-tree. The so-called Australian tea-tree is much employed in the colonies for making rough brooms, and for roofing plant sheds, etc.

Durabbe.—SYZYGIUM MOOREI. (Natural Order, MYRTACEÆ.) See chapter 'Australian Vegetation,' p. 91.

E

Edging or Border Box.—BUXUS SEMPERVIRENS. (Natural Order, EUPHORBIACEÆ.) Pp. 30, 194.—The dwarf variety of this plant is well known throughout civilised countries from its very extensive use in forming edges or borders to flower-beds, especially to those laid out in the formal, or geometric style. The Box Tree varies in height from 3 to 30 feet. The wood is hard, heavy, and close-grained; and these characteristics, combined with its light colour, cause it to be esteemed by engravers beyond all other woods. Trials of various colonial woods recently made by the writer lead to the hope that it is possible to find an Australian wood which will answer for all except the finest line engraving, thus supplying a great want, for boxwood is both scarce and expensive.

Eel-Grass or Spring-plant.—VALLISNERIA SPIRALIS. (Natural Order, HYPOCHARIDEÆ.) P. 64.—A curious grass-like aquatic found in rivers, lakes, etc. The spiral flower-stalks, which are sent up sometimes from a great depth, resemble the springs of a carriage lamp, hence the common name 'Spring-plant.' The name Eel-grass is probably applied from the fact that eels either feed on, or shelter themselves under the leaves.

Elæocarpus.—(Natural Order, TILIACEÆ.) See chapter 'Australian Vegetation,' p. 91.

Elder.—SAMBUCUS. (Natural Order, CAPRIFOLIACEÆ.) Pp. 38, 185.—A well-known shrub or tree, the bark and leaves of which are used in medicine; the berries, besides producing elderberry wine, are frequently used to adulterate port wine.

Elderberry Ash. — PANAX SAMBUCIFOLIUS. (Natural Order, ARALIACEÆ.) P. 29.—A very handsome shrub, or small glossy-leaved tree, with pinnate foliage; chiefly found in the underwood of deep forest glens and rich mountain slopes of Victoria, New South Wales, and Tasmania. From its resemblance to the common Mountain Ash—or Rowan Tree—(*Pyrus aucuparia*) it is known in some parts by the former name. The wood, which is light, yet tough, is used by splitters for making axe handles.

Elkhorn Fern. — PLATYCERIUM ALCICORNE. (Natural Order, FILICES.) Pp. 59, 90.—This singular but beautiful epiphytal fern is indigenous to temperate Australia. It, however, extends farther to the southward, and is more common in New South Wales. Some hundreds of fine specimens exist in the Melbourne Botanic Gardens; those growing on the British Oak rivalling those on the Moreton Bay Fig, though the latter tree is certainly the more favourable to their growth in a natural state.

Elm.—ULMUS. (Natural Order, URTICEÆ.) Pp. 25, 194.—An extensive genus of large trees, chiefly valuable for their timber, and in Australia, for shade and avenue planting; the cool, green, umbrageous foliage of these deciduous trees affording a grateful shelter from the fierce glare of the summer sun. The common Elm (*Ulmus campestris*), a valuable tree, attains great longevity. It is this tree which is principally used in Victoria for avenues, etc. The American Elm (*Ulmus Americana*) has much the same appearance as the English species, but its leaves are larger. The Cork Elm (*Ulmus suberosa*) is so named from a corky excrescence produced on its trunk and branches. The Wych Elm (*Ulmus montana*) is the only species indigenous to Scotland.

Ergot of Rye.—CLAVICEPS PURPUREA. (Natural Order, FUNGI.) P. 59.—A fungus belonging to the above-named order, principally attacking rye, but occasionally other grasses. It is very destructive to the crop on which it makes its appearance, and is poisonous.

Eupomatia.—(Natural Order, ANONACEÆ.) See chapter 'Australian Vegetation,' p. 90.—Commonly called Moreton Bay Scrub Jasmine, on account of its delicious perfume.

F

Fan Palms. — CHAMÆROPS AND CORYPHA. (Natural Order, PALMÆ.)—The name Fan Palm is principally applied to the genus Chamærops, but occasionally to Corypha (*Livistona*). Pp. 25, 90. The latter has already been mentioned under the head of Cabbage Palm. The Chamærops is found farther north than any other member of the Palm family. It comprises about a dozen kinds. The Hemp Palm (*Chamærops excelsa*), one of the finest of its tribe, succeeds well in Victoria.

Fennel.—FŒNICULUM VULGARE. (Natural Order, UMBELLIFERÆ.) Pp. 38, 187.—Native of temperate Europe and Western Asia; a tall rank-growing perennial, the stems rising to about 6 feet in height. It grows wild around Melbourne, having escaped from cultivation. Besides its medicinal properties, it is used for culinary purposes.

Fieldia.—(Natural Order, GESNERACEÆ.) See chapter 'Australian Vegetation,' p. 80.

Fig. — FICUS. (Natural Order, URTICEÆ.) Pp. 17, 28, 89, 185.—The history of the Fig dates from the earliest period. Besides the cultivated Fig (*Ficus carica*), which is a deciduous tree, there are nearly 600 species, many of them evergreens. Such are the Moreton Bay Fig (*Ficus macrophylla*), so well known in the gardens of Australia by its noble appearance and dark glossy leaves; the Banyan Tree (*Ficus indica*), India-rubber Tree (*Ficus elastica*), and many others. Of the Australian species, the most remarkable for their huge size are *Ficus macrophylla* and *Ficus Cunninghamii*. The roots of these two species extend for a considerable distance along the surface of the ground, forming abutments large enough to conceal twenty or thirty persons when standing erect.[1] The girth of some of these

---

[1] The frontispiece to this work represents one of these giants of the forest, sketched from the living specimen by the writer, at Cudgen,

trees exceeds 80 feet. The thickened sap of the Moreton Bay Fig is converted into a kind of India-rubber. The fruit of another Queensland species — the Cluster Fig (*Ficus glomerata*)—is edible.

Firethorn Nightshade. — SOLANUM PYRACANTHUM. (Natural Order, SOLANEÆ.) P. 30.—A beautiful purple-flowered shrub, indigenous to Madagascar. The leaves and branches bear numerous reddish-brown spines: the former are covered with a downy substance. There are several species of Nightshade indigenous to the Australian colonies, and many of which are notoriously poisonous.

Flagellaria.—(Natural Order, LILIACEÆ.) See chapter 'Australian Vegetation,' p. 90.

Flame Tree. — STERCULIA (BRACHYCHITON) ACERIFOLIA. (Natural Order, STERCULIACEÆ.) Pp. 30, 53, 87, 191. — One of the most magnificent trees in existence, bearing a profusion of scarlet coral-like racemes of flowers, and large bright green leaves. The bark, which, like that of most of the tribe, is composed of concentric layers, yields by maceration a lace-like bast of fine texture, which can be converted into cordage, ropes, mats, etc. The tree is found on many parts of the eastern coast of Australia; seldom far inland. In the Illawarra district, fifty or sixty miles south of Sydney, it is very plentiful. Commencing at the Macleay River, it is found in the brush lands of most of the northern rivers of New South Wales—

Tweed River, on the borders of Queensland and New South Wales, in 1871. The surroundings give a faithful representation of the spot where this enormous *Ficus macrophylla* was growing, and will furnish some idea of the exuberant vegetation of the brush lands. See chapter 'Australian Vegetation,' p. 88.

the Bellenger, the Clarence, the Richmond, the Brunswick, and the Tweed. On the banks of some of the Queensland rivers it may occasionally be found. For several weeks during the summer season this tree presents a most gorgeous sight. From the splendour and profuseness of its bloom it derives its common name. At Illawarra the finest specimens occur. When in flower one could imagine portions of the landscape to be on fire. The foliage sheds itself to give room for the profuse inflorescence. The Lasiopetalums (*Velvet-flower*) belong to this order. One of the tallest growing *Lasiopetalum Tepperi*—a most beautiful shrub with pink flowers—attains a height of 5 or 6 feet, and is found at Yorke's Peninsula, South Australia.

Fringe Lilies.[1] — THYSANOTUS and ARTHROPODIUM. (Natural Order, LILIACEÆ.) Pp. 35, 49, 207. —These pretty, purple-flowered, fleshy-rooted perennials are very abundant throughout Victoria and other parts of Australia, imparting a purple tinge to grass lands during spring and the early part of summer. A white-flowered species (*Arthropodium cirrhatum*), which is very beautiful when in full bloom, is found in New Zealand. One of the Victorian species (*Thysanotus Patersoni*) is a slender twiner, and is often found ascending young Gums and Wattles. It is also very plentiful on moist heath grounds.

Fuchsia.—(Natural Order, ONAGRARIEÆ.)—This beautiful plant, numerous varieties of which are common in Australian gardens, has been fully described in Lesson VI. Pp. 19, 38, 40, 43, 48, 49, 53, 55, 56, Plate V. p. 37. Of the New Zealand Fuchsias, *Fuchsia excorticata* grows

---

[1] These genera are often known under the name of *Fringe Violet* in Victoria, New South Wales, and Tasmania.

to 30 feet in height. Its flowers are of a dark purplish red. It is commonly found in the damp forests.

Fungus.—Pp. 57, 59.—Applied to a large family of flowerless plants (Fungi), including mushrooms, toadstools, mould, mildew, smut or rust in corn, and the excrescence, known as Punk, on Gum trees. The Fungi have by some eminent botanists been divided into more than a dozen natural orders. There are 600 genera and between 4000 and 5000 described species. Many of the diseases affecting plants and animals are caused or accompanied by species of Fungi. There is yet much to learn in this branch of botany. Some of the Fungi present very beautiful forms when viewed under the microscope. By far the greater proportion are of a poisonous nature; but some, as the Mushroom and the Truffle, are used as food or as condiments.

G

Garden Celery.—APIUM GRAVEOLENS. (Natural Order, UMBELLIFERÆ.) Pp. 38, 182.—A well-known esculent. Cultivation has removed certain poisonous qualities peculiar to the plant in its wild state.

Garden Parsley.—PETROSELINUM SATIVUM. (Natural Order, UMBELLIFERÆ.) Pp. 38, 183.—A common biennial herb, largely used for culinary purposes.

Garden Sage.—SALVIA OFFICINALIS. (Natural Order, LABIATÆ.) P. 18.—A small shrub, in extensive use as a pot-herb.

Giant Gum.—EUCALYPTUS AMYGDALINA, var. REGNANS. (Natural Order, MYRTACEÆ.) See chapter 'Australian Vegetation.'

Gleichenia.—(Natural Order, FILICES.) See chapter 'Australian Vegetation,' p. 80.

Golden Wattle. — ACACIA PYCNANTHA. Pp. 35, 54, 198.

Gooseberry.—RIBES GROSSULARIA. (Natural Order, SAXIFRAGEÆ.) Pp. 52, 53, 185.—A popular fruit, of which there are many varieties. This shrub flourishes best in cold climates; but though it adapts itself to warmer regions, the fruit produced under the latter circumstances, though larger, is inferior in flavour. In the locality of Ballarat, however, very fine gooseberries are grown.

Gourd. — CUCURBITA. (Natural Order, CUCURBITACEÆ.) Pp. 53, 185.—There are several species of this plant under cultivation, amongst others the Snake Gourd (*Trichosanthes anguina*), Pumpkin Gourd (*Cucurbita Pepo*), Viper Gourd (*Trichosanthes colubrina*), and many other kinds, grown either as edible, or for domestic use, or ornament.

Grape Vine. — VITIS. (Natural Order, AMPELIDEÆ.) Pp. 18, 53, 185.—The common Grape Vine (*Vitis vinifera*), one of the species of the family, is cultivated in all suitable climates; the description of wine produced from the grapes greatly varying; some districts being celebrated for a heavy, full-bodied vintage, while others are as famous for wines of a lighter character. Soil, climate, and many other circumstances are studied by vinegrowers in making choice of varieties suitable to particular localities; and when long in cultivation in a particular spot, a vine has been known to become changed in character from the circumstances just mentioned. Vine culture is one of the staple industries of Australia, and the growth of the grape in these colonies is continually the subject of pamphlets and newspaper articles. The vines of Tabilk, the Murray and Hunter districts, and numbers of other Australian localities, have achieved a European reputation.

Grass Lily.—(Natural Order, LILIACEÆ.) Pp. 17, 206. —This name is indiscriminately applied to two genera of Liliaceous plants, natives of Australia. One (*Arthropodium strictum*) is a tall perennial, bearing panicles of purple flowers. It is plentiful in the fields around Melbourne; the other (*Cæsia vittata*) is a pretty, blue-flowered, dwarfish plant, quite as common as the Arthropodium. Two species of the latter—*A. paniculatum* and *A. minus*—are common in some parts of South and West Australia.

Grevillea.—(Natural Order, PROTEACEÆ.) Pp. 42, 53, 171.—A very large genus, comprising some interesting and beautiful Australian flowering shrubs and trees. Nearly 200 species have been described, all, with one or two exceptions, indigenous to Australia, and two-thirds of that number belong to Victoria. They are chiefly admired and cultivated for their flowers; some of them are of a dwarf heath-like habit; others are trees of a considerable size. The most noticeable is the 'Silky Oak' (*Grevillea robusta*), a grand timber-producing species, bearing large masses of comb-shaped orange flowers. It is a native of New South Wales and Queensland, where on rich alluvial river banks it often attains a height of over 100 feet.

Gum, or Eucalyptus.—(Natural Order, MYRTACEÆ.) Pp. 16, 18, 20, 26, 32, 40, 81, 85, 86, 87, 88, 195, 199.—Though it is to be regretted that a more appropriate common name than that of 'Gum tree' was not in the first instance bestowed upon this extensive family, comprising the principal timber and most stately trees of Australia, still the term has now become so widely spread that only partial success could be expected to attend any sudden attempt to alter it. Under its popular name, therefore, each species will be mentioned. The substance which exudes from the tree is known all over the world as 'Kino.' The Tasmanian Blue Gum (*Eucalyptus globulus*) is widely known, and is very common in Victoria.[1] It is a quick-growing tree, attaining in favourable situations a height exceeding 300 feet, and producing very hard and durable wood, in great request for shipbuilding, fencing, railway sleepers, and many other purposes, where toughness and staunchness in the material employed are indispensable. This tree has lately attracted considerable attention from its alleged power of counteracting malaria, and the weight of testimony goes to prove the truth of the statement. From this fact the Blue Gum is known in Southern Europe as the Fever tree. The Red Gum [2] (*Eucalyptus rostrata*) (the 'Blue Gum' of New South Wales) is common in Victoria and South Australia, and is principally found in low, moist situations. Its wood has been held by experts to be superior even to that of the Tasmanian Blue Gum for durability. The Jarrah (*Eucalyptus marginata*), native of West Australia, Ironbark (*Eucalyptus leucoxylon*), and Karri (*Eucalyptus diversicolor*), are also famed for their splendid timbers, which are valuable for jetty piles, shipbuilding, etc. The Stringy-

---

[1] The 'South Australian *Blue* Gum' is *Eucalyptus viminalis*, and is common in Victoria, where it is known as the 'Manna Gum.'

[2] The 'Red Gum' of New South Wales, known as such to the earliest settlers, which is by far their best wood for fuel, and the resinous gum of which is used for various purposes, is a species of *Angophora*, and is still one of the commonest 'Gum trees' on the north shore, etc., Sydney.

bark (*Eucalyptus macrorrhyncha*) and Messmate (*Eucalyptus obliqua*) are two of the tribe most plentiful in Victoria; and though their timber is not very durable, it is largely employed for fence rails, quartering, battens, shingles, palings, etc.; whilst the bark is used for roofing by the settlers, and also converted into pulp for the use of the upholsterer and papermaker. A volatile oil is distilled from Eucalyptus leaves, those of the BLUE GUM and GIANT GUM of the mountains being principally used for this purpose. The latter tree, it is said, has been known to attain the exceedingly great height of 400 feet, having a diameter approaching 23 feet. It is found in its most noble proportions in Gippsland. The Karri of Western Australia rivals the Giant Gum in height. The ALPINE GUM (*Eucalyptus alpina*) is a small but well-shaped shrubby specimen of the family, and is very hardy. The YELLOW BOX (*Eucalyptus melliodora*) is attractive to bees, from the quantity of nectar secreted by its flowers. Under the name Ironbark, four or five species of the Eucalypts are comprised, the principal of which are *Eucalyptus siderophloia* (New South Wales) and *E. leucoxylon*, common in several of the Australian colonies. In point of beauty, however, as distinguished from the towering height and stately appearance which mark other members of the family, the gorgeous SCARLET FLOWERING GUM (*Eucalyptus ficifolia*) stands without a rival.[1] This beautiful tree, a native of Broke's

[1] There is a scarlet flowering variety of *Eucalyptus calophylla* indigenous to West Australia which is very beautiful, and resembles in many respects the *Eucalyptus ficifolia*, but it is nevertheless quite distinct in colour of blossom and form of seed, though the capsules are almost identical. Young specimens of both may be seen in the Melbourne Botanic Gardens.

Inlet, Western Australia, is sometimes met with in groups or single specimens on the hill-sides, and frequently in the valleys. Its handsome tufted heads of bright scarlet bloom, in contrast with the dark green of the foliage, renders it a most attractive object in the landscape. There are upwards of 150 species of Eucalypts confined to Australia and some neighbouring islands, but none are known in New Zealand. For further particulars concerning this genus, see also chapter on 'Australian Vegetation.'

H

Hakea.—(Natural Order, PROTEACEÆ.) Pp. 26, 32, 42, 79, 204.—A very large, widely-spread genus, distributed throughout the Australian continent, and particularly plentiful in Western Australia. About one hundred kinds have been enumerated, all indigenous to this continent; of these a few only belong to Victoria. Eleven species are said to be found in South Australia. None of the tribe are remarkable for any special qualities, though all are objects of interest from a garden point of view, on account of their peculiar foliage, flowers, and seed-vessels. A few kinds are used as hedge plants in the bush. The genus is peculiar to Australia.

Hawthorn.—CRATÆGUS. (Natural Order, ROSACEÆ.) Pp. 35, 43.—The Hawthorn bears a fragrant flower, and is commonly known in England by the name of May or Hawberry, May being the month when the plant puts forth its fragrant white or pink blossoms. It grows freely in Australia, and is often used for hedges.

Hazel.—CORYLUS. (Natural Order, CUPULIFERÆ) Pp. 51, 53.—This genus comprises the Hazel, Filbert, and Cob-nuts, the latter variety including the well-known Barcelona Nut of commerce. They succeed well in the elevated districts of Victoria, New South Wales, and Tasmania, producing nuts of good quality in abundance.

Heliotrope.— HELIOTROPIUM. (Natural Order, BORAGINEÆ.) P. 29.—The Garden Heliotrope (*Heliotropium Peruvianum*) originally came from South America. It is also known as *Cherry Pie*, from the peculiar odour of its blossoms.

Holly.—ILEX. (Natural Order, ILICINEÆ.) P. 62.— A family of plants, about one hundred in number, peculiar to both tropical and temperate regions. The common Holly (*Ilex aquifolium*), a native of Europe, grows freely in Victoria. The Holly is a beautiful plant for hedges and ornamental purposes, its glossy green leaves contrasting most agreeably with its vivid scarlet berries. Birdlime is produced from its bark, and the wood is largely used for fine cabinet-work and ornamental turning. Some species are used in medicine.

Horse Chestnut.—ÆSCULUS HIPPOCASTANUM. (Natural Order, SAPINDACEÆ.) Pp. 30, 62.—A very stately tree, with umbrageous foliage, and pyramidal masses of flowers coloured yellow and red.

Hyacinth.--HYACINTHUS. (Natural Order, LILIACEÆ.) Pp. 17, 20.—A beautiful family of plants, in much request for ornamental purposes, producing delicate flowers. It is well known in the colonies, and is extensively cultivated.

Hymenophyllum.—(Natural Order, FILICES.) See chapter 'Australian Vegetation,' p. 80.

I

Indian Corn (Maize).—ZEA MAYS. (Natural Order, GRAMINEÆ.) Pp. 3, 20, 54, 183.—A native of America, but now cultivated for its useful grain in most warm countries. A tall, stout-growing plant, more resembling a cane than a grass, and reaching a height of over six feet, the stalks surmounted by thick heads or cobs of grain, contained in a sheath. Australia, particularly the northern and western parts of New South Wales, is well suited to its cultivation, and it is extensively grown in those districts. In Victoria it furnishes large quantities of green fodder for cattle, and is also cultivated as a grain crop in the Bairnsdale district.

Iris.—IRIS FLORENTINA, *'Fleur de lis.'* (Natural Order, IRIDEÆ.) Pp. 17, 189.—The rhizomes of this plant furnish the principal supply of orris-root, used by perfumers. It is the large, white-flowered Flag Lily of gardens, and is common in Victoria. This and a purple-flowered variety are also naturalized in New South Wales and South Australia. Notwithstanding the abundance of roots that could be propagated, they have never been turned to account in any of the colonies, and the supply of this root has still to be imported.

Iron Barks.—(EUCALYPTUS SIDEROPHLOIA, E. MELANOPHLOIA, E. CREBRA, AND E. LEUCOXYLON.) See chapter 'Australian Vegetation;' also Glossary, 'Gum.'

Ivy.—HEDERA HELIX. (Natural Order, ARALIACEÆ.) Pp. 14, 17, 43.—A native of Britain, but acclimatised and very abundant in Australia, where its dark, glossy, green foliage may be seen creeping over and hiding old walls, buildings, etc.

Ixia.—See 'African Corn Lily,' pp. 17, 97.

J

Japanese Anemone. — ANEMONE JAPONICA. (Natural Order, RANUNCULACEÆ.) P. 30. — An attractive herbaceous perennial, producing large, purplish-red flowers. A white-flowered variety is also cultivated in gardens.

Jasmine.—JASMINUM. (Natural Order, JASMINEÆ.) P. 29. — This order includes a large number of species, esteemed and largely cultivated for their beautiful and fragrant flowers, from which a valuable essential oil is obtained. There are many species in Australia; most of them prove hardy. They are variously woody climbers, or slender shrubs, producing flowers abundantly. The English Lilac, Ash, and Ligustrum or Privet belong to the same order.

Jerusalem Artichoke.—HELIANTHUS TUBEROSUS. (Natural Order, COMPOSITÆ.) P. 29.—The tubers of this plant, before the introduction of the potato into England, were used as food. It is now grown chiefly as an ornamental plant. Correctly speaking, it is not an artichoke, nor did it originally come from Jerusalem; thus affording another instance of the occasional ludicrous misapplication of common names.

Jonquil.—NARCISSUS JONQUILLA. (Natural Order, AMARYLLIDEÆ.) P. 49.—A pretty, rush-leaved, bulbous-rooted perennial, flowering early in spring. Many kinds blossom throughout the winter in New South Wales and Victoria.

K

Kangaroo Apple.—SOLANUM AVICULARE. (Natural Order, SOLANEÆ.) P. 53.—A handsome, bluish-purple flowered plant, indigenous to Victoria and most of the other Australasian colonies. It is frequently found on the banks of creeks and rivers, also in moist sandy soil, ascending to sub-alpine heights. It is also common around Melbourne. The plant is of very quick growth, and of shrubby habit. The first year it produces flowers and fruit in great abundance, the latter generally of a deep orange colour. After the first year it seems to become herbaceous; the branches die down to the ground, and are annually replaced by a fresh growth. The Gunyang (*Solanum vescum*) is another variety found in Victoria. The berries of the Kangaroo Apple, like most solanaceous plants, possess poisonous properties.

Kangaroo Grape.—VITIS (CISSUS) ANTARCTICA. (Natural Order, AMPELIDEÆ.) P. 30.—An evergreen, woody climber, with ovate glabrous leaves. It bears an abundance of black, globular berries, about the size of a currant. They are edible, but rather harsh. The plant is usually found on the banks of rivers, and is very common in parts of New South Wales. It is also found in the Moreton Bay district, Queensland.

Kangaroo Grass.—ANTHISTIRIA CILIATA. (Natural Order, GRAMINEÆ.) Pp. 17, 54, 208.—This strong, coarse grass grows to a height of 2 or 3 feet in suitable situations. It is indigenous to all parts of Australia, affording excellent pasture for cattle and horses. Mr. Bacchus, a recognised authority on our native grasses, says of it—' The finest and most useful of all indigenous grasses. Here (Victoria) it commences to vegetate early in November, when all stock should be taken away until it is in flower. From then until winter it proves an excellent fattening grass. It keeps green during the summer, but turns a little brown in autumn, when its nutritive qualities are at the highest. In the early days of the colony I have ridden the same horse twenty to forty miles daily, on a journey of several hundred miles, turning him out to graze on pasture of which this grass formed the principal part, and the horse kept his condition.'

Kidney Fern. — TRICHOMANES RENIFORME. (Natural Order, FILICES.) P. 30.—A pretty dwarf Fern, with thick, leathery, kidney-shaped leaves, a native of New Zealand. It is cultivated as a greenhouse plant in Australia.

Kidney Weed.—DICHONDRA REPENS. (Natural Order, CONVOLVULACEÆ.) P. 30.—A small, creeping herb, with kidney-shaped leaves and insignificant yellow flowers. It is very common throughout Australia, and is frequently met with at the butts of Wattles and other trees.

L

Lactaria.—(Natural Order, APOCYNEÆ.) See chapter 'Australian Vegetation,' p. 91.

Lantern Flower.—ABUTILON. P. 19.

Larkspur.—DELPHINIUM. (Natural Order, RANUNCULACEÆ.) P. 53.—These plants are cultivated for the beauty of their flowers. The common Larkspur (*Delphinium consolida*) is an annual, and is a great favourite in all cottage gardens. Some of the perennial kinds are very beautiful. The Monkshood belongs to this order.

Laurel. — PRUNUS LAURO-CERASUS. (Natural Order, ROSACEÆ.) P. 53.—This well-known evergreen shrub has no claim to the name under which it is generally known and cultivated in gardens. Its proper designation is Cherry Laurel, and as such it is always spoken of in medical works, etc. The plant thrives exceedingly well in Victoria, parts of New South Wales, and South Australia, especially in rich alluvial soil in the upland districts, where the frosts are not too severe, nor the hot winds too fierce. Its leaves, which are highly poisonous, are used for making cherry-laurel water.

Laurustinus.—VIBURNUM TINUS. (Natural Order, CAPRIFOLIACEÆ.) P. 38.—This handsome, free-flowering, evergreen shrub is now in general cultivation. It has a very effective appearance when planted singly on lawns or in shrubberies, and forms fine ornamental hedges.

Lavender.—LAVANDULA. (Natural Order, LABIATÆ.) Pp. 34, 187.—Three or four kinds of Lavender are cultivated in gardens as ornamental border plants, and for the sake of their leaves and flowers. Lavender succeeds well in many parts of Victoria. The climate of Phillip Island (Western Port), where it grows with great luxuriance, would be particularly suited to its cultivation for commercial purposes.

Lawyer Palm.—CALAMUS. (Natural Order, PALMÆ.) See chapter 'Australian Vegetation,' p. 90.

Lichens. — USNEA AND STICTA. (Natural Order, LICHENES.) See 'Lesson on Acotyledons,' p. 57.—Lichens are found upon almost all kinds of substances, and are considered injurious to fruit and other trees in orchards and plantations. About 3000 species, included in 60 or 70 genera, have been described.

Lightwood, p. 194.—See also chapter 'Australian Vegetation,' p. 85.

Lilac. — SYRINGA VULGARIS. (Natural Order, JASMINEÆ.) P. 35.—A well-known odorous shrub, acclimatised in Australia.

Lily.—LILIUM. (Natural Order, LILIACEÆ.) Pp. 17, 49. — The typical genus of the large and beautiful order to which it belongs. The most common garden species are: —Orange Lily (*Lilium bulbiferum*), common White Lily (*Lilium candidum*), Tiger Lily (*Lilium tigrinum*), Lance-leaved Lily (*Lilium lancifolium*), Golden-striped Lily, (*Lilium auratum*), Slender-leaved Lily (*Lilium tenuifolium*). There are others, less common, but equally beautiful.

Lily-Pillies or Lillipillies. — EUGENIA SMITHII. (Natural Order, MYRTACEÆ.) See chapter 'Australian Vegetation,' p. 82.

Lindsaya, p. 209.—(Natural Order, FILICES.) See also chapter 'Australian Vegetation,' p. 80.

Lonchocarpus.—THE LANCE-POD. (Natural Order, LEGUMINOSÆ.) See chapter 'Australian Vegetation,' p. 90.

Looking-glass Bush.—COPROSMA LUCIDA. (Natural Order, RUBIACEÆ.) P. 28.—An attractive, glabrous-leaved, pale-barked shrub, or small, much-branched tree, indigenous to New Zealand. Known by its common name in many Australian gardens. A congener (*Coprosma hirtella*), known as 'native Coffee,' occurs in many parts of Victoria and South Australia.

Loquat.—ERIOBOTRYA JAPONICA. (Natural Order, ROSACEÆ.) Pp. 53, 185. Also called Japan Medlar.— A straggling tree, with large serrated leaves; cultivated for its well-known fruit, which in Victoria ripens about the end of

November. In the neighbourhood of Sydney and farther north the Loquat is a very common fruit, and ripens from August to November.

Lotus Lily.—NELUMBIUM SPECIOSUM. (Natural Order, NYMPHÆACEÆ.) P. 30.—An aquatic plant found in Asia and Northern Australia—*the Sacred Lily of India*. The large and magnificent rosy-pink flowers of this plant are borne on stems which stand erect 2 or 3 feet above the water. The leaves, which are peltate, and rather more than 18 inches in diameter, have long petioles, and stand up parasol-like far above the flowers. The seeds are used as food, both raw and cooked, by the Chinese; they are wholesome, as are also the roots, which are used for food in India and by the natives of North Australia. It thrives in stagnant or still water, and blooms well in the Sydney climate. There are some magnificent specimens of this plant in the ponds of the Brisbane Botanic Gardens.

Lyonsia.—(Natural Order, APOCYNEÆ.) See chapter 'Australian Vegetation,' p. 80.

M

Magnolia. — (Natural Order, MAGNOLIACEÆ.) P. 30. —This order contains some of the most gorgeous and beautifully-flowered trees and shrubs. Several of the Magnolias, from their brilliant inflorescence, are termed Tulip Trees. There is one representative of the order indigenous to Australia—the native Pepper Tree (*Drimys aromatica*). Most of the Magnoliaceæ succeed well in the open air in Australia.

Maiden-Hair Fern. — ADIANTUM ASSIMILE AND

ÆTHIOPICUM. (Natural Order, FILICES.) P. 209. See chapter 'Australian Vegetation,' p. 80.

Maize.—See 'Indian Corn,' p. 130.

Mallee. — EUCALYPTUS. See chapter 'Australian Vegetation,' p. 87.

Mangrove. — RHIZOPHORA MANGLE. (Natural Order, RHIZOPHOREÆ.) P. 17.—This strange tree grows to a height of 40 or 50 feet, principally along the seashores of tropical countries, forming dense forests, commonly called Mangrove swamps. Its roots rise some feet above the ground, supporting the trunk, as it were, upon piles. An allied species (*Rhizophora mucronata*) is very plentiful along the coast of Queensland and North Australia. Our Native Mangrove (*Avicennia officinalis*), however, belongs to a different order, *Verbenaceæ*. It is an evergreen shrub, or small tree, growing to a height of from 10 to 20 feet; it is very common along several parts of the coast. It abounds on the shores of Western Port Bay; is found at the Clarence, Richmond, Brunswick, and Tweed Rivers, in New South Wales, and sometimes extends for miles along the creeks and inlets.

In South Australia it extends from Le Fevre's Peninsula, Torrens Island, along the eastern shore of St. Vincent Gulf to Port Wakefield. The wood is very hard and tough; it is used for underground purposes and waterworks. Like the true Mangrove, its bark is used in tanning. There is also another kind of Mangrove or pseudo-Mangrove generally found growing in company with Avicennia in New South Wales, and both have been looked upon as valuable for staying and consolidating the mud flats of tidal rivers and estuaries, and preventing the malarial effects of such localities in climates of too low a temperature for the true Mangrove to be made available. The pseudo-Mangrove alluded to is *Ægiceras majus*, and belongs to the order *Myrsineæ* or *Ardisiads*.

Manna Gum.—EUCALYPTUS VIMINALIS. (Natural Order, MYRTACEÆ.) P. 199. See chapter 'Australian Vegetation,' p. 88.

Marigold.—CALENDULA OFFICINALIS. (Natural Order, COMPOSITÆ.) P. 34.—Commonly called Pot Marigold. A well-known herb, bearing a bright yellow flower; common, and very hardy. Employed in cookery and for medicinal purposes. There are many hybrid varieties of this plant cultivated in gardens.

Melon.—CUCUMIS MELO. (Natural Order, CUCURBITACEÆ.) Pp. 53, 186, 187.—A very common plant, extensively cultivated in warm regions. The Rock and Water Melons are the best known kinds. The Water Melon (*C. citrullis*) is well known in Australia, and some of its varieties have become naturalised. The Cucumber (*Cucumis sativus*) and the Pumpkin (*Cucurbito pepo*) also belong to this natural order, and are largely grown in Australia, the latter particularly so in New South Wales, where some of its varieties are employed as fodder for cattle. The Pig or Pie Melon is found in quantities on the banks of the Murrumbidgee and other rivers.

Messmate.—See chapter 'Australian Vegetation,' p. 85; also Glossary, 'Gum.'

Mignonette.—RESEDA ODORATA. (Natural Order, RESEDACEÆ.) P. 35.—A common fragrant herb almost universally acclimatised, and a great favourite.

Mildew.—ERYSIPHE. See 'Fungus,' p. 57.

Mistletoe.—LORANTHUS. (Natural Order, LORAN-

THACEÆ.) Pp. 59, 200.—A true parasitical plant, chiefly found in forests. The Mistletoes, like most parasites, are indiscriminate in their selection of trees, and gradually destroy them. The genus is represented in Australia by about twenty species, some of them very beautiful, bearing scarlet flowers. They are generally found on the Eucalypts, Acacias, tea-tree, etc. Those curious bunches of leaves so often seen at the end of Gum-tree branches are well-developed specimens of this plant. One of the most common of the Australian Mistletoes is *Loranthus celastroides*, frequently found on the Sheoak or Forest-oak (*Casuarina*). The Mistletoe is troublesome in orchards and other plantations; apple and pear trees are particularly liable to become its hosts.

Moreton Bay Fig.—See Frontispiece; also Glossary, 'Fig.'

Moreton Bay Trumpet Jasmine.—TECOMA JASMINOIDES. (Natural Order, BIGNONIACEÆ.) P. 29.—A beautiful, glabrous, evergreen climber, common on the river banks of Queensland and New South Wales. It bears a profusion of trumpet-shaped flowers, generally of a delicate white or flesh colour, the centre being of a purplish crimson.

Moreton Bay Pine.—ARAUCARIA CUNNINGHAMII. (Natural Order, CONIFERÆ.) P. 23.—A magnificent timber tree, frequently met with on the banks of rivers at their confluence with the sea, but often found a considerable distance inland in the colonies of Queensland and New South Wales. Its timber is largely used for flooring-boards, etc. In favourable situations it reaches 200 feet in height. It is of quick, though erratic growth; sometimes making shoots 8 or 10 feet long during a season, without throwing out lateral branches; at others, branching at a distance of 2 or 3 feet.

Moss.—SPHAGNUM. (Natural Order, MUSCI or MOSSES.)

Pp. 7, 57.—Generally known as Bog Moss, from its peculiarity of growth, being the principal agent in forming the turf or peat found in bogs; its upper portions growing continually for indefinite periods, while the lower as continually die and decay. It is largely used for packing plants or cuttings, also in the artificial growth of orchids, especially those of aerial habit. Plants known as Mosses are of several natural orders. There are Scale-mosses, Split-mosses, Urn-mosses, and some even approaching to the fern tribes, as the Club-mosses or Lycopods.

Murray Pine. — FRENELA ROBUSTA. Variety, VERRUCOSA. (Natural Order, CONIFERÆ.) P. 55. See also 'Australian Vegetation,' p. 85.—This handsome evergreen tree, best known as the *Callitris verrucosa*, is a native of the desert regions of the Murray River, from which fact, combined with its appearance, it is sometimes called the desert Cypress. It attains from 60 to 90 feet in height, furnishing excellent timber and a kind of gum sandarac, producing excellent varnish.

Mushroom. — AGARICUS CAMPESTRIS. (Natural Order, FUNGI.) Pp. 7, 10.—The common Mushroom is found in a natural state in all parts of the world. It is abundant during spring and autumn, especially after mild showers of rain. It is also cultivated to a very great extent. It grows spontaneously and abundantly here and throughout Australia.

Myall.—ACACIA HOMALOPHYLLA AND A. PENDULA. P. 195. See also chapter 'Australian Vegetation,' p. 86.

Myrtle (Australian).—EUGENIA SMITHII AND E. MYRTIFOLIA. See chapter 'Australian Vegetation,' p. 82.

N

Nasturtium.—TROPÆOLUM. (Natural Order, Geraniaceæ.) P. 30. — The common Nasturtiums of the garden (*Tropæolums majus* and *minus*) are well-known annuals, bearing helmet-shaped flowers of different bright hues. The fruit is used as a pickle, and for other culinary purposes. It is also known as Indian Cress. The leaves are pungent and pleasant to the taste, and are often used as a salad.

Native Apple Tree.—EUCALYPTUS STUARTIANA. (Natural Order, Myrtaceæ.) See chapter 'Australian Vegetation,' p. 88.

Native Bower Spinach.—TETRAGONA IMPLEXICOMA. (Natural Order, Ficoideæ.) P. 30.—A trailing or climbing perennial plant, with ovate or more frequently rhomboid leaves. It is found in a wild state along the coast, trailing over rocks, or ascending shrubs, which it completely envelopes in a dense mass of leafage, the pendant stems having in many instances a pretty effect, forming natural bowers which, from the succulent nature of the leaves and branches, afford a cool and pleasant retreat in hot weather. The plant is very eligible for trailing over rockwork, or covering bowers and fences. This plant, like its congener, *Tetragona expansa*, is of some value as a drought-enduring pasture plant of a sodic and saline nature, in which it resembles the 'salt-bush,' and is therefore specially desirable for sheep, preventing fluke, etc. It will thrive in most arid regions. *Tetragona expansa*, although a native of Australia and found along the north - eastern coast almost as far as Carpentaria, is generally known as 'New Zealand Spinach' or 'Spinage.' It is cultivated in Victoria, New South Wales, and also in England as a culinary vegetable. The 'Bower Spinach' is also edible, and is a perennial. *T. expansa* is an annual.

Native Box. — EUCALYPTUS. See chapter 'Australian Vegetation,' p. 85.

Native Box-wood, Prickly Box, or Pouch-thorn.—BURSARIA SPINOSA. (Natural Order, PITTOSPOREÆ.) Pp. 19, 197.—A very common shrub, with blackish myrtle-like small shining green leaves, and dense spikes of white flowers followed by small fruits resembling a pouch or purse. The ends of the branchlets form sharp thorns, the more numerous the poorer the soil. It is found from the sea-coast to mountain ridges—on plains, in forests and scrubs, but never in swamps—in Victoria, South Australia (where it is also called 'Black-bush'), and parts of New South Wales, Queensland, and Tasmania.

Native Buttercup or 'Cocksfoot.'—RANUNCULUS LAPPACEUS. (Natural Order, RANUNCULACEÆ.) Pp. 54, 196.—This pretty perennial is very plentifully distributed throughout Victoria. It is found in moist, sandy flats, and ascends also to alpine elevations, being often found on the tops of the highest mountains. It is indigenous to other parts of Australia; a variety of it is common in New Zealand. Its flowers are of a bright yellow.

Native Celery.—APIUM PROSTRATUM. (Natural Order, UMBELLIFERÆ.) Pp. 38, 200.—A very common Australian herbaceous plant, usually found in moist places near the coast.

Native Cherry.—EXOCARPUS CUPRESSIFORMIS.

(Natural Order, SANTALACEÆ.) Pp. 39, 205.—A handsome tree of Cypress-like habit and appearance, its generic name derived from the kernel or seed being situated on a fleshy receptacle, hence the saying that the stone of the Native Cherry is outside. The timber, like that of all the order, is very close and beautifully grained; it is of a rich brown colour when polished, and affords one of the best species of charcoal for goldsmiths' work. It is also used for crayons. The branches of *E. cupressiformis* are stiff and upright, which distinguish it at once from the 'Desert Cherry' (*E. Sparten*), with slender pendant branches. The fruits of both are edible, but not so those of the shrubby leafless *E. aphylla*, which occurs in company with the preceding in the Mallee country. The tree is indigenous to Victoria and other Australian colonies.

Native Convolvulus.—IPOMŒA BONA-NOX. (Natural Order, CONVOLVULACEÆ.) See chapter 'Australian Vegetation,' p. 90.

Native Currant.—LEUCOPOGON RICHEI. (Natural Order, EPACRIDACEÆ.) Pp. 39, 202.—A struggling, rough-barked shrub, very frequent along the coast of extra-tropical Australia. It seems to thrive best on steep banks and rocky declivities. The berries, which are about the size of a currant, are edible. The wood is of a deep orange colour, very heavy, hard, and close-grained. It is useful for rustic work, and the knees of boats. The common name is also applied to *Coprosma Billardieri*, a small-leaved, myrtle-like shrub, which grows abundantly on the banks of rivers and creeks; it is very common on the banks of the Yarra. *Leptomeria acida* is the Native Currant of New South Wales, but it belongs to the order *Santalaceæ*.

Native Daisy. — BRACHYCOME. (Natural Order, COMPOSITÆ.) Pp. 32, 200.—A large genus of annual or perennial herbs, closely allied to the common Field Daisy (*Bellis*). *Brachycome multifida* has attractive purple flowers. It is indigenous to Victoria and New South Wales, and is found on the lowlands, and ascending to sub-alpine elevations. It may often be seen on the tops of mountains, where bush fires have occurred, carpeting the blackened and calcined surface of the earth with its bright green foliage and pretty flowers. *Brachycome iberidifolia* is known as the Swan River Daisy. In the hills near Adelaide, *B. diversifolia* —the diverse-leaved Brachycome—is very abundant in September and October. The flowers are rather large and white, and their stalks from six to twelve inches high. Another species, *B. ciliaris*, is abundant in the Mallee scrubs of Yorke's Peninsula, having very narrowly divided leaves and purplish flowers. Other species are minute, and form a dense carpet with other plants. The genus is confined to Australia and New Zealand.

Native Elder.—SAMBUCUS. (Natural Order, CAPRIFOLIACEÆ.) P. 38.—Two species of Elder occur in Australia, of which *Sambucus xanthocarpa* bears yellow berries; it is a tall shrub, or small tree, indigenous to New South Wales and Moreton Bay; principally met with on the banks of streams, and not unlike the common Elder in habit and appearance. The other species, *Sambucus Gaudichaudiana*, is a perennial, throwing up stems of from 3 to 5 feet annually, which after the fruit is ripe die down to the root-stock. This plant is invariably found in moist valleys, on mountain slopes, and banks of watercourses. Its large bunches of succulent white semi-transparent berries, somewhat resembling white currants, look very pretty when the plant is in full bearing. It is found in the Macedon and Otway ranges, Victoria, and is abundant in the adjoining colonies.

Native Flax Lily. — DIANELLA. (Natural Order, LILIACEÆ.) Pp. 28, 207.—A genus of pretty grass or sword-leaved perennials, usually blue-flowered, very plentiful throughout many parts of Australia. Their leaves afford a fibre of fair strength, which emits a fragrant odour after being prepared. The aborigines plait them into baskets, mats, etc., and also use them for fishing-lines. One species, *Dianella cærulea*, is known as the Paroo Lily. The commonest species in South Australia is *Dianella revoluta*, found in the hills and scrub; its leaves roll themselves lengthwise together when drying, hence the name. The stalk attains a height of 2 to 3 feet, with many branches and more buds, but only a single flower of dark-blue petals and yellow stamens occurs at the time on each branch; the berries are of a beautiful purple tint; the leaves frequently exceed the stalk in length, and are very tough in fibre.

Native Foxtail. — TRICHINIUM. (Natural Order, AMARANTACEÆ.) Pp. 34, 204.—A large genus of herbs or undershrubs, confined to Australia. Six or seven species are found in Victoria, *Trichiniums spathulatum* and *macrocephalum* being the most common. The most beautiful species known is *Trichinium Manglesii*, from West Australia.

Native Fuchsia.—CORREA. (Natural Order, RUTACEÆ.) Pp. 19, 29, 30, 36, 38, 39, 43, 47, 48, 49, 55.—A pretty shrub, usually hairy, much branched, and variously erect or trailing; mostly found near the coast; leaves generally orbicular, or rotund; flowers either white, flesh-coloured, or red. Indigenous to Victoria, New South Wales, Tasmania, and South

Australia, and is very plentiful along their eastern shores, though it occurs in the Murray scrub east of Callington more than forty miles from the shore. The term 'Native Fuchsia' is applied to most of the species. *Correa speciosa* and its varieties produce crimson or greenish-white, bell-shaped flowers. The white variety, *C. alba*, is common near Melbourne, especially on heath grounds. The name 'Native Fuchsia' is in many other parts of Australia often applied popularly to several other plants distinct from either the Correa or real Fuchsia; for instance, the genus *Eremophila* (or *Stenochilus*),—order Myoporineæ,—of which there are many beautiful species diffused over the great western interior; amongst the best known and most beautiful are *E. longifolia, E. maculata, E. polyclada, and E. Sturtii*. In New South Wales the *Epacris grandiflora* is sometimes termed 'Native Fuchsia,' but in Victoria is always known as the 'Native Heath.'

Native Furze.—HAKEA ULICINA. (Natural Order, PROTEACEÆ.) P. 204. See also chapter 'Australian Vegetation,' p. 79.

Native Geranium.—PELARGONIUM AUSTRALE. (Natural Order, GERANIACEÆ.) Pp. 38, 197.—A very pretty perennial, varying much in the shape of its leaves and form of inflorescence. It is common on banks of creeks and rivers, but is usually met with on sandy heath grounds, especially near the coast, ascending also to sub-Alpine elevations. Indigenous to Victoria and the neighbouring colonies. Another species (*Pelargonium Rodneyanum*) is also found in Australia. The flowers of both are purplish-lilac. There is a true Geranium found in various parts of Australia, the tapering roots of which are eaten by the natives. It is sometimes called 'Native Radish.'

Native Gooseberry.—BILLARDIERA. (Natural Order, Pittosporeæ.) Pp. 53, 197.—A genus of handsome, usually undertwining shrubs, principally met with in damp forests, shady ravines, and on banks of streams, and also in the Mallee scrub of South Australia. The genus is confined to Australia and Tasmania. Some species—such as *Billardieras scandens* and *longiflora*, both indigenous to Victoria—produce yellowish-white, bell-shaped flowers. Others—for instance, *Billardieras cymosa* and *variifolia*, the former a native of Victoria, the latter of Tasmania—bear beautiful blue flowers, succeeded by oblong or cylindrical succulent berries.

Native Grape Vine.—VITIS. (Natural Order, Ampelideæ.) P. 39.—*Vitis hypoglauca*, an evergreen climber, is the Native Grape Vine of East Gippsland. It is found abundantly on the banks of watercourses, especially in New South Wales. All the Australian species were; and probably are still, best known by the obsolete term *Cissus*.

Native Grass Tree. — XANTHORRHŒA. (Natural Order, Juncaceæ.) Pp. 32, 34, 207.—A very curious and interesting genus, confined to Australia. Two species are indigenous to Victoria and New South Wales—*Xanthorrhœa australis* and *X. minor. Xanthorrhœa quadrangulata* and *X. semiplana*, as also the two species previously mentioned, are found in South Australia. *X. australis* has a tree-like form, the trunk rarely exceeding 6 feet in height in Victoria, but in parts of New South Wales often 15 feet, and having outwardly a great resemblance to some of the Cycads. *X. minor* grows in large, grass-like tussocks, especially in poor, damp ground; it is very plentiful about Dandenong. *Xanthorrhœa australis* usually occupies the slopes of hills on clayey soils, often presenting a weird appearance. A fragrant resin is obtained from the base of the decayed leaves, and also a yellow colouring matter, used for imparting a fine dye to silk. The resin is known as Botany Bay or Acaroid resin.

Native Hazel.—POMADERRIS APETALA. (Natural Order, RHAMNEÆ.) See chap. 'Australian Vegetation,' p. 79.

Native Heath.—EPACRIS. (Natural Order, EPACRIDEÆ.) Pp. 19, 20, 202.—Although the genus *Epacris* has very much the aspect of the true Heath (*Erica*), and in many respects resembles it, yet they are placed by botanists for good reasons in different families. The Epacrideæ is essentially Australian, and the species are numerous and widely dispersed. Only one or two of the true Heath family (*Ericaceæ*) have been discovered in Australia. The genus *Gaultheria* is found in Tasmania. See also chapter 'Australian Vegetation,' p. 79.[1]

Native Holly.—LOMATIA FRASERI. (Natural Order, PROTEACEÆ.) P. 204. See chapter 'Australian Vegetation.'

Native Honeysuckle.—BANKSIA. (Natural Order, PROTEACEÆ.) Pp. 42, 204. See also chapter 'Australian Vegetation,' p. 86.—Nearly fifty species are described, principally natives of Western Australia, which seems to be richer in this order than any of the other Australian colonies. They generally inhabit poor, sandy ground, and are remarkable for their singular flowers, resembling those of the Bottlebrush (*Callistemon*) family. The wood of the common Victorian Honeysuckle (*Banksia integrifolia*) is beautifully grained, and suitable for cabinet-work, though too perishable for outside work.

Native Hop.—DAVIESIA. (Natural Order, LEGUMINOSÆ.) P. 198. See also chapter 'Australian Vegetation,' p. 79.—(*Another kind of so-called Native Hop is Goodenia.*)

---

[1] The genus *Epacris* is also found in New Zealand.

Native Hop Tree (Wedge-leaved). — DODONÆA CUNEATA. (Natural Order, SAPINDACEÆ.) P. 32.—A tall, bushy shrub, usually inhabiting the banks of watercourses and scrubby localities in mountainous districts. The winged seed-vessels somewhat resemble hops, hence the common name. The wood of all the Dodonæas is very close-grained and hard, that of *Dodonæa viscosa* and its varieties particularly so. One form or variety of the latter (*Dodonæa conferta*) is the Native Lignum-Vitæ of Phillip Island and New Zealand. *Dodonæa viscosa* and about a dozen other species inhabit the southern parts of South Australia, several of which are very ornamental in appearance, notably the small *Dodonæa humilis* and *D. stenozyga*, resembling small pine trees crowded together. Both are found in the Mallee scrubs of Yorke's Peninsula and elsewhere.

Native Hoya.—HOYA AUSTRALIS. (Natural Order, ASCLEPIADEÆ.) See chapter 'Australian Vegetation,' p. 90.

Native Mint.—MENTHA AUSTRALIS, ETC. (Natural Order, LABIATÆ.) P. 203. See also chapter 'Australian Vegetation,' p. 80.

Native Mint Bush (Round-leaved). — PROSTANTHERA ROTUNDIFOLIA. (Natural Order, LABIATÆ.) P. 30.—A pretty shrub, attaining a height of from 5 to 8 feet; the leaves usually dark green, flowers dark violet, borne in racemes. When bruised, the leaves emit a powerful and fragrant odour, resembling that of mint. The plant is indigenous to Victoria and other Australian colonies. It is principally found in mountainous localities, occupying stony places and the banks of streams. The commonest species in South Australia is *Prostanthera coccinea*, a dwarf species with red flowers found in sandy hill ridges. It is also found in the Grampian range, Victoria.

Native Mistletoe.—P. 200.   See also 'Mistletoe.'

Native Mulberry.—HEDYCARYA ANGUSTIFOLIA. (Natural Order, MONIMIACEÆ.) P. 64. See also chapter 'Australian Vegetation,' p. 81.

Native Musk.—OLEARIA (EURYBIA) ARGOPHYLLA. (Natural Order, COMPOSITÆ.) See chapter 'Australian Vegetation,' p. 83.

Native Nettle.—URTICA INCISA. (Natural Order, URTICEÆ.) P. 205. See also chapter 'Australian Vegetation,' p. 81.—A tall perennial, principally met with on scrubby swamp land and the banks of watercourses, where its stems often attain a length of 8 or 10 feet. The leaves are usually lanceolate, and deeply serrated. It is very common on the banks of the Yarra, and is found in other parts of Australia. Paper of very fine texture has been prepared from its stems. The sting of the glandular hairs with which the plant is armed is very painful, but may be counteracted by an application of the root of the 'Nile Lily' (*Calla Æthiopica*) or any of the Taro (*Alocasia*) family to the affected parts. The leaves or roots of the latter are applied by the blacks of Queensland and Northern New South Wales, with good effect, as a cure for the sting of the great Tree Nettle (*Laportea gigas*).

Native Paper Grass.—POA AUSTRALIS. (Natural Order, GRAMINEÆ.) P. 19.—There are several varieties of this coarse paper grass. It is found on river banks and swampy ground, usually on heavy black soils, growing in tussocks. Though not a very nutritious pasture grass, it has the merit of withstanding drought well, hence it affords sustenance to cattle at seasons when most grasses fail. It yields a good pulp for papermaking.

Native Parsnip. — TRACHYMENE AUSTRALE. (Natural Order, UMBELLIFERÆ.) Pp. 17, 200.—A common annual or biennial weed, found in moist, sandy ground, especially along the eastern shores of Port Philip. In the neighbouring colonies it often ascends to considerable elevations, though it is usually a coast plant.

Native Passion-flower. — PASSIFLORA (DISEMMA) BANKSII. (Natural Order, PASSIFLOREÆ.) See chapter 'Australian Vegetation,' p. 90.—A glabrous climber, bearing very conspicuous flowers of a dull red hue. It is indigenous to Queensland, Norfolk Island, and New Caledonia, and is usually found near the sea.

Native Pear.—XYLOMELUM PYRIFORME. (Natural Order, PROTEACEÆ.) P. 39.—A medium-sized tree common in the neighbourhood of Port Jackson and the Darling Downs, Queensland. The fruit is like a common pear, reversed on the stalk, but consists of a hard, woody substance. It is locally known as the Wooden Pear.

Native Pepper Tree.—DRIMYS (TASMANNIA) AROMATICA. (Natural Order, MAGNOLIACEÆ.) See chapter 'Australian Vegetation,' p. 79.

Native Pine.—See 'Murray Pine.'

Native Rose Apple. — EUGENIA MYRTIFOLIA (JAMBOSA AUSTRALIS). (Natural Order, MYRTACEÆ.) See chapter 'Australian Vegetation,' p. 82.

Native Rosewood.—SYNOUM (TRICHILIA) GLANDULOSUM. (Natural Order, MELIACÆ.) See chapter 'Australian Vegetation,' p. 92.

Native or Spurious Sarsaparilla.—HARDENBERGIA

MONOPHYLLA. (Natural Order, LEGUMINOSÆ.) Pp. 30, 35, 54, 198.—This pretty climber is very common throughout Victoria. It is most frequently found growing on rocky hills in stiff soils, and is abundant on the Yarra, in the Dandenong and other ranges. It has ovate leaves, and very handsome violet or lilac flowers. A white-flowered variety, of more shrubby habit, is common around Melbourne. The root is supposed by some to possess properties similar to those of the American Sarsaparilla (*Smilax*), and is often used as a domestic medicine in the bush; but the idea is erroneous. The species is also found in other parts of Australia. It is mistaken for the true Australian Sarsaparilla (*Smilax glycyphylla*), to which its leaves have at first sight some resemblances, and in company with which it is frequently found throughout Eastern New South Wales. It cannot possess any of the medicinal properties belonging to the Sarsaparilla, and its effects are more likely to be injurious than beneficial, judging from its affinities. *Muehlenbeckia adpressa*, a pretty climber common throughout Australia, is known as *Native Sarsaparilla* in South Australia.

Native Scarbush.—PULTENÆA SCABRA. (Natural Order, LEGUMINOSÆ.) P. 32.—A rough-leaved, much-branched mountain shrub, from 4 to 5 feet high, indigenous to Victoria and New South Wales.

Native Scarlet-runner.—KENNEDYA PROSTRATA. (Natural Order, LEGUMINOSÆ; sub-order, PAPILIONACEÆ.) P. 54.—This trailing plant has bright scarlet flowers, and usually hairy obovate leaflets. It is plentifully distributed throughout Victoria and several of the other Australian colonies. It is common on low lands near the sea, and also on sub-Alpine elevations, usually on heavy, dry, clayey soils.

It can be gathered in the fields around Melbourne and Adelaide.

Native Seaberry. — RHAGODIA. (Natural Order, CHENOPODIACEÆ.) Pp. 30, 64, 204.—Usually soft-wooded climbers or shrubs, generally found along the coast, on the banks of creeks, and in scrubby places. Their leaves are mostly rhomboid or hastate, berries scarlet or yellowish, and very succulent. The commonest species is *R. nutans*, with greyish-green, halbert-shaped leaves and small red berries. It is generally found on rocks.

Native Sheathed Rush. — JUNCUS VAGINATUS. (Natural Order, JUNCACEÆ.) P. 17.—A large and also a small form of this Rush are found in Victoria. The former reaches 4 feet in height in favourable situations. The latter is a slender variety, and rarely exceeds 2 feet. Both kinds yield a strong fibre, good pulp for papermaking, and lamp-black of superior quality. They are generally found on wet, sandy soil.

Native Smooth Holly. — MYRSINE VARIABILIS. (Natural Order, MYRSINEÆ.) See chapter 'Australian Vegetation,' p. 82.

Native Snow Bush.—OLEARIA (EURYBIA) STELLULATA. (Natural Order, COMPOSITÆ.) P. 202. See also chapter 'Australian Vegetation,' p. 83.

Native Snowdrop.—ANGUILLARIA AUSTRALIS. (Natural Order, LILIACEÆ.) Pp. 17, 64, 206.—The earliest of all our indigenous spring flowering plants. Three very distinct forms or varieties are met with, often growing side by side, and frequently mistaken by casual observers for separate species. In early spring our fields are white with the flowers of this pretty little bulbous-rooted plant. It is especially abundant in damp, sandy soils, and it is a notable feature that in poor or worn-out pastures it often takes the place of the grasses. It is found all over extra-tropical Australia.

Native Star of Bethlehem. — CHAMÆSCILLA CORYMBOSA. (Natural Order, LILIACEÆ.) Pp. 35, 207. —A blue-flowered, tuberous, or fleshy-rooted perennial; very plentiful in spring, and often associated with the last-mentioned plant. It was formerly classed with *Cæsia*, to which its flowers have a great resemblance, both in form and colour. The plant is found in all the Australian colonies excepting Queensland.

Native Sundew. —DROSERA. (Natural Order, DROSERACEÆ.) Pp. 17, 29, 32, 199.—These exquisite little plants chiefly grow in damp ground, some being semi-aquatic. The generic name is from *Droseros*, signifying 'dewy,' applied from the fact that the leaves are covered with glandular hairs, from the ends of which is discharged a transparent, sticky juice, resembling drops of dew. These hairs are sensitive to the touch of insects, and make prisoners of small flies, etc., by closing on them.

Drosera Whitakeri is one of the most common species around Melbourne. It is often found on dry ground; the leaves are generally of a spathulate form; the flowers often of a delicate white, and very large in proportion to the size of the plant, resembling a primrose. One of the most beautiful and singular of the species is *Drosera binata*, usually an aquatic plant. Its leaves have the appearance of the sides of a lyre. The roots of several afford a brown dye. There are upwards of forty species indigenous to Australia, several of which are also found in New Zealand. It is considered an unfavourable sign for the quality of a sheep-run when the Sundews are found flourishing upon it, though the statement that the plant itself is actively injurious to sheep needs confirmation. *Drosera binata* is more generally known under the specific name *dichotoma*. It is to be found in almost every swamp, morass, or marsh in the Blue Mountains of New South Wales and other places near by, and was formerly common on the Botany swamps, Sydney, New South Wales.

Native Tea Tree. — MELALEUCA AND LEPTOSPERMUM. (Natural Order, MYRTACEÆ.) Pp. 23, 53, 199.—The name Tea Tree is said to have originated in the fact of the early Australian colonists having used an infusion of the leaves of some species of the above genera as a substitute for tea. The common name is now applied to the plants comprised in both genera, but the species most commonly so employed belonged to *Leptospermum*. *Leptospermum* possesses flowers with well-developed petals, while those of *Melaleuca* are generally devoid of them. Both contain volatile oils of curative property. That of *Melaleuca uncinata* is said to cure coughs and colds.

Native Woodbine or Coffee-bush. — COPROSMA HIRTELLA. (Natural Order, RUBIACEÆ.) See chapter 'Australian Vegetation,' p. 83.

Native Wood Sorrel. — OXALIS CORNICULATA. (Natural Order, GERANIACEÆ.) P. 30.—A prostrate perennial, rooting at the joints; leaflets of a light-green colour; flowers, yellow. It is usually found on sandy ground near the coast, and is indigenous to all the Australian colonies. Being green and fresh during the heat, the plant sometimes proves a great boon to the thirsty traveller, the pleasant acidity of the leaves offering a relief to his sufferings.

Native Yam.—MICROSERIS FORSTERI. (Natural Order, COMPOSITÆ.) Pp. 17, 26, 201.—A tuberous or fleshy-rooted, yellow-flowered perennial, common in the neighbourhood of Melbourne and other parts of Victoria, also in Tasmania and South Australia. Its presence is indicative of good, though heavy, soil. The tubers are edible.

Nectarine.—AMYGDALUS. (Natural Order, ROSACEÆ.) Pp. 53, 186.—A plant originally a native of Persia, but now extensively cultivated for its luscious fruit, which is merely a smooth-skinned variety of the common peach. There are many varieties in cultivation.

Nettle.—URTICA. (Natural Order, URTICEÆ.) Pp. 29, 42.—A large genus of plants, principally distinguished for the virulence of the sting caused by their glandular hairs. Some of the species yield beautiful and valuable fibre. The New South Wales Tree Nettle (*Laportea gigas*) grows to a height of 100 feet. The sting from its leaves is so great as to create severe inflammation. Cattle brushing against its branches have been known to run absolutely mad until the pain subsided. The bark of this tree affords a strong fibre, which the natives convert into fishing lines and nets. The Common Nettle (*Urtica dioica*) is a perennial, cosmopolitan weed, being either indigenous or naturalized in most civilised countries.

New South Wales Fig.—FICUS AUSTRALIS. (Natural Order, URTICEÆ.) P. 17.—This large tree, which in habit somewhat resembles the Banyan of India, is plentiful in some parts of the colony, from which it derives its common name.

New Zealand Laurel.—CORYNOCARPUS LÆVIGATUS. (Natural Order, ANACARDIACEÆ.) Pp. 28, 30.

—A beautiful, glabrous-leaved tree, of quick growth; in favourable situations attaining a height of from 30 to 40 feet. It has large shining, oblong or elliptical leaves, inconspicuous green-hued flowers, and large oblong fruit. The pulp of the latter is eaten by the Maoris, by whom the tree is called 'Karaka,' meaning 'church,' and probably having some reference to the early days of the missionaries' open-air preaching in its shade.

Nile Lily.—CALLA (RICHARDIA) ÆTHIOPICA. (Natural Order, AROIDEÆ.) Pp. 30, 35.—This well-known plant is aquatic, but also grows in ordinary garden soil. Its large, deep, creamy-white flowers, with orange-coloured spadix, form an attractive contrast. It is often called the Trumpet Lily, from the shape of its flowers. It is a native of Africa.

Norfolk Island Pine.—See 'Araucaria.'

O

Oat.—AVENA SATIVA. (Natural Order, GRAMINEÆ.) Pp. 54, 183.—There are numerous species of Oats, such as the White, Black, Potato, etc. The oat thrives best in cold regions; in Victoria, New South Wales, and Tasmania it is principally grown as a hay crop.

Oidium Tuckeri (FUNGI) or 'WHITE MILDEW.' P. 59.—This is the parasite producing one of the diseases in Grape Vines. Sulphur dusted on the leaves offers a complete cure. Some grasses are attacked by kindred species.

Old Maid.—See 'Periwinkle.'

Oleander.—NERIUM OLEANDER. (Natural Order,

APOCYNEÆ.) P. 32.—This handsome, evergreen shrub, bearing a beautiful flower, is in much request for ornamental gardening. It is sometimes called the Rose Bay. The plant is poisonous.

Olive.—OLEA. (Natural Order, OLEACEÆ, included in the JASMINEÆ.) Pp. 35, 53, 186.—This plant was originally introduced into Europe from Asia. The cultivated species, from which the valuable fruit and oil are obtained, are much-branched, evergreen trees, living to a great age. Chalky soils, near the coast, seem best adapted for the culture of the Olive. Excellent Olive oil has been prepared from fruit grown in the Melbourne Botanic Gardens. The climate of many parts of Australia is well adapted for its cultivation. In South Australia its culture is, at the present time, an industry of considerable importance. Oil of great excellence has been frequently produced from Olives grown in New South Wales during the past forty years, but the culture has never developed into importance.

Onion.—ALLIUM CEPA. (Natural Order, LILIACEÆ.) Pp. 17, 183.—An esculent, with qualities too well known to need description.

Orange.—CITRUS AURANTIUM. (Natural Order, RUTACEÆ.) Pp. 1, 2, 4, 52, 55, 63, 186.—There are many varieties of this genus; amongst those best known are the Sweet, Blood (or Maltese), Mandarin, Seville (or Bitter), and Bergamot Oranges; from the latter the well-known perfume is obtained. The warmer parts of Australia are suited to the culture of this delicious fruit. The trees thrive tolerably well around Melbourne; but at Paramatta, near Sydney, their cultivation has been for many years a systematic industry, and the orangeries of that locality are one of the principal attractions to visitors. In Adelaide also there are some very fine Orange groves.

Orchid. — (Natural Order, ORCHIDEÆ.) Pp. 17, 44, 205, 206. See also chapter 'Australian Vegetation,' p. 89. —Orchids are herbaceous plants, perennial in nature, sometimes growing in the earth, at other times aerial in their habit, attaching themselves to rocks and trees. Their flowers are of various shapes, and often emit an exceedingly attractive perfume. The peculiar construction of Orchids is worthy of the student's close attention, and should be sought for in the best available works on the subject, assisted by the numerous beautiful specimens to be obtained in Australia. Some of the tribe are insect-catchers. Orchids are well represented in Australia—in the temperate localities by terrestrial or ground varieties, and in the warmer regions by both terrestrial and epiphytal species, principally the latter. In Victoria there are at least between sixty and seventy species, and in South Australia almost as many, none of which are, however, epiphytal. In most parts of Queensland and New South Wales, however, both epiphytal as well as terrestrial kinds occur.[1]

Osier.—See 'Salix.'

P

Pæony.—PÆONIA. (Natural Order, RANUNCULACEÆ.) P. 53.—A family of handsome herbaceous plants, producing large flowers, mostly white, red, or purple. There are some beautiful double varieties. *Pæonia officinalis* is the

---

[1] The student of Australian Orchids should consult the magnificent illustrated work of R. D. Fitzgerald, Esq., F.L.S., of Sydney, N.S.W., a gentleman who has devoted many years to the study of the subject.

most common of the species. The Chinese Tree Pæony or Moutan (*Pæonia Moutan*) is a shrub bearing very beautiful flowers.

Panax. — (Natural Order, ARALIACEÆ.) See chapter 'Australian Vegetation,' p. 92.

Parsnip. — PASTINACA SATIVA. (Natural Order, UMBELLIFERÆ.) Pp. 38, 183.—A common, edible vegetable. Parsnip wine is made from the tap root.

Passion-flower.—(Scarlet): TACSONIA MANICATA. (Pink): TACSONIA MORTI. (Natural Order, PASSIFLOREÆ.) Pp. 30, 63.—This genus has several botanical differences from the true Passion-flower or Passion fruit (*Passiflora edulis*). The fruits of several kinds are eaten, and their handsome flowers render them great favourites as climbing plants. They are hardy about Melbourne, but will not thrive out of doors in elevated situations, from their susceptibility to frost.

Pea.—PISUM. (Natural Order, LEGUMINOSÆ.) Pp. 2, 5, 6, 41, 50, 51, 54, 183.—There are many kinds of Peas, being widely different in form, etc. The common garden Pea is well known, and may be easily obtained for dissection. It is one of the most valuable vegetables in general use.

Peach.—AMYGDALUS PERSICA. (Natural Order, ROSACEÆ.) Pp. 53, 186.—A short-lived tree, undersized in its natural state. Cultivation has made the Peach one of the most luscious and esteemed of fruits. It grows well in some parts of Australia, and very plentifully in the northern island of New Zealand, where Peach groves are common. The Maoris distil a kind of brandy from the fruit.

Pear. — PYRUS COMMUNIS. (Natural Order, ROSACEÆ.) Pp. 25, 52, 53, 67, 186.—Cultivation has produced numerous varieties of this esteemed fruit. The tree is long-lived, and the wood of matured specimens highly valued for many purposes.

Pelargonium. — (Natural Order, GERANIACEÆ.) Pp. 29, 30, 39, 197.—A few kinds only of this extensive genus are indigenous to Australia. The cultivated garden plants are known as Geraniums, though materially different in botanical points from that genus. Pelargoniums are divided into several sub-genera. The well-known garden Scarlet Geranium belongs to the Pelargoniums. Of the other sub-divisions of the order *Geraniaceæ*, viz. Geraniums and Erodiums, only two are indigenous here.

Periwinkle. — VINCA. (Natural Order, APOCYNEÆ.) P. 30. — A pretty, continuous-flowering little trailer, an evergreen, and very hardy. Both *Vincas major* and *minor* are natives of Britain. *Vinca rosea*, a greenhouse plant, is a native of the tropics. It is a great favourite, being almost constantly in bloom. 'Old Maid' is its common name in the West Indies. *Vinca major* is found to survive all other plants, when a garden has gone to ruin. In fact, it is one of the most hardy of plants known.

Phlox.—(Natural Order, POLEMONIACEÆ.) P. 18.—A tribe of herbaceous plants, annual or perennial, producing very beautiful flowers of different colours, and largely cultivated. 'Texan Pride' (*Phlox Drummondi*) and 'Pride of Columbia' (*Phlox speciosa*) are two of the best known.

Pimelea.—(Natural Order, THYMELEÆ.) Pp. 23, 205.— A large genus of shrubs, undershrubs, or herbaceous plants, confined to Australia and New Zealand. Of the Australian species, nearly twenty are found in Victoria, many of them producing beautiful flowers. In South Australia there are said to be seventeen species, of which *Pimelea glauca* ('Sea-green Pimelea') is one of the most beautiful. Western Australia is the richest in species celebrated for their bloom. The robust Victorian species are principally found in damp forests, on banks of rivulets, and in upland districts. The bark of several kinds is very tough, from which fact they are sometimes called 'Tough Barks.' The aborigines apply the name Kurrajong, or Currijong, to some; but it would appear that this native name is indiscriminately given to any plant possessing a tough bark. The bark of *Pimeleas axiflora* and *pauciflora*, both mountain shrubs, furnish a strong fibre, an excellent paper material, and also a fine brown dye. Daphne (*Wickstrœmia*) indica, a closely allied plant, and much cultivated in gardens, is not uncommon in the mountains and coast regions of New South Wales and Queensland. It possesses a fibrous bark of extraordinary strength. This plant is also common in Norfolk Island, where in the time of its penal occupation it was called '*Kurrajong*,' and the bark was used for whip-lashes and other purposes in lieu of string or cord.

Pine.—PINUS. (Natural Order, CONIFERÆ.) Pp. 55, 195.—The true pines are chiefly confined to the temperate and cold regions, being rarely found in the tropics. The family is a very numerous one, including the Stone Pine (*Pinus pinea*), which produces an edible seed, called 'Pine-nut.' Some species of the pine family attain a very great size. They are principally valued for their timber and turpentine. The foreign pines would require a lengthened description, from their number and immense commercial value. Many of them grow freely in Australia.

Pineapple. — ANANASSA. (Natural Order, BROME-

LIACEÆ.) P. 186.—A well-known fruit, which has been greatly improved in Europe by cultivation. The plant is a triennial, and requires great care. It is grown with success out of doors in the northern part of Australia, in favourable situations. The Victorian and New South Wales markets are plentifully supplied from the South Sea Islands, the Clarence River, New South Wales; and Queensland.

Pine Cone.—'See Pine.'

Pithecolobium.—(Natural Order, LEGUMINOSÆ.) See chapter 'Australian Vegetation,' p. 91.

Pittosporum.—(Natural Order, PITTOSPOREÆ.) Pp. 20, 21, 194.—A large genus of handsome, evergreen trees and shrubs, generally glabrous. The greater number are found in Australia and New Zealand. Most of the Australian kinds are large, leafy shrubs, or slender trees. They are generally found growing on river banks, and in moist, shady ravines, in upland districts. The timber of *Pittosporum bicolor*, a native of the mountains of Victoria, is very handsome, and is commercially known as Cheesewood. The Victorian Laurel (*Pittosporum undulatum*) is perhaps the finest of all. It is also found in Southern New South Wales. It grows to a considerable height (between 35 and 40 feet) in Victoria; furnishes excellent timber; and a valuable perfume is distilled from its flowers. This and most of the New Zealand species form fine ornamental hedges; hence the name 'Hedge Laurel' has been given to them. The Diamond-leaf Laurel of Queensland (*Pittosporum rhombifolium*) is a handsome tree, producing large corymbs of jasmine-scented flowers, and afterwards masses of yellow fruit in great profusion. A fragrant water has lately been distilled from its flowers at the Melbourne Botanic Gardens laboratory. In South Australia *Pittosporum phillyræoides* is very common, and frequents the sea-coast (Yorke's Peninsula) and Mallee scrubs. It grows to a height of 10 or 15 feet. All the species are worthy of cultivation. See 'Victorian Laurel.'

Plane Tree. — PLATANUS. (Natural Order, PLATANACEÆ.) P. 30. — A genus of deciduous trees, generally having lofty, massive stems and thick foliage. The bark, like that of many of the Eucalyptus tribe, is annually shed. The wood is extensively used by carpenters and joiners. The Oriental Plane (*Platanus orientalis*) and *Platanus acerifolia* often approach 100 feet in height, with trunks from 13 to 15 feet in diameter. There are other species of less importance. Planes are generally cultivated as shade-trees, from their umbrageous habit. They succeed well in Victoria if they receive a moderate supply of water during the summer months. Like most deciduous trees, however, the leaves are apt to become scorched by hot winds, and fall off, leaving the branches bare at the season when shade is most required.

Plum. — PRUNUS DOMESTICA. (Natural Order, ROSACEÆ.) Pp. 51, 53, 186. — A well-known family of fruit-producing trees, comprising many varieties, all of which thrive well in Australia.

Poplar. — POPULUS. (Natural Order, SALICINEÆ.) P. 64. — A large genus of deciduous trees, natives of temperate climes, and having a wide geographical range. The genus is largely represented in Europe, Asia, and America. Those most commonly cultivated are P. fastigiata, 'the Lombardy or upright poplar;' P. monolifera, 'the black Italian poplar;' P. alba, the 'white or Abele poplar;' P. tremula, the 'aspen;' P. nigra, the 'black or spreading poplar;'

and P. balsamifera, the 'Tacamahac' of North America. They are all noted for celerity of growth.

Poppy.—PAPAVER. (Natural Order, PAPAVERACEÆ.) Pp. 42, 52, 53, 189.—The brilliant flowers of the Field or Corn Poppy (*Papaver Rhœas*) are familiar to all who have seen a growing crop of wheat in England. The Opium Poppy (*Papaver somniferum*) is the species from which the drug opium is prepared. *Papavers orientale* and *bracteatum* are perennial plants, bearing glossy red flowers of singular beauty. The only Australian species of Poppy is *Papaver aculeatum*, a small plant with scarlet flowers.

Potato.—SOLANUM TUBEROSUM. (Natural Order, SOLANEÆ.) Pp. 17, 18, 53, 183.—The Potato may be called a universal vegetable. Its estimable qualities are too well known to need comment. The district of Warrnambool in this colony (Victoria) and also Tasmania are noted for their excellent quality of the Potato crops. Starch, whisky, and a gum called 'dextrine' are made from the tubers.

Pothos. — (Natural Order, AROIDEÆ.) See chapter 'Australian Vegetation,' p. 90.

Pot Marigold.—See 'Marigold,' p. 138.

Prickly Wattle.—ACACIA JUNIPERINA. P. 198.

Privet.—LIGUSTRUM. (Natural Order, JASMINEÆ.) Pp. 19, 35.—A shrub, rarely exceeding 10 feet in height, largely used in the formation of hedges to gardens, but in Victoria superseded in a great measure by the more attractive Pittosporums.

Pteris. — (Natural Order, FILICES.) P. 209. See also chapter 'Australian Vegetation,' p. 80.

Pumpkin.—CUCURBITA PEPO. (Natural Order, CUCURBITACEÆ.) Pp. 53, 186.—A common trailing plant, the fruit of which is largely used in some countries. It is a favourite article of diet in many parts of Australia, and is generally cultivated, particularly in New South Wales.

Q

Queensland Cigar Cassia. — CASSIA (CATHARTO-CARPUS) BREWSTERI. (Natural Order, LEGUMINOSÆ.) Pp. 54, 89.—A fair-sized tree, with pinnate foliage, sometimes exceeding 30 feet in height. In the brush lands, and upon the banks of rivers and creeks in Northern New South Wales and Queensland, this tree is often a striking object bearing long racemes of golden-yellow flowers. It is perhaps the most attractive of the genus.

Queensland Laurel.—(DIAMOND-LEAF.) P. 30.—See also Pittosporum.

Queensland Native Plum.—ACHRAS. (Natural Order, SAPOTACEÆ.) See chapter 'Australian Vegetation,' p. 89.

Queensland 'Spurge Holly.' — CŒLEBOGYNE (ALCHORNEA) ILICIFOLIA. (Natural Order, EUPHORBIACEÆ.) P. 47.—A glabrous, holly-like shrub, native of Northern New South Wales and Queensland, usually found near the coast.

Queensland Tulip Tree. — STENOCARPUS SINUATUS. (Natural Order, PROTEACEÆ.) P. 30.—A tall-growing, pinnatifid-leaved, timber tree, found on the banks of rivers in Northern New South Wales and Queensland, where, under favourable circumstances, it attains a height of 100 feet. The flowers are of a fiery red, and are borne in umbels. The wood is beautifully grained, and very durable.

Quince. —CYDONIA VULGARIS. (Natural Order, ROSACEÆ.) Pp. 30, 41, 53, 186.—The common Quince-tree is widely scattered. It is deciduous, grows from 15 to 20 feet in height, and produces the large and well-known fruit, of which there are several varieties. It flourishes in many parts of Australia. The Orient is its native home.

R

Radish.—RAPHANUS SATIVUS. (Natural Order, CRUCIFERÆ.) Pp. 17, 54, 183.—A common annual, well known in kitchen gardens. The Red and White Turnip Radishes are merely varieties; the Black and White Spanish are winter sorts.

Rafflesia Arnoldii. — (Natural Order, RAFFLESIACEÆ.) P. 41.—A most singular plant, first discovered in Sumatra. It is a parasite, possessing neither leaf, branch, nor stem. Its enormous flower, which after a few days' expansion sends forth a most putrid odour, has been known to measure more than a yard across; and the nectarium or flower-cup will sometimes hold six quarts of water.

Red Cedar. — CEDRELA TOONA. (Natural Order, MELIACÆ.) P. 195. See also chapter 'Australian Vegetation,' p. 92.

Rhododendron.—(Natural Order, ERICACEÆ.) Pp. 20, 63. —This handsome shrub, sometimes called the Tree Rose, is well known in Victoria, where it is largely cultivated, growing freely in the open air with moderate attention, and producing exquisite fragrant flowers, relieved by glossy green foliage. There are many varieties, all of them favourites in our public and private gardens.

Rib Grass.— PLANTAGO. (Natural Order, PLANTAGINEÆ.) Pp. 34, 203. — The Greater Plantain or Rib-grass (*Plantago major*) is a very common weed on roadsides and in cultivated fields. It is cosmopolitan in habit; has broad, prominently-ribbed leaves, and long flower-stalks terminating in cylindrical spikes of greenish-coloured flower. It is common in these colonies, having probably been introduced with grass seeds. Sheep and cattle are fond of it. The common Rib-grass (*Plantago lanceolata*) is extensively used for laying down mixed pastures. It is a good fodder plant.

Rice-paper Plant.—ARALIA PAPYRIFERA. (Natural Order, ARALIACEÆ.) P. 30.—From the stems of this plant a very fine snowy pith is obtained, from which rice-paper is made. It is a native of the island of Formosa, where it flourishes in the swampy forests; and is largely exported to China for utilisation in various manufactures. It is very common in ornamental plantations throughout the colonies, and its large palmate leaves are very effective in scenic embellishments when employed skilfully. The plant will probably be found of industrial importance in the future of these colonies.

Ripogonum.—(Natural Order, LILIACEÆ.) See chapter 'Australian Vegetation.' p. 90.

Rock Rose. — CISTUS. (Natural Order, CISTINEÆ.) P. 41.—A family of attractive shrubs; the flowers, resembling those of the dog-rose, die within a few hours after expansion. The species known as Gum Cistus is most esteemed.

Rose. — ROSA. (Natural Order, ROSACEÆ.) Pp. 26, 28, 29, 39, 41, 54, 63.—This beautiful plant, the theme of poets from the earliest days, has, by cultivation and hybridization, been indefinitely multiplied into varieties in all parts of the civilised world. Volumes have been written upon this Queen of Flowers, yet something new and interesting always remains to be added. The Rose, though requiring attention, grows freely in the open air in Australia. Some of our public and private gardens possess superb collections of this plant in most of its beautiful species and varieties. The weeds known as *Acæna ovina* and *A. sanguisorba* with green pinnatifid leaves and burr-like fruits, which adhere to the clothes of the passer-by, belong to this order.

Rose Bay.—See 'Oleander.'

Royal Water Lily.—VICTORIA REGIA. (Natural Order, NYMPHÆACEÆ.) Pp. 25, 30, 41.—The astonishing dimensions and great beauty of this tropical plant render it an object of the greatest interest. It can only be grown in this colony in a hothouse—requiring the utmost care and attention; but its broad expanse of leaf, floating on the water, and the fragrance of its flower when it is in bloom, have delighted all who have had the opportunity of seeing it. The leaves have been known to approach 7 feet in diameter, and the flowers to measure 15 inches across. The Melbourne Botanic Garden contains a fine specimen under glass, also the Adelaide Botanic Garden, the Director of which, Dr. Schomburgk, first introduced this noble plant into Australia.

Rush.—JUNCUS. (Natural Order, JUNCACEÆ.) Pp. 17, 191, 192, 207.—An extensive order, widely distributed; common in bogs and marshy spots, particularly where the soil is sandy. The pith and stems of many species are employed for useful purposes, such as the manufacture of paper, etc. It might be advantageously used in the manufacture of pith hats for summer wear.

Rust.—TRICHOBASIS (UREDO) RUBIGO. (Natural Order, FUNGI.) P. 59.—A deadly enemy to cereals. Rust in wheat is one of the greatest plagues to farmers. It is a parasitical fungus.

Rye.—SECALE CEREALE. (Natural Order, GRAMINEÆ.) P. 34.—A cereal, cultivated for its grain, and well known in these colonies.

S

Sassafras (Victorian). — ATHEROSPERMA MOSCHATA. (Natural Order, MONIMIACEÆ.) P. 64.—New South Wales Sassafras, *Doryphora Sassafras.* See chapter 'Australian Vegetation,' p. 92.

Scarlet Geranium.—See 'Pelargonium.'

Screw Pine.—PANDANUS. (Natural Order, PANDANACEÆ.) Pp. 22, 192.—A tribe of over thirty known kinds; partial to the sea-coast, and forming dense masses of vegetation over considerable areas. One species, the Vacona of Mauritius, is utilised for the manufacture of bags from its leaves. Several species are found in tropical Australia. *Pandanus Forsteri*, a native of Lord Howe's Island, is called the Tent-tree from its spreading habit. One species, *Pandanus pedunculatus*, reaches far north in Queensland, but scarcely south of the Clarence, New South Wales. It is called *native bread fruit* by the settlers, and by the aborigines, *inam*. The leaves, like those of the Vacona, might be utilized for sugar and other mats.

Scrub Box.—HYMENANTHERA DENTATA. (Natural Order, VIOLARIEÆ.) See chapter 'Australian Vegetation,' p. 83.

Scrub-vine. — CASSYTHA MELANTHA. (Natural Order, LAURINEÆ.) — A leafless parasitical twiner, very common on Melaleuca ericifolia, the swamp tea tree, Eucalypti, Acacias, etc.

Seaweed. — ALGÆ. Pp. 57, 59, 65. — Curious specimens of marine vegetation; many of them possessing useful qualities, as, for instance, Iodine. — A curious form is *Harmonia Agardhi*, the *Sea Grape*, named so on account of the grape-like floating bladders which burst with a crash when trod upon. It is common on our coasts.

Sensitive Mimosa. — MIMOSA SENSITIVA. (Natural Order, LEGUMINOSÆ.) P. 28. — A tropical plant, worthy of cultivation in hothouses on account of its peculiar sensitiveness to the touch.

Sheoak. — CASUARINA. (Natural Order, CASUARINEÆ.) Pp. 21, 55, 205. See also chapter 'Australian Vegetation,' p. 85. — The black, gloomy appearance of these singular trees is familiar to dwellers in the Australian bush, where their leafless branches form one of the most striking features of the landscape. A few kinds only are indigenous to Victoria, *Casuarina suberosa* (erect Sheoak or Victorian Beefwood) being the most common. The shrubby species *Casuarina distyla* and seven others, including *C. quadrivalvis*, are abundantly scattered through Southern Australia. Like many other names given by the earliest settlers, the term oak was given to this genus because when worked up the wood had some resemblance to that of the English oak, and in fact was used like it for staves, for buckets, kegs, tubs, etc. The species most common around Melbourne is known in New South Wales as 'Forest Oak.'

Silky Oak. — See 'Grevillea Robusta,' pp. 53, 125. — The most noticeable of the numerous species of this genus known in Australia. It is a grand timber tree, bearing large masses of comb-shaped, highly-perfumed yellow or orange coloured flowers. It is a native of Northern New South Wales and Queensland, found on rich alluvial river banks, where it often attains to a height of 100 feet. It is considered the best Australian stavewood.

Silver Wattle.—See 'Acacia Dealbata,' pp. 54, 197.

Snowflake.—LEUCOJUM. (Natural Order, AMARYLLIDEÆ.) Pp. 17, 49.—An attractive, bulbous-rooted plant, resembling the snowdrop, but somewhat larger. The Snowflake grows from 12 to 18 inches in height, producing spikes of white flowers, tipped with green.

Soap Aloe.—ALOE SAPONARIA. (Natural Order, LILIACEÆ.) P. 188.—Drugs obtained from this beautiful genus of plants are in great use in medicine. They are natives of most warm countries. The Soap Aloe produces a lather when rubbed between the hands, like soap; hence its common name.

Spotted Thistle.—CARDUUS MARIANUS. (Natural Order, COMPOSITÆ.) Pp. 29, 201.—Also called the Holy Thistle; a plant having large, glossy leaves with white veins. Its seeds are eaten with avidity by many birds. This Thistle is better known in pastoral and agricultural districts as the variegated thistle; also known as the 'Artichoke Thistle.'

Staghorn Fern.—PLATYCERIUM GRANDE. (Natural Order, FILICES.) Pp. 59, 90.—A handsome, epiphytal fern, found in many parts of Australia, and though not indigenous to Victoria, it grows freely, when cultivated on the trunks of trees. In the Queensland forests the stems of giant specimens of Ficus and Tree Ferns are profusely decked with these curious plants, which derive their nourishment from the moisture falling from the trees on which they grow.

Starwort.—STELLARIA. (Natural Order, CARYOPHYLLACEÆ.) P. 62.—A large genus of annual or perennial herbs, widely distributed; five or six species occur in Australia. One of the latter, the common Chickweed (*Stellaria media*), is very abundant. The name Starwort is also applied to the genus Aster, of the order Compositæ.

Stock.—MATTHIOLA. (Natural Order, CRUCIFERÆ.) Pp. 35, 54. — Some kinds of this family of cruciferous plants, notably the Brompton Stock and Stock-gilliflower, are well known in our gardens.

Stone Pine.—See 'Pine,' p. 162.

Strawberry.—FRAGARIA. (Natural Order, ROSACEÆ.) Pp. 17, 30, 50, 186.—A well-known plant, throwing out runners which take root in their turn. Cultivation has brought this delicious fruit to great perfection as regards flavour and the number of varieties. It thrives in the colonies.

Stringy Bark.—Pp. 18, 126. See also chapter 'Australian Vegetation,' p. 85.

Sunflower.—HELIANTHUS. (Natural Order, COMPOSITÆ.) P. 29.—A common annual, principally cultivated for its seeds, which in some countries are used for fattening poultry and stock; a very useful oil is also expressed from them. The flowers are much sought after by bees, on account of the quantity of nectar they contain. The Sunflower is well suited for planting at the back of flower-beds, or in the foreground of shrubberies, from its tall and ornamental appearance. Its culture is much to be recommended on account of its oil, for which there exists an almost unlimited market. There are many varieties, suitable for different soils, localities, etc.

Swamp-weed. — SELLIERA RADICANS. (Natural Order, GOODENIACEÆ.) Pp. 17, 202.—A creeping perennial, partial to moist ground, and generally found near the coast. It is indigenous to Victoria, and very common in some of the adjoining colonies, especially New South Wales.

Sweet William.—DIANTHUS. (Natural Order, CARYOPHYLLACEÆ.) P. 35.—The Sweet William (*Dianthus barbatus*) is so old a favourite in our gardens as to render description unnecessary. There are many varieties, single and double; the flowers are variously coloured, from white to dark purple.

Sword Lily.—GLADIOLUS. (Natural Order, IRIDEÆ.) P. 17. — A genus of beautiful plants, acclimatised and flourishing vigorously throughout Australia. The flowers are produced in long spikes, are of large size, and infinitely variegated hues. The plant is also known as the Corn Flag. There are a very great number of varieties.

Sword Rush.— LEPIDOSPERMA. (Natural Order, CYPERACEÆ.) Pp. 19, 208.—A very large tribe of tufted, sword-leaved grass, or rush-like plants, usually found on the banks of watercourses. The Common or Coast Sword Rush (*Lepidosperma gladiatum*) grows very plentifully along the eastern coast of Victoria, and on the islands in Western Port Bay. It has become celebrated, both here and in Europe, for its paper-producing qualities. Many of the other species yield good fibre and paper pulp.

Sycamore.—ACER PSEUDO-PLATANUS. (Natural Order, SAPINDACEÆ.) Pp. 30, 54. — This tree is known as the Scotch Plane-tree. It is a large and picturesque tree, its broad leaves affording a pleasant shade. Its timber is valued for many purposes.

Syzygium.—(Natural Order, MYRTACEÆ.) See chapter 'Australian Vegetation,' p. 91.

T

Tasmanian Tea Bush. — LEPTOSPERMUM SCOPARIUM. (Natural Order, MYRTACEÆ.) P. 199. See also chapter 'Australian Vegetation,' p. 79.

Thistle.—CARDUUS. (Natural Order, COMPOSITÆ.) Pp. 29, 54, 200.—A very numerous family, some kinds of which have, since their introduction into Australia, proved great pests to our farmers; so much so, indeed, that legislation has been found necessary to provide for their periodical destruction. It is most difficult—in fact, practically impossible —to eradicate them when they have once gained a hold on a district, their downy seeds being carried by the wind to all quarters. Since the last great drought in New South Wales, many settlers have come to the conclusion that some of the varieties are valuable fodder plants as a 'stand by' in starvation times. In South Australia the encroachment of this plant was so much dreaded that a law was enacted with a view to its extermination; but experience has shown that it is more worthy of protection than of destruction, and the law, although not repealed, is not enforced. The proper period for destroying thistles is just before the seed commences to mature. The Spear Thistle (*Carduus lanceolatus*) is the plant generally supposed to be the emblem of Scotland. Bushmen in Australia frequently use the thistle as a vegetable and antiscorbutic.

Thorn Apple.—DATURA STRAMONIUM. (Natural Order, SOLANEÆ.) P. 53.—A coarse plant, bearing large white, pink, or purple flowers; seed capsules covered with spines. It possesses poisonous properties, and its poison is sometimes used in medicine in cases of epilepsy or falling sickness. It is said, upon good authority, that asthma has been alleviated by the patient inhaling the smoke from the leaves of this plant, used as tobacco.

Tobacco.—NICOTIANA TABACUM. (Natural Order, SOLANEÆ.) P. 29.—Tobacco, which is a native of America, since it came into general use, has never ceased to furnish matter for fierce controversy between its opponents and admirers. The various species are largely cultivated in countries suitable to their growth, and some parts of Australia, from the Murray River northwards, now produce large quantities of the leaf; the manufacture of tobacco and cigars being a leading colonial industry. Nicotine is a deadly poison contained in tobacco, and it is asserted that by its absorption into the system, through excessive smoking, it enfeebles the brain and produces paralysis. On the other hand, the soothing qualities of tobacco, when used in moderation, are universally admitted; and it is probable that the abuse, and not the use, creates the evil. The power of a pipe of tobacco in temporarily alleviating hunger is a philosophical fact at which Australian bushmen have arrived by practical experience. Tobacco is frequently cultivated as an ornamental plant.

Todea.—(Natural Order, FILICES.) See chapter 'Australian Vegetation,' p. 80.

Tomato.—SOLANUM LYCOPERSICUM. (Natural Order, SOLANEÆ.) Pp. 53, 185.—This useful plant is common in Victoria, and its fruit is very largely used, especially in the manufacture of sauces and other relishes. It is very wholesome, and is said to be useful in cases of indigestion and derangement of the liver. The fruit is also known as the Love-apple. It requires a liberal share of warm weather to bring it to perfection.

Treasure Flower.—GAZANIA. (Natural Order, COMPOSITÆ.) Pp. 32, 34.—A hardy perennial, flowering almost continuously, and well adapted for covering bare patches under trees where other vegetation will not grow.

Tree Fern.—(Natural Order, FILICES.) Pp. 19, 20, 57, 58.—These noble representatives of the Fern tribe form a special feature in Australian and New Zealand vegetation, often attaining a height exceeding 80 feet. *Dicksonia antarctica* and *Alsophila australis* are the two most frequently met with in Victoria; the former is the pride of our fern gullies, and is found only in the most shady and well-watered localities. The latter is often encountered growing on mountain-tops, its feathery fronds waving in the breeze. It is known as the Mountain Tree Fern and Umbrelia Fern.

Trumpet Flower.—TECOMA RADICANS. (Natural Order, BIGNONIACEÆ.) P. 18.—A woody climber, bearing large bunches of orange-red flowers of a shape from which its common name is derived. It is well suited to ornament walls, dead trees, and fronts of houses.

Tuberose.—POLIANTHES TUBEROSA. (Natural Order, LILIACEÆ.) P. 17.—A handsome plant, bearing on a stalk of a few feet in length white funnel-shaped flowers, emitting a most agreeable odour.

Tulip.—TULIPA. (Natural Order, LILIACEÆ.) Pp.

17, 49.—This gaudy-flowering, bulbous-rooted plant is generally known. Large quantities of bulbs are yearly exported by the Dutch, who are the principal growers.

Turnip.—BRASSICA RAPA. (Natural Order, CRUCIFERÆ.) Pp. 54, 183.—A very common esculent, some varieties of which are largely used for feeding stock. It thrives well in Victoria.

V

Valerian.—CENTRANTHUS. (Natural Order, VALERIANEÆ.) Pp. 32, 190.—Red Valerian succeeds very well in Victoria. It is a small plant, bearing little flowers in panicles. Another variety, the White Valerian, also does well here.

Vegetable Marrow. — CUCURBITA SUCCADA. (Natural Order, CUCURBITACEÆ.) Pp. 53, 187.—A common esculent; very easily cultivated.

Verbena.—(Natural Order, VERBENACEÆ.) Pp. 29, 33, 63.—The Vervain (*Verbena officinalis*) had formerly a great medicinal reputation, but it has survived it. The so-called Lemon-Scented Verbena, though of the same order, belongs to the genus Lippia, but is almost universally known as Aloysia. It is the most highly esteemed of all herbal remedies by the Spanish. A few of the dried leaves mixed in tea or coffee not only greatly improve the flavour of those beverages, but is considered a remedy against headache and other nervous ailments. The garden Verbenas produce flowers of the most brilliant and varied colours.

Victorian Crocus.—HYPOXIS GLABELLA. (Natural Order, AMARYLLIDEÆ.) Pp. 17, 206.—A pretty little herbaceous plant, with bulbous root-stocks and yellow flowers; abundant round Melbourne and in other parts of the colony.

Victorian Plum Wood. — PERSOONIA AND NOTELÆA. See chapter 'Australian Vegetation,' p. 82.

Vine Disease. — OIDIUM. P. 59. — The celebrated Oidium Tuckeri, which has worked such havoc in some of our vineyards, is a form of this disease. Sulphur is used to stay its ravages, but when it has obtained a firm hold the vines have to be destroyed root and branch.

Violet. — VIOLA. (Natural Order, VIOLARIEÆ.) Pp. 17, 30, 53, 197. — A genus of beautiful plants, widely differing in some botanical points, but most of them familiar to lovers of flowers. The Violet is a common garden plant in the colonies. There are four species of Viola found in Australia and Tasmania. Of these three are indigenous to Victoria, and one is found only in Tasmania.

W

Walking-Stick Palm. — KENTIA (ARECA) MONOSTACHYA. (Natural Order, PALMÆ.) See chapter 'Australian Vegetation.'

Wallflower. — CHEIRANTHUS. (Natural Order, CRUCIFERÆ.) Pp. 35, 39, 41, 46, 54, 63. — A very common garden plant. Cultivation has produced double flowers of various tints, having a sweet odour, particularly towards the close of the day.

Watercress. — NASTURTIUM-OFFICINALE. (Natural Order, CRUCIFERÆ.) Pp. 54, 183. — This useful perennial grows abundantly throughout the Australian colonies and New Zealand. It is not only grateful to the palate, but very wholesome and purifying to the blood. The Native Watercress (*Nasturtium palustre*) is common to these colonies. In New South Wales it is called Native Cabbage, and is used as a pot herb.

Wattles.—ACACIA. See 'Black Wattle,' pp. 54, 103; 'Silver Wattle,' pp. 54, 172; 'Golden Wattle,' pp. 54, 124; 'Blackwood,' or Lightwood, p. 194; also chapter 'Australian Vegetation,' p. 85.

Wheat.—TRITICUM. (Natural Order, GRAMINEÆ.) Pp. 6, 16, 51, 62, 67, 183.—Probably the most valuable of all cereals, and upon which the prosperity of South Australia greatly depends. It is cultivated now in hundreds of varieties, and almost every year new ones appear. They are produced by very careful selection of seeds from plants that show a tendency to vary in the direction desired, and cultivate separately till the result is obtained.

White Cedar.—MELIA AUSTRALIS. (Natural Order, MELIACEÆ.) See chapter 'Australian Vegetation,' p. 92.

Willow.—SALIX. (Natural Order, SALICINEÆ.) Pp. 25, 42, 46, 64.—This graceful deciduous tree, with its pendulous boughs, is thoroughly acclimatised in Australia, and very abundant in our public and private gardens where the soil is suitable to its growth. It requires moist ground, and is seen to the best advantage growing on the banks of rivers and watercourses. The wood and twigs are used for a number of purposes. The Weeping Willow (*Salix Babylonica*) is the finest growing species. The willows used for basket-making are called Osiers—*Salix Viminalis, S. Forbeyana, S. Rubra, S. Vitellina*, etc.; and their cultivation in moors and along rivulets, where scarcely anything else could be grown profitably, is much to be recommended, on account of the demand for basket manufacture.

Wistaria.—(Natural Order, LEGUMINOSÆ.) See p. 35, and chapter 'Australian Vegetation,' pp. 70, 90.

Wonga Wonga Vine. — TECOMA AUSTRALIS. (Natural Order, BIGNONIACEÆ.) P. 29. — This hardy, evergreen, pinnate-leaved climber is also known in some parts of Victoria as the Churchill Island Jasmine or creeper. In habit it closely resembles the Moreton Bay Trumpet Jasmine (*Tecoma jasminoides*). It grows very quickly, and forms a handsome bower-plant. Two or three varieties occur, differing in size of foliage and flowers. It is one of the most common climbers in New South Wales, and is especially abundant on the North Shore, Sydney; the Paramatta River, Ashfield, Burwood, etc.

Wood-sorrel.—OXALIS. (Natural Order, GERANIACEÆ.) Pp. 17, 30.—A numerous family, principally herbaceous plants, some of them pleasant to the palate, and considered useful in cases of scurvy.

Z

Zamia.—(Natural Order, CYCADEÆ.) Pp. 2, 55. See also chapter 'Australian Vegetation,' p. 89.—Very graceful plants, suitable for lawns and other ornamental gardening where an effect is required from a single specimen, and also in groups; all the Australian species have been referred to Macrozamia. They are partial to marshy places bordering on the coast. Some beautiful tropical effects may be gained by grouping with them hardy palms, bamboos, reeds, and tree ferns.

PRINCIPAL PLANTS OF ECONOMIC VALUE.

1. PLANTS USED AS FOOD, YIELDING ESCULENT ROOTS, LEAVES, Etc.

Common Name.	Botanical Name.	Native Country.
Arrowroot, Purple or East Indian	*Canna edulis*	India
Arrowroot, West Indian	*Maranta arundinacea*	Tropical America and West Indies
Arrowroot, South Sea Island	*Tacca pinnatifida*	South Sea Islands
Artichoke	*Cynara Scolymus*	South Europe and Africa
Asparagus	*Asparagus officinalis*	Europe, Asia, and Africa
Barley	*Hordeum*	Unknown
Bean	*Faba vulgaris*	Egypt
Beet	*Beta vulgaris*	South Europe
Cabbage	*Brassica oleracea*	Europe
Carrot	*Daucus Carota*	,,
Cauliflower	*Brassica oleracea* (*variety*)	,,
Celery	*Apium graveolens*	,,
Chive	*Allium Schænoprasum*	,,
Endive	*Cichorium Endiva*	Asia
Garden Cress	*Lepidium sativum*	Persia
Garlic	*Allium sativum*	South Europe
Hop	*Humulus Lupulus*	Europe, Asia, and North America
Horse Radish	*Cochlearia Armoracea*	Europe and Asia

PRINCIPAL PLANTS OF ECONOMIC VALUE.

Common Name.	Botanical Name.	Native Country.
Jerusalem Artichoke	*Helianthus tuberosus*	Brazil
Kidney Bean	*Phaseolus vulgaris*	India
Lettuce	*Lactuca sativa*	South Asia
Maize, or Indian Corn	*Zea Mays*	South America
Oat	*Avena sativa*	Europe and Asia
Onion	*Allium Cepa*	Unknown
Parsley	*Petroselinum sativum*	Sardinia
Parsnip	*Pastinaca sativa*	Britain
Pea	*Pisum sativum*	Supposed to be South Europe
Potato	*Solanum tuberosum*	Chili and Peru
Radish	*Raphanus sativus*	Asia
Rhubarb	*Rheum*	,,
Rice	*Oryza sativa*	South Asia
Sago Palm	*Sagus farinifera*	Moluccas
Samphire	*Crithmum maritimum*	Europe, Asia, and Africa
Sea-Kale	*Crambe maritima*	Europe and Africa
Sorrel	*Rumex acetosa*	Europe, Asia, and North America
Spinach, or Spinage	*Spinacea oleracea*	Supposed to be Western Asia
Sugar Cane	*Saccharum officinarum*	India, China, and South Sea Islands
Tea	*Thea chinensis*	China and Assam
Turnip	*Brassica Rapa*	Europe
Water Cress	*Nasturtium officinale*	,,
Wheat	*Triticum vulgare*	South Europe and Asia
Yam	*Dioscorea, various species*	India, China, Japan, South Sea Islands, West Indies, and Queensland

2. YIELDING EDIBLE FRUITS, NUTS, Etc.

Common Name.	Botanical Name.	Native Country.
Almond	*Amygdalus communis*	Barbary
American Papaw	*Asimina triloba*	North America
Apple	*Pyrus malus*	Europe and Asia
Apricot	*Prunus Armeniaca*	Armenia
Assai Palm	*Euterpe edulis*	Brazil
Avocado, or Alligator Pear	*Persea gratissima*	Tropical America and West Indies
Bael, or Bela	*Ægle marmelos*	India
Banana, or Plantain	*Musa, various species*	Tropics
Barberry	*Berberis communis*	Europe
Belote Oak	*Quercus ballota*	Barbary
Bilimbi	*Averrhoa Bilimbi*	India
Blackberry	*Rubus fruticosus*	Europe, Asia, Africa
Brazil Nut	*Bertholletia excelsa*	Tropical America
Bread Fruit	*Artocarpus incisa*	South Sea Islands
Bread Nut	*Brosimum Alicastrum*	West Indies
Caimito	*Lucuma Camaito*	Peru
Cape Gooseberry	*Physalis Peruviana*	Peru
Cashew Nut	*Anacardium occidentale*	West Indies and Mexico
Cassava Sweet	*Manihot Api*	Tropical America
Cassava, or Tapioca	*Manihot ultissima*	South America
Cherimoyer	*Anona cherimolia*	Peru
Cherry	*Prunus cerasus*	Britain
Chestnut	*Castanea vesca*	Europe, Asia, and North America
Chilian Guava	*Eugenia Ugni*	Chili
Citron	*Citrus medica*	Asia
Cob Nut	*Corylus Avellana*	Europe and Asia
Cocoa, or Cacao Tree	*Theobroma Cacao*	Guiana, Brazil, and Trinidad
Cocoa, or Coco-Nut Palm	*Cocos nucifera*	Sea-shores of Southern India, Malayan and South Sea Islands

PRINCIPAL PLANTS OF ECONOMIC VALUE.

Common Name.	Botanical Name.	Native Country.
Coffee	*Coffea Arabica*	Abyssinia
Cranberry	*Vaccinium Oxycoccus*	Europe, Asia, and North America
Cucumber	*Cucumis sativus*	Asia and Africa
Currant	*Ribes rubrum* and *R. nigrum*	Europe, Asia, and North America
Custard Apple	*Anona reticulata*	West Indies
Date Palm	*Phœnix dactylifera*	North Africa
Date Plum	*Diospyros Kaki*	China and Japan
Durion	*Durio zibethinus*	Malay Islands
Earth, or PeaNut	*Arachis hypogæa*	South America
Elderberry	*Sambucus nigra*	Europe, Asia, Africa
Fig	*Ficus carica*	Levant
Filbert	*Corylus Avellana*	Europe and Asia
Gooseberry	*Ribes Grossularia*	Europe, North Africa, and Nepaul
Gourd	*Cucurbito Pepo* (variety)	Astrachan
Granadilla	*Passiflora quadrangularis*	South America
Grape	*Vitis vinifera*	Asia
Guava	*Psidium* (various species)	West Indies and Tropical America
Guava Berry	*Eugenia lineata*	Island of Tortolo, West Indies
Herbert River Cherry	*Antidesma Dallachiana*	Queensland
Jambolana	*Eugenia jambolana*	Australia and India
Jujube	*Zizyphus jujuba*	Tropical Asia, Africa, and Australia
Lausa, or Beejetlan	*Lausium domesticum*	India
Lemon	*Citrus medica,* var. *Limonium*	Southern Asia
Limes	*Citrus medica,* var. *Limetta*	Southern Asia
Litchii	*Nephelium Litchii*	China
Longan	*Nephelium Longan*	China
Loquat	*Eriobotrya japonica*	China and Japan
Love Apple, or Tomato	*Solanum Lycopersicum*	Jamaica, and Mexico to Brazil
Mabola	*Diospyros mabola*	Philippine Islands

Common Name.	Botanical Name.	Native Country.
Malay Apple	*Eugenia Malaccensis*	India
Mango	*Mangifera indica*	East Indies
Mangosteen	*Garcinia mangostana*	Malayan Islands
Medlar	*Mespilus germanica*	Europe
Melon	*Cucumis Melo*	Countries bordering on the Caspian Sea
Mulberry	*Morus nigra*	Persia and Asia Minor
Nectarine	*Amygdalus Persica, var. Nectarina*	Persia
Olive	*Olea Europea, and its varieties*	Asia
Orange	*Citrus Aurantium*	Southern Asia
Otaheite Walnut	*Aleurites Moluccana*	Ceylon, Moluccas, etc.
Papau	*Carica Papaya*	South America
Peach	*Amygdalus Persica*	Persia
Pear	*Pyrus communis*	Europe
Persimon, or States Date Plum	*Diospyros Virginianæ*	United States, America
Pigeon Pea	*Cajanus indicus*	India
Pine Apple	*Ananassa sativa*	South America
Pine Apple Arum	*Monstera deliciosa*	Mexico
Pistacia Nut	*Pistacia lentiscus*	South Europe
Plum	*Prunus domestica*	Asia
Pomegranate	*Punica granatum*	Africa and Asia
Pumpkin	*Cucurbito Pepo, variety*	Astrachan
Quince	*Cydonia vulgaris*	Europe, Asia, and Africa
Rambeh, or Choopa	*Pierardia dulcis*	Malay Islands
Rambutan	*Nephelium lappaceum*	Malay Archipelago
Raspberry	*Rubus Idæus*	Europe and Asia
Rose Apple	*Eugenia Jambos*	India
Strawberry	*Fragaria vesca*	Europe and America
Sweet Raisin Tree	*Hovenia dulcis*	China and Japan
Tamarind	*Tamarindus indica*	East Indies, Africa, and West Indies

PRINCIPAL PLANTS OF ECONOMIC VALUE.

Common Name.	Botanical Name.	Native Country.
Vegetable Egg Tree, or Natural Marmalade	*Lucuma mammosa*	Tropical America and N.W. Australia
Vegetable Marrow	*Cucurbito Pepo, var. Ovifera*	Astrachan
Walnut	*Juglans regia*	Europe and Asia
Wampee	*Cookia punctata*	China and Indian Archipelago
Water Melon	*Cucumis citrullus*	Levant
Zante Currant	*Vitis vinifera (variety)*	Mediterranean

3. SPICE AND CONDIMENT PLANTS, Etc.

Anise	*Pimpinella Anisum*	South Europe, Asia, and Africa
Basil	*Ocimum Basilicum*	Tropical Africa, India
Black Pepper	*Piper nigrum*	East Indies
Caper	*Capparis spinosa*	South Europe, Asia, and Africa
Caraway Seed	*Carum Carui*	Europe and Asia
Cayenne, or Red Pepper	*Capsicum annuum, etc.*	E. and W. Indies and S. America
Cinnamon	*Cinnamomum zeylanicum and C. verum*	India and Ceylon
Clove	*Caryophyllus aromaticus*	Moluccas
Coriander	*Coriandrum sativum*	S. Europe and Asia
Fennel	*Fœniculum vulgare*	Mediterranean
Ginger	*Zingiber officinale*	Tropical Asia
Lavender	*Lavandula vera*	South Europe, Asia, and North Africa
Marjoram	*Origanums Majorana and vulgare*	Europe, Asia, and Africa
Mint	*Mentha viridis*	Europe, Asia, and North America
Nutmeg	*Myristica fragrans*	Indian Archipelago

Common Name.	Botanical Name.	Native Country.
Pepper (Jamaica), or Allspice	*Eugenia Pimenta*	West Indian Islands
Peppermint	*Mentha piperita*	Europe
Rosemary	*Rosmarinus officinalis*	Mediterranean
Sage	*Salvia officinalis*	South Europe
Thyme	*Thymus vulgaris*	,,
Vanilla	*Vanilla aromatica and planifolia*	Mexico

4. MEDICINAL PLANTS.

Aloes	*Aloe socotrina, saponaria, and vulgaris*	East and West Indies
Anise, or Aniseed	*Pimpinella Anisum*	Asia and Africa
Arbutus, or Bearberry	*Arbutus (Arctostaphylos) uva-ursi*	Europe, Asia, and North America
Arum, or Wake Robin	*Arum maculatum*	Britain
Asafœtida	*Narthex Asafœtida*	Tibet
Camomile, or Chamomile	*Anthemis nobilis*	Europe
Castor-oil Plant	*Ricinus communis*	India
Catechu, or Cutch	*Acacia Catechu*	India, Ceylon, Burmah, and Tropical Eastern Africa
Colchicum, or Meadow Saffron	*Colchicum autumnale*	Europe
Colocynth	*Cucumis (Citrullus) Colocynthis*	Europe, Asia, and Africa
Croton Oil	*Croton Tiglium*	Malabar, Tenasserim
Cubebs	*Piper Cubeba*	
Dandelion	*Taraxacum officinale*	Temperate regions of the Globe
Deadly Nightshade	*Atropa Belladonna*	Europe and Asia

PRINCIPAL PLANTS OF ECONOMIC VALUE.

Common Name.	Botanical Name.	Native Country.
Fenugreek	*Trigonella Fœnum-græcum*	Mediterranean regions
Foxglove	*Digitalis purpurea*	Europe
Gamboge	*Garcinia Morella*	Siam and Cochin China
Gentian	*Gentiana lutea*	Alps of Europe
Guaiacum	*Guaiacum officinale*	West Indies and Tropical South America
Hellebore, or Christmas Rose	*Helleborus niger*	Europe
Hemlock	*Conium maculatum*	Europe, Asia, Africa
Henbane	*Hyoscyamus niger*	Europe, Asia, Africa
Horehound	*Marrubium vulgare*	Europe and Asia
Ipecacuanha	*Cephaëlis Ipecacuanha*	South America
Jalap	*Ipomœa (Exogonium) purga*	Mexican Andes
Lettuce	*Lactuca virosa*	Europe
Mandrake	*Mandragora officinarum*	Europe and Asia
Mezereon	*Daphne Mezereum*	Europe
Nux-Vomica	*Strychnos Nux-vomica*	India, Cochin China, and North Australia
Opium	*Papaver somniferum*	Asia
Orris-Root	*Iris germanica and Florentina*	Europe and Asia
Peruvian, or Officinal Bark	*Cinchona officinalis, etc.*	South America
Physic Nut, or Pinhœn Oil Plant	*Jatropha curcas*	South America
Quassia	*Quassias amara and excelsa*	South America and West Indies
Queensland Fever Bark	*Alstonia constricta*	Queensland
Rhubarb	*Rheum officinale and other species*	China
Rue	*Ruta graveolens*	Levant
Sarsaparilla	*Smilax, various species*	South America, India, China, Australia
Sassafras	*Laurus sassafras*	North America
Scammony	*Convolvulus Scamonia*	South Europe, Asia, and North Africa

Common Name.	Botanical Name.	Native Country.
Scurvy Grass	*Cochlearia officinalis*	Europe, Asia, and North America
Senna	*Cassia, various species*	East Africa, Arabia, Egypt, Punjaub, etc.
Snakeroot, or Birthwort	*Aristolochia Serpentaria*	North America
Stramonium, or Thorn Apple	*Datura Stramonium*	All over the warmer portions of the Globe
Squill	*Urginia (Scilla) maritima*	S. Europe, Asia, Africa
Sweet Flag	*Acorus Calamus*	Asia and North America
Tormentil	*Potentilla Tormentilla*	Europe
Valerian	*Valeriana officinalis*	Europe and North Asia
Wolf's-bane, or Monkshood	*Aconitum Napellus*	Europe, Asia, and North America
Wormwood	*Artemisia Absinthium*	Europe, Asia, and Africa
Yarrow, or Milfoil	*Achillea millefolium*	Europe, Asia, and North America

5. YIELDING GUMS, RESINS, AND BALSAMS.

Common Name	Botanical Name	Native Country
Balm of Gilead	*Balsamodendrons - Opobalsamum and Gileadense*	Arabia
Balsam of Peru	*Myroxylon (Myrospermum) Pereiræ*	Central America
Balsam of Tolu	*Myroxylon Toluifera*	Tropical America
Benzoin, or Benjamin Tree	*Styrax Benzoin*	Sumatra
Copaiva Tree	*Copaifera officinalis*	South America and West Indies
Galbanum	*Ferulas galbaniflua and rubricaulis*	Persia
Gum Arabic	*Acacias verek, Seyal and others*	Africa
Gum Elemi	*Icica and Colophonia*	South America and West Indies
Indian-Rubber Tree, or Caoutchouc	*Siphonia and Ficus elastica*	Tropical America and India

PRINCIPAL PLANTS OF ECONOMIC VALUE. 191

Common Name.	Botanical Name.	Native Country.
Mastic Tree	*Pistacia lentiscus*	Mediterranean
Opopanax	*Opopanax Chironium*	South Europe
Storax, or Styrax	*Styrax officinale*	Mediterranean
Sweet Gum	*Liquidambar Styraciflua*	North America
Tragacanth	*Astragalus*, various species	South Europe and Asia
Turpentine Tree	*Pistacia Terebinthus*	Asia and North Africa

6. FIBRE PLANTS USED IN THE MANUFACTURE OF CLOTHING, CORDAGE, AND PAPER.

Common Name	Botanical Name	Native Country
Areng, or Gomuti Palm	*Arenga Sacchifera*	Malayan Archipelago
Bowstring Hemp	*Sansevierus zeylanica* and *Roxburghiana*	India and Ceylon
Bulrush	*Typha angustifolia*	All over the World
Cape Wedding-Flower	*Dombeya natalensis*	Natal
Club, or Palm Lily	*Cordyline* (*Dracæna*), various species	India, China, South Sea Islands, New Zealand, Australia, etc.
Coast Rush	*Juncus maritimus*	All temperate climes
Cotton	*Gossypium*, various species	South America, East and West Indies
Cuba Bast	*Paritium elatum*	West Indies
Danubian, or Bamboo Reed	*Arundo Donax*	South Europe
Dragon Tree	*Dracæna Draco*	Canary Islands
Esparto.-Grass, or Atocha	*Stipa* (*Macrochloa*) *tenacissima*	Spain and Portugal
Flame Tree	*Sterculia* (*Brachychiton*) *acerifolium*	New South Wales and Queensland
Flax (common)	*Linum usitatissimum*	Supposed to have originated in the East
Flax (New Zealand)	*Phormium tenax*	New Zealand
Galingale Rush	*Cyperus lucidus*, and other species.	Throughout the World

Common Name.	Botanical Name.	Native Country.
Grasscloth Plant (Chinese)	*Bœhmeria nivea*	China, Japan, and India
Grasscloth (Queensland)	*Pipturus argenteus*	Queensland, South Sea Islands, and Indian Archipelago
Hemp	*Cannabis sativa*	Asia
Indian Rose Hemp	*Hibiscus mutabilis*	East Indies
Jute	*Corchorus càpsularis and C. olitorius*	Asia
Lace Bark (New Zealand)	*Hoheria populnea*	New Zealand
Maddoo Grass	*Cycas circinalis*	Malayan Islands
Manilla Hemp	*Musa textilis*	Philippine Islands
Muddar Plant	*Calotropis gigantea*	India
Papyrus, or Paper Reed	*Cyperus (Papyrus) antiquorum*	South Europe and the East
Peruvian Hemp	*Buonapartea juncea*	Peru
Petre Hemp	*Yucca gloriosa*	Southern United States of America
Pita Hemp	*Agave americana*	South America and West Indies
Queensland Hemp	*Sida retusa*	Queensland, Asia, Africa, and America
Queensland Hollyhock Tree	*Hibiscus splendens*	Queensland and New South Wales
Ribbon Tree of Otago	*Plagianthus betulinus*	New Zealand
Rosella Hemp	*Hibiscus sabdariffa*	East and West Indies
Screw Pine	*Pandanus, various species*	Mauritius, Pacific Isles, Australia, Java, etc.
Sea Mallow	*Lavatera maritima*	South Europe
Sesal Hemp	*Fourcroya gigantea*	South America and West Indies
Sheathed Rush	*Juncus vaginatus*	New South Wales
Spear Lily	*Doryanthes excelsa*	Queensland and New South Wales
Sunn Hemp	*Crotalaria juncea*	Tropical Australia, S. Asia, and Jamaica

Common Name.	Botanical Name.	Native Country.
Victorian Hemp	*Plagianthus pulchellus*	Victoria, New South Wales, and Tasmania
Victorian Bottle Tree, or Currajong	*Sterculia diversifolia*	Victoria, New South Wales, and Queensland

7. PLANTS USED FOR DYEING.

Arnatto, or Annotto	*Bixa Orellana*	Tropical America and West Indies
Brazil Wood	*Cæsalpinia Sappan, and other species*	East Indies
Dyers' Broom, or Woadwaxen	*Genista tinctoria*	Europe
Avignon, or French Berries	*Rhamnus infectorius*	Mediterranean
Fustic	*Maclura tinctoria*	Jamaica and South America
Henna, or Henne	*Lawsonia albia*	South Africa, Arabia, Persia, and India
Indigo	*Indigofera tinctoria*	East Indies
Logwood	*Hæmatoxylon campechianum*	Central America
Madder	*Rubia tinctoria*	Mediterranean
Officinal Croton, or Turnsole	*Croton tinctoria*	South Europe
Safflower, or Bastard Saffron	*Carthamus tinctorius*	Asia and Africa
Sumach, or Shumach	*Rhus coriaria*	Mediterranean
Turmeric	*Curcuma longa*	Southern Asia
Woad	*Isatis tinctoria*	South Europe

8. PRINCIPAL TIMBER TREES OF COMMERCE.

Common Name.	Botanical Name.	Native Country.
Ash	*Fraxinus excelsior*	Europe, Asia, and Africa
Beech (common)	*Fagus sylvatica*	Europe and Asia
Beech (Australian), or Myrtle Tree	*Fagus Cunninghamii*	Victoria and Tasmania
Birch	*Betula alba*	Europe and Asia
Blue Gum	*Eucalyptus globulus*	Victoria and Tasmania
Blackwood, or Lightwood	*Acacia melanoxylon*	Victoria, New South Wales, South Australia, and Tasmania
Box	*Buxus sempervirens*	Europe, Asia, and Africa
Cheesewood	*Pittosporum bicolor*	Victoria and Tasmania
Cedar of Lebanon	*Cedrus Libani*	Mounts Lebanon and Taurus
Cypress	*Cupressus sempervirens*	South Europe and Levant
Ebony	*Diospyros Ebenum*	Ceylon
Elm	*Ulmus campestris*	South Europe and Asia
Hickory	*Carya, various species*	North America
Jarrah, or Mahogany Gum	*Eucalyptus marginata*	Western Australia
Karri, or West Australian Gum	*Eucalyptus diversicolor*	Western Australia
Kauri Pine	*Dammara australis*	New Zealand
Lancewood	*Guatteria (Oxandra) virgata*	Jamaica, Cuba, and Hayti
Lime, or Linden Tree	*Tilia europæa*	Europe and Asia
Lignum-vitæ	*Guaiacum officinale*	Jamaica, Cuba, and Venezuela
Mahogany	*Swietenia Mahogani*	Mexico, Central America, and West Indies
Maple	*Acer campestre*	Europe and Asia

PRINCIPAL PLANTS OF ECONOMIC VALUE.

Common Name.	Botanical Name.	Native Country.
Myall (Fragrant)	*Acacia homalophylla*	Victoria and New South Wales
Myall (Weeping)	*Acacia pendula*	Victoria and New South Wales
Norway Spruce	*Pinus (Abies) excelsa*	Europe
Oak	*Quercus Robur and others*	Europe and Asia
Pine, or Deal-wood	*Pinus, various species*	Europe, Asia, and North America
Red Gum	*Eucalyptus rostrata*	Victoria, New South Wales, and South Australia
Rosewood	*Dalbergia nigra, etc.*	South America
Sandal-wood (South Sea Islands)	*Santalum obtusifolium*	New Caledonia, Aneitum, etc.
Sandal-wood (Australian)	*Santalum acuminatum*	West Australia
Sandal-wood (Yellow)	*Santalum Freycenetianum*	Sandwich Islands
Sandal-wood (White)	*Santalum album*	India
Sydney or Red Cedar	*Cedrela Toona, Syn. C. australis*	New South Wales, Queensland, and India
Teak	*Tectona grandis*	Southern Asia

WILD PLANTS

Found around MELBOURNE, many of which are common in NEW SOUTH WALES, QUEENSLAND, SOUTH AUSTRALIA, and TASMANIA, arranged in their various orders in sequence.[1]

NATURAL ORDER.	BOTANICAL NAME.	VERNACULAR NAME.
Ranunculaceæ	*Clematis microphylla*	Australian Virgin's Bower
,,	,, *aristata*	Native Supple Jack
,,	*Myosurus minimus*	Small Mouse Tail
,,	*Ranunculus lappaceus*	Burdock-like Crowfoot
,,	,, *parviflorus*	Small-flowered Crowfoot
,,	,, *rivularis*	Water Crowfoot
Dilleniaceæ	*Hibbertia acicularis*	Pointed-leaved Hibbertia
,,	,, *fasciculata*	Bundle-flowered Hibbertia
,,	,, *sericea*, variety *densiflora*	Dense-flowered Hibbertia
,,	,, *stricta*	Erect-growing Hibbertia
Cruciferæ	*Cakile maritima*	Sea Rocket
,,	*Capsella bursa-pastoris*	Shepherd's Purse
,,	*Cardamine parviflora*	Small-flowered Lady's Smock
,,	*Lepedium ruderale*	Rubble Pepperwort
,,	*Senebiera coronopus*	Buckhorn Wart Cress

[1] Those marked with an asterisk have been introduced from Europe, etc., and are now naturalized here.

Natural Order.	Botanical Name.	Vernacular Name.
Cruciferæ	*Stenopetalum lineare*	Narrow-leaved Stenopetalum
Violaceæ	*Viola betonicæfolia*	Betony-leaved Violet
,,	,, *hederacea*	Ivy-leaved Violet
,,	*Viola hederacea*, variety *Sieberiana*	Sieber's Violet
Pittosporeæ	*Billardiera scandens*	Climbing Native Gooseberry
,,	*Bursaria spinosa*	Prickly Box, or French Island Myrtle
Tremandreæ	*Tetratheca ciliata*	Purple Heath Flower
Polygaleæ	*Comesperma ericina*	Heath-like Comesperma
,,	,, *volubile*	Common Blue Creeper
Caryophylleæ	*Sagina procumbens*	Creeping Pearlwort
,,	*Silene gallica	French Catch-fly
,,	**Spergula arvensis*	Corn Spurrey
,,	*Spergularia rubra*	Red-flowered Spergularia
Portulaceæ	*Claytonia Australasica*	Australian Claytonia
,,	*Portulaca oleracea*	Common Purslane
Hypericineæ	*Hypericum gramineum*	Grass-leaved St. John's Wort
Malvaceæ	*Modiola Caroliniana*	Carolina Modiola
,,	*Plagianthus pulchellus*	Victorian Hemp-bush
Sterculiaceæ	*Lasiopetalum ferrugineum*	Rusty Lasiopetalum
Lineæ	*Linum marginale*	Native Flax
Geraniaceæ	*Erodium cicutarium*	Hemlock-leaved Cranesbill
,,	*Geranium dissectum*	Divided-leaved Geranium
,,	*Oxalis corniculata*	Native Wood-Sorrel
,,	*Pelargonium Australe*	Native Storksbill
,,	,, *Rodneyanum*	Rodney's Storksbill
Rutaceæ	*Correa alba*	White Native Fuchsia
,,	,, *speciosa*, variety *normalis*	Common Native Fuchsia
Stackhousieæ	*Stackhousia monogyna*	One-styled Stackhousia
Leguminosæ	*Acacia armata*	Prickly Acacia
,,	,, *dealbata*	Silver Wattle

Natural Order.	Botanical Name.	Vernacular Name.
Leguminosæ	*Acacia decurrens*, var. *mollissima*	Common or 'Black Wattle
,,	,, *juniperina*	Prickly Wattle
,,	,, *longifolia*	Long-leaved Wattle
,,	,, ,, variety *Sophoræ*	Coast Wattle
,,	,, *oxycedrus*	Juniper Wattle
,,	,, *pycnantha*	Golden Wattle
,,	,, *suaveolens*	Sweet-scented Wattle
,,	*Aotus villosus*	Hairy Aotus
,,	*Bossiæa cinerea*	Ash-grey Bossiæa
,,	,, *prostrata*	Trailing Bossiæa
,,	*Daviesia corymbosa*	Native Hop
,,	,, *ulicina*	Furze-leaved Native Hop
,,	*Dillwynia cinerascens*	Ashy Dillwynia
,,	*Glycine Latrobeana*	Governor La Trobe's Glycine
,,	*Gompholobium Huegeli*	Hugel's Gompholobium
,,	*Hardenbergia monophylla*	Victorian Sarsaparilla
,,	*Hovea heterophylla*	Various-leaved Hovea
,,	*Indigofera australis*	Native Indigo or Lilac
,,	*Kennedya prostrata*	Native Scarlet Runner, or Scarlet Pea
,,	*Lotus corniculatus*	Small-horned Birdsfoot Trefoil
,,	*Medicago denticulata*	Toothed Medick
,,	*Melilotus officinalis*	Common Melilot, or King's Clover
,,	*Platylobium obtusangulum*	Victorian Flat Pea
,,	*Pultenæa dentata*	Tooth-bracted Pultenæa
,,	,, *paleacea*	Chaffy Pultenæa
,,	,, *tenuifolia*	Slender-leaved Pultenæa
,,	*Sphærolobium vimineum*	Twiggy Sphærolobium
,,	*Trifolium filiforme*	Thread-like Clover
,,	* ,, *repens*	White Clover
,,	* ,, *tomentosum*	Woolly Clover
,,	*Viminaria denudata*	Swamp Oak, or Broom
Rosaceæ	*Acæna ovina*	Sheep's-Burr

Natural Order.	Botanical Name.	Vernacular Name.
Rosaceæ	*Acæna sanguisorba*	Burnet-leaved Sheep's-Burr
Crassulaceæ	*Tillæa macrantha*	Large-flowered Tillæa
,,	,, *recurva*	Recurved Tillæa
,,	,, *verticillaris*	Whorled Tillæa
Droseraceæ	*Drosera auriculatus*	Ear-like Sundew
,,	,, *glanduligera*	Gland-bearing Sundew
,,	,, *Menziesii*	Menzies' Sundew
,,	,, *peltata*	Shield-shaped Sundew
,,	,, *pygmæa*	Dwarf Sundew
,,	,, *spathulata*	Spathulate-leaved Sundew
,,	,, *Whittakeri*	Whittaker's Sundew
Halorageæ	*Callitriche verna*	Water Starwort
,,	*Haloragis micrantha*	Small-flowered Haloragis
,,	,, *tetragyna*	Four-styled Haloragis
,,	*Myriophyllum varii folium*	Various-leaved Water Milfoil
,,	,, *verrucosum*	Warted Water Milfoil
Myrtaceæ	*Eucalyptus amygdalina*	Victorian Peppermint
,,	,, *melliodora*	Victorian Yellow Box
,,	,, *polyanthemos*	Victorian Bastard Box
,,	,, *rostrata*	Victorian Red Gum
,,	,, *viminalis*	Victorian Manna Gum
,,	*Leptospermum flavescens*	Yellowish Leptospermum
,,	,, *lævigatum*	Coast Tea Tree or Sand-stay Bush
,,	,, *myrsinoides*	Myrsine-like Leptospermum
,,	,, *scoparium*	Tasmanian Tea Bush
,,	*Melaleuca ericifolia*	Common Tea Tree
,,	,, *parviflora*	Small-flowered Tea Tree
,,	,, *squarrosa*	Victorian Yellow-Wood, or Yellow Bottlebrush
Lythrarieæ	*Lythrum salicaria*	Purple Willow Herb, or Loose Strife
Onagrarieæ	**Epilobium tetragonum*	Square-stalked Willow Herb

Natural Order.	Botanical Name.	Vernacular Name.
Ficoideæ	*Mesembryanthemum australe*	Common Victorian Noon-flower, or Pig's-face
,,	,, *tegens*	Clothing Noon-flower, or Pig's-face
,,	*Tetragona implexicoma*	Victorian Bower Spinach
Umbelliferæ	*Apium australe*	Native Celery
,,	*Daucus brachyatus*	Native Carrot
,,	*Hydrocotyle callicarpa*	Beautiful-fruited Pennywort
,,	,, *laxiflora*	Loose-flowered Pennywort
,,	*Siebiera ericoides*	Heath-like Siebera
,,	*Trachymene australis*	Native Parsnip
,,	*Xanthosia dissecta*	Divided-leaved Xanthosia
,,	,, *pusilla*	Dwarf Xanthosia
Loranthaceæ	*Loranthus celastroides*	Celastrus-like Mistletoe
,,	,, *pendulus*	Hanging Mistletoe
,,	,, *Quandang*	Hoary Mistletoe
Rubiaceæ	*Asperula conferta*	Crowded Woodruff
,,	*Coprosma Billardieri*	Victorian Native Currant
,,	,, *hirtella*	Victorian or Native Coffee-plant
,,	*Galium Gaudichaudiana*	Gaudichaud's Galium
,,	*Opercularia varia*	Changing Opercularia
Compositæ	*Angianthus eriocephalus*	Woolly-headed Angianthus
,,	,, *Preissianus*	Preiss' Angianthus
,,	*Brachycome cardiocarpa*	Heartshaped-fruited Native Daisy
,,	,, *diversifolia*	Various-leaved Native Daisy
,,	,, *graminea*	Grass-like Native Daisy
,,	*Calocephalus Brownii*	Garland Flower
,,	,, *lacteus*	Milky Garland Flower
,,	*Calotis scapigera*	Scape-bearing Calotis

Natural Order.	Botanical Name.	Vernacular Name.
Compositæ	*Carduus marianus*	Spotted Thistle
,,	*Centaurea Melitensis*	Maltese Centaury
,,	*Cirsium lanceolatum*	Spear Thistle
,,	*Cotula australis*	Southern Cotula
,,	,, *coronopifolia*	Buckhorn-leaved Cotula
,,	*Craspedia Richei*	Riche's Craspedia
,,	*Cryptostemma calendulacea*	Cape Weed
,,	*Cymbonotus Lawsonianus*	Lawson's Cymbonotus
,,	*Erecthites arguta*	Quaint Erecthites
,,	,, *quadridentata*	Four-toothed Erecthites
,,	*Gnaphalium japonicum*	Japanese Gnaphalium
,,	* ,, *luteo alba*	Yellowish-white Gnaphalium
,,	*Helichrysum apiculatum*	Pointed-leaved Everlasting Flower
,,	,, *bracteatum*	Common Australian Everlasting Flower
,,	,, *cinereum*	Ash-grey Everlasting Flower
,,	,, *ferrugineum*	Rusty Everlasting Flower
,,	,, *scorpioides*	Scorpion-like Everlasting Flower
,,	,, *semi-papposa*	Partly Downy Everlasting Flower
,,	*Helipterum dimorpholepis*	Sun Wing
,,	*Hypochæris glabra*	Smooth Cat's-ear
,,	* ,, *radicata*	Rooting Cat's-ear, Spurious Dandelion, or Sheep Tonic
,,	*Lagenophora Billardiera*	Labillardiere's Bottle Thistle
,,	,, *emphysopus*	The Bottle Thistle
,,	*Leptorhynchus squamatus*	Scaly Leptorhynchus, or Slender Beak
,,	,, *tenuifolius*	Slender-leaved Leptorhynchus
,,	*Microseris Forsteri*	Native Yam
,,	*Millotia tenuifolia*	Slender-leaved Millotia

Natural Order.	Botanical Name.	Vernacular Name.
Compositæ	*Myriogyne minuta*	Small Myriogyne
,,	*Olearia axillaris*	Axillary-flowered Olearia
,,	,, *stellulata*	Native Snow Bush
,,	*Podolepis acuminata*	Pointed-leaved Podolepis
,,	*Rutidosis pumilo*	Dwarf Rutidosis
,,	*Senecio australis*	Australian Groundsel
,,	,, *vagus*	Straggling Groundsel
,,	**Sonchus oleraceus*	Milk or Sow Thistle
,,	*Stuartina Muelleri*	Mueller's Stuartina
,,	*Vittadenia australis*	Southern Vittadenia
,,	*Xanthium spinosum*	Bathurst Burr
Stylideæ	*Levenhookia dubia*	
,,	*Stylidium despectum*	Despised Stylewort
,,	,, *gramineum*	Grass-leaved Stylewort
Goodenovieæ	*Brunonia australis*	Native Forget-me-not, or Ladies' Button
,,	*Goodenia geniculata*	Jointed Goodenia
,,	,, *heteromera*	Various-stemmed Goodenia
,,	,, *ovata*	Ovate-leaved Goodenia
,,	*Goodenia pinnatifida*	Pinnate-leaved Goodenia
,,	*Selliera radicans*	Victorian Swamp Weed
,,	*Velleia paradoxa*	Paradoxical Velleia
Campanulaceæ	*Isotoma fluviatalis*	River Isotoma
,,	*Lobelia anceps*	Double-headed Lobelia
,,	,, *gibbosa*	Swollen Lobelia
,,	*Pratia platycalyx*	Broad-calyxed Pratia
,,	*Wahlenbergia gracilis*	Native Blue Bell
Epacrideæ	*Acrotriche serrulata*	Notch-leaved Acrotriche
,,	*Astroloma humifusa*	Creeping Native Cranberry
,,	*Epacris impressa*	Common Native Heath
,,	,, *obtusifolia*	Blunt-leaved Native Heath
,,	*Leucopogon Richei*	Tasmanian Native Currant

Natural Order.	Botanical Name.	Vernacular Name.
Epacrideæ	*Leucopogon virgatus*	Twiggy Leucopogon
,,	*Monotoca scoparia*	Broom Monotoca
,,	*Sprengelia incarnata*	Flesh-coloured Sprengelia
Primulaceæ	**Anagallis arvensis*	Common Pimpernel
,,	*Samolus repens*	Creeping Brookweed
Apocyneæ	*Alyxia buxifolia*	Tonga Bean Wood
Loganiaceæ	*Mitrasacme paradoxa*	Paradoxical Mitrasacme
Gentianeæ	*Erythræa australis*	Native Centaury
,,	*Sebæa albidiflora*	White-flowered Sebæa
,,	,, *ovata*	Ovate-leaved Sebæa
,,	*Villarsia reniformis*	Kidney-leaved Marsh Buttercup
Boragineæ	*Cynoglossum suaveolens*	Sweet-scented Hound's tongue
Convolvulaceæ	*Convolvulus erubescens*	Pink Convolvulus
,,	,, *sepium*	Great Hedge Bindweed
,,	*Dichondra repens*	Kidney Weed
,,	*Wilsonia humilis*	Dwarf Wilsonia
Solaneæ	*Nicotiana suaveolens*	Native Tobacco
,,	*Solanum nigrum*	Black-fruited Nightshade
Schrophularineæ	*Euphrasia speciosa*	Showy Euphrasia
,,	*Gratiola Peruviana*	Victorian Hedge Hyssop
,,	*Mimulus repens*	Creeping Monkey Flower
,,	*Veronica gracilis*	Slender Speedwell
Lentibularieæ	*Utricularia dichotoma*	Lady's Satchel, or Hooded Milfoil
,,	,, *lateriflora*	Side-flowered Hooded Milfoil
Myoporineæ	*Myoporum serratum*	Common Blueberry Tree
Labiatæ	*Ajuga australis*	Native Bugle
,,	*Mentha australis*	Native Mint
,,	*Scutellaria humilis*	Dwarf Skull-cap
,,	*Teucrium corymbosum*	Corymb-flowered Germander
Plantagineæ	*Plantago coronopis*	Star of the Earth
,,	* ,, *lanceolata*	Common Rib Grass

Natural Order.	Botanical Name.	Vernacular Name.
Pantagineæ	*Plantago major*	Greater Plantain
,,	,, *varia*	Changing Plantain
Chenopodiaceæ	*Atriplex patula*	Spreading Orache
,,	,, *semi-baccata*	Berry-bearing Salt Bush
,,	**Chenopodium album*	White Goosefoot
,,	,, *carinatum*	Keeled Goosefoot
,,	** ,, murale*	Wall Goosefoot
,,	*Enchylæna villosa*	Hairy Euchylæna
,,	*Kochia sedifolia*	Sedum-leaved Broom Cypress
,,	*Rhagodia Billardieri*	Labillardiere's Sea-berry
,,	,, *linifolia*	Flax-leaved Sea-berry
,,	,, *nutans*	Nodding Sea-berry
,,	*Salicornia arbuscula*	Shrubby Glasswort
,,	,, *australe*	Southern Glasswort
,,	*Suæda maritima*	Sea Goosefoot
Amarantaceæ	*Alternanthera denticulata*	Toothed Joy Weed
,,	*Trichinium spathulatum*	Native Foxtail
Polygonaceæ	*Polygonum aviculare*	Wire Grass or Bird's Polygonum
,,	,, *lapathifolium*	Dock-leaved Redshanks
,,	**Rumex acetosella*	Common Sorrel
,,	,, *Brownii*	Swamp Dock
,,	,, *crispus*	Common Dock
Laurineæ	*Cassytha melantha*	Common Scrub Vine, or Dodder Laurel
,,	,, *glabella*	Smooth Scrub Vine, or Dodder Laurel
Proteaceæ	*Banksia integrifolia*	Common, or Hill Honeysuckle
,,	,, *marginata*	Coast Honeysuckle
,,	*Grevillea ericifolia*	Heath-leaved Grevillea
,,	*Hakea ulicina*	Native Furze
,,	*Isopogon ceratophyllus*	Buckshorn-leaved Isopogon
,,	*Lomatia Fraseri*	Native Holly
,,	*Persoonia juniperina*	Juniper-like Persoonia
Thymeleæ	*Pimelea curviflora*	Curved-flowered Tough Bark, or Rice Flower

WILD PLANTS.

Natural Order.	Botanical Name.	Vernacular Name.
Thymeleæ	*Pimelea humilis*	Dwarf Tough Bark, or Rice Flower
,,	,, *octophylla*	Eight-leafleted Tough Bark, or Rice Flower
,,	,, *phylicoides*	Phylica-like Tough Bark, or Rice Flower
Euphorbiaceæ	*Amperea spartioides*	Broom-like Amperea
,,	*Poranthera microphylla*	Small-leaved Poranthera
,,	*Ricinocarpus pinifolius*	Pine-leaved Ricinocarpus
Urticeæ	*Australina pusilla*	Dwarf Australina
,,	*Urtica incisa*	Native Nettle
Casuarineæ	*Casuarina distyla*	Stunted Sheoak
,,	,, *stricta*	Coast, or Drooping Sheoak
,,	,, *suberosa*	Common Sheoak, or Beefwood
Santalaceæ	*Exocarpus cupressiformis*	Native Cherry
Hydrocharideæ	*Ottelia ovalifolia*	Oval-leaved Ottelia
Orchideæ	*Acianthus fornicatus*	Arched Acianthus
,,	*Caladenia barbata*	Bearded Caladenia
,,	,, *carnea*	Flesh-coloured Caladenia
,,	,, *fimbriata*	Fringed Caladenia
,,	,, *latifolia*	Broad-leaved Caladenia
,,	,, *Menziesii*	Menzies' Caladenia
,,	,, *Patersonii*	Paterson's Caladenia
,,	*Calochilus campestris*	Field Calochilus
,,	*Corysanthes fimbriatus*	Fringed Corysanthes
,,	*Cyrtostylis reniformis*	Kidney-leaved Cyrtostylis
,,	*Diuris longifolia*	Long-leaved Diuris
,,	,, *maculata*	Spotted Diuris
,,	,, *pedunculata*	Long-stalked Diuris
,,	,, *punctata*	Dotted Diuris
,,	,, *sulphurea*	Dog's-eye Orchid
,,	*Eriochilus autumnalis*	Autumn Flowering Eriochilus
,,	*Glossodia major*	Large Tongue Orchid

Natural Order.	Botanical Name.	Vernacular Name.
Orchideæ	*Lyperanthus nigricans*	Native Flower of Sadness
,,	*Microtis porrifolius*	Leek-leaved Microtis
,,	*Orthoceras strictum*	Upright-growing Orthoceras
,,	*Prasophyllum alatum*	Tall Prasophyllum
,,	*Pterostylis aphylla*	Leafless Frog's-mouth Orchid
,,	,, *barbata*	Bearded Frog's-mouth Orchid
,,	,, *concinna*	Neat Frog's-mouth Orchid
,,	,, *cucullata*	Hooded Frog's-mouth Orchid
,,	,, *longifolia*	Long-leaf Frog's-mouth Orchid
,,	,, *mutica*	Shortened Frog's-mouth Orchid
,,	,, *nutans*	Nodding Frog's-mouth Orchid
,,	,, *præcox*	Tall Frog's-mouth Orchid
,,	*Thelymitra antennifera*	Native Hyacinth
,,	,, *aristata*	Awned Ladies' Cap Orchid
,,	,, *carnea*	Flesh-coloured Ladies' Cap Orchid
,,	,, *epipactoides*	Epipactis-like Ladies' Cap Orchid
,,	,, *ixioides*	Ixia-like Ladies' Cap Orchid
,,	,, *longifolia*	Long-leaved Ladies' Cap Orchid
Irideæ	*Patersonia glauca*	Native Swamp Flag
,,	,, *longiscapa*	Native Purple Lily
Amaryllideæ	*Hypoxis glabella*	Victorian Crocus
Liliaceæ	*Anguillaria dioica*	Victorian Snowdrop
,,	*Arthropodium minus*	Small Grass Lily
,,	*Bulbine bulbosa*	Bulbous-rooted Bulbine

Natural Order.	Botanical Name.	Vernacular Name.
Liliaceæ	*Burchardia umbellata*	Australian Colchicum
,,	*Cæsia parviflora*	Small-flowered Cæsia
,,	,, *vittata*	Blue-striped Grass Lily
,,	*Chamæscilla corymbosa*	Native Star of Bethlehem
,,	*Dianella lævis*	Smooth-leaved Flax Lily
,,	,, *revoluta*	Curled Flax Lily
,,	*Dichopogon strictus*	Common Grass Lily
,,	*Laxmannia sessiliflora*	Stemless-flowered Laxmannia
,,	*Thysanotus Patersonii*	Twining Fringe Lily
,,	,, *tuberosus*	Tuberous-rooted Fringe Lily
,,	*Tricoryne elatior*	Tall Tricoryne
Xyrideæ	*Xyris gracilis*	Slender Xyris
Juncaceæ	*Juncus bufonius*	Toad Rush
,,	,, *capitatus*	Headed Rush
,,	,, *maritimus*	Common Coast Rush
,,	,, *prismatocarpus*	Prism-shape fruited Rush
,,	,, *vaginatus*	Sheathed Rush
,,	*Luzula campestris*	Wood Rush, or Glow-worm Grass
,,	*Xanthorrhœa minor*	Dwarf Grass Tree
,,	*Xerotes filiformis*	Thread-shape Mat Rush
,,	,, *longifolia*	Native Tussack Grass, or Mat Rush
Typhaceæ	*Typha angustifolia*	Native Cat's-tail, or Bulrush
Naiadeæ	*Potomogeton crispum*	Curled Pond-weed
,,	,, *natans*	Floating Pond-weed
Centrolepideæ	*Aphelia gracilis*	Slender Aphelia
,,	,, *pumilio*	Dwarf Aphelia
,,	*Centrolepis aristata*	Awned Centrolepis
,,	,, *fascicularis*	Bundle-flowered Centrolepis
,,	,, *strigosa*	Hairy Centrolepis
Restiaceæ	*Hypolæna fastigiata*	Pyramidal Hypolæna

Natural Order.	Botanical Name.	Vernacular Name.
Restiaceæ	*Hypolæna lateriflora*	Side-flowering Hypolæna
Cyperaceæ	*Carex clorantha*	Green-flowered Sedge Grass
,,	,, *pseud-cyperus*	False Galingale Rush
,,	*Cladium articulatum*	Jointed Cladium
,,	,, *filum*	Thread-like Cladium
,,	*Cyperus lucidus*	Shining Galingale Rush
,,	,, *rotundus*	Round-rooted Galingale Rush
,,	*Gahnia radula*	Cutting Grass, or Black Reed
,,	*Heleocharis acuta*	Pointed Heleocharis
,,	,, *multicaulis*	Many-stemmed Heleocharis
,,	,, *spacelata*	Withered Heleocharis
,,	*Lepidosperma gladiatum*	Coast Sword Rush
,,	,, *tenuissimum*	Slender Sword Rush
,,	*Scirpus maritimus*	Coast Club Rush
Gramineæ	*Agropyrum Scabrum*	Rough Agropyrum
,,	*Aira caryophylla*	Wheat-eared Aira
,,	*Anthistiria ciliata*	Kangaroo Grass
,,	**Anthoxanthemum odoratum*	Sweet Vernal Grass
,,	*Aristida vagans*	Spreading Aristida
,,	**Avena fatua*	Wild Oats
,,	**Briza major*	Large Quaking or Quivering Grass
,,	* ,, *minor*	Smaller Quaking or Quivering Grass
,,	*Cynodon dactylon*	Indian Doub, or Couch Grass
,,	*Danthonia racemosa*, var. *penicillata*	Wallaby Grass
,,	,, *semi-annularis*	Partly-ringed Danthonia
,,	*Deyeuxia Forsteri*	Forster's Deyeuxia
,,	,, *quadriseta*	Four-bristled Deyeuxia
,,	*Dichelachne crinita*	Mouse Grass
,,	*Distichlis maritima*	Native Couch Grass

Natural Order.	Botanical Name.	Vernacular Name.
Gramineæ	*Echinopogon ovatus*	Ovate Echinopogon
,,	*Eragrostis Brownii*	Australian Love Grass
,,	*Lepturus cylindricus*	Cylindrical Lepturus
,,	,, *incurvatus*	Incurved Lepturus
,,	*Microlæna Stipoides*	Stipa-like Microlæna
,,	*Panicum Sanguinale*	Reddish Panic Grass
,,	*Paspalum distichum*	Swamp Couch Grass
,,	*Phalaris canariensis*	Canary Grass
,,	*Phragmitis communis*	Common Reed
,,	*Poa cæspitosa, var. australis*	Native Paper Grass
,,	*Polypogon monspiliensis*	Montpelier Polypogon
,,	*Spinifex hirsutus*	Hairy Spinifex
,,	*Sporobolus indicus*	Indian Sporobolus
,,	*Stipa flavescens*	Yellowish Feather Grass
,,	,, *semi-barbata, var. mollis*	Partly-bearded Soft Feather Grass
,,	,, *setacea*	Bristled Feather Grass
Filices	*Adiantum Æthiopicum*	Maiden Hair Fern
,,	*Cheilanthes tenuifolia*	Slender Grass Fern
,,	*Schizæa bifida*	Forked Schizæa
,,	*Pteris aquilina, var. esculenta*	Common Bracken
,,	*Lindsaya linearis*	
Lycopodiaceæ	*Selaginella uliginosa*	Swamp Moss

LIST OF NATURAL ORDERS OF PLANTS REPRESENTED IN AUSTRALIA.[1]

WITH REFERENCES TO EXAMPLES WHERE THEY OCCUR IN PRECEDING PAGES.

Class I. — Dicotyledons.

Sub-Class I.—Polypetaleæ.

ORDER
- I. Ranunculaceæ, 104, 112, 131, 133, 142, 159, 196.
- II. Dilleniaceæ, 196.
- III. Magnoliaceæ, 136, 151.
- IV. Anonaceæ, 119.
- V. Menispermaceæ.
- VI. Nymphæaceæ, 136, 169.
- VII. Papaveraceæ, 109, 165.
- VIII. Cruciferæ, 105, 109, 167, 173, 178, 179, 196.
- IX. Capparideæ.
- X. Violarieæ, 170, 179.
- XI. Bixineæ.
- XII. Pittosporeæ, 142, 147, 163, 197.
- XIII. Tremandreæ, 197.
- XIV. Polygaleæ, 197.
- XV. Frankeniaceæ.
- XVI. Caryophylleæ, 197.
- XVII. Portulaceæ, 197.
- XVIII. Elatineæ.
- XIX. Hypericineæ, 197.
- XX. Guttiferæ.

ORDER
- XXI. Malvaceæ, 197.
- XXII. Sterculiaceæ, 99, 121, 197.
- XXIII. Tiliaceæ, 118, 135.
- XXIV. Lineæ, 197.
- XXV. Malpighiaceæ.
- XXVI. Zygophyllaceæ.
- XXVII. Geraniaceæ, 141, 146, 155, 161, 181, 197.
- XXVIII. Rutaceæ, 145, 158, 197.
- XXIX. Simarubæ.
- XXX. Burseraceæ.
- XXXI. Meliaceæ, 167, 180.
- XXXII. Olacineæ.
- XXXIII. Ilicineæ, 129.
- XXXIV. Celastrineæ.
- XXXV. Stackhousieæ, 197.
- XXXVI. Rhamneæ, 148.
- XXXVII. Ampelideæ, 124, 132, 147.
- XXXVIII. Sapindaceæ, 129, 149, 174.
- XXXIX. Anacardiaceæ, 156.
- XL. Leguminosæ, 102, 107, 108, 115, 135, 148, 152, 160, 163, 166, 171, 181, 197, 198.

[1] Compiled from *Flora Australiensis*.

LIST OF NATURAL ORDERS OF PLANTS.

ORDER
    Sub-Orders.
  1. Papilionaceæ.
  2. Cæsalpineæ.
  3. Mimosæ.

- XLI. Rosaceæ, 97, 98, 110, 128, 134, 135, 156, 160, 164, 167, 168, 173, 198, 199.
- XLII. Saxifrageæ, 113, 124.
- XLIII. Crassulaceæ, 112, 199.
- XLIV. Droseraceæ, 199.
- XLV. Halorageæ, 199.
- XLVI. Rhizophoreæ, 137.
- XLVII. Combretaceæ.
- XLVIII. Myrtaceæ, 103, 123, 125, 135, 138, 141, 151; 199.
- XLIX. Melastomaceæ.
- L. Lythrarieæ, 199.
- LI. Onagrarieæ, 122, 199.

ORDER
- LII. Samydaceæ.
- LIII. Passifloreæ, 151, 160.
- LIV. Cucurbitaceæ, 113, 124, 138.
- LV. Ficoideæ, 141, 200.
- LVI. Umbelliferæ, 108, 120, 123, 142, 150, 160, 200.
- LVII. Araliaceæ, 118, 130, 160, 168.
- LVIII. Cornaceæ.
- LIX. Loranthaceæ, 139, 200.
- LX. Caprifoliaceæ, 118, 134, 144.
- LXI. Rubiaceæ, 135, 155, 200.
- LXII. Compositæ, 98, 107, 108, 112, 114, 115, 131, 138, 144, 150, 153, 156, 173, 175, 177, 200, 201, 202.

Sub-Class II.—Monopetaleæ.

ORDER
- LXIII. Stylideæ, 202.
- LXIV. Goodenovieæ, 202.
- LXV. Campanulaceæ, 202.
- LXVI. Ericaceæ, 167.
- LXVII. Epacrideæ, 143, 148, 202, 203.
- LXVIII. Plumbagineæ.
- LXIX. Primulaceæ, 203.
- LXX. Myrsineæ, 153.
- LXXI. Sapotaceæ, 166.
- LXXII. Ebenaceæ.
- LXXIII. Styracaceæ.
- LXXIV. Jasmineæ, 99, 131, 134, 165.
- LXXV. Apocyneæ, 133, 136, 157, 161, 203.
- LXXVI. Asclepiadeæ, 149.
- LXXVII. Loganiaceæ, 203.
- LXXVIII. Gentianeæ, 203.
- LXXIX. Hydrophyllaceæ.
- LXXX. Boragineæ, 103, 129, 203.

ORDER
- LXXXI. Convolvulaceæ, 112, 133, 142, 203.
- LXXXII. Solaneæ, 110, 120, 132, 165, 176, 203.
- LXXXIII. Scrophularineæ, 115, 203.
- LXXXIV. Lentibularieæ, 203.
- LXXXV. Orobanchaceæ.
- LXXXVI. Gesneraceæ, 120.
- LXXXVII. Bignoniaceæ, 139, 177, 180.
- LXXXVIII. Acanthaceæ.
- LXXXIX. Pedalineæ.
- XC. Myoporineæ, 203.
- XCI. Selagineæ.
- XCII. Verbenaceæ, 178.
- XCIII. Labiatæ, 116, 123, 134, 149, 203.
- XCIV. Plantagineæ, 168, 203, 204.
- XCV. Phytolaccaceæ.

ORDER
XCVI. Chenopodiaceæ, 153, 204.
XCVII. Amarantaceæ, 145, 204.
XCVIII. Paronychiaceæ.
XCIX. Polygonaceæ, 115, 204.
C. Nyctagineæ.
CI. Myristiceæ.
CII. Monimiaceæ, 150, 170.
CIII. Laurineæ, 102, 110, 204.
CIV. Proteaceæ, 125, 128, 146, 148, 151, 166, 204.
CV. Thymeleæ, 161, 205.

ORDER
CVI. Elæagnaceæ.
CVII. Nepenthaceæ.
CVIII. Euphorbiaceæ, 108, 117, 166, 205.
CIX. Urticeæ, 103, 119, 120, 150, 156, 164, 205.
CX. Casuarineæ, 171, 205.
CXI. Piperaceæ.
CXII. Aristolochiaceæ.
CXIII. Cupuliferæ, 95, 129.
CXIV. Santalaceæ, 143, 205.
CXV. Balanophoreæ.
CXVI. Coniferæ, 98, 103, 109, 114, 139, 140, 162.
CXVII. Cycadeæ, 113, 181.

Class II.—Monocotyledons.

ORDER
CXVIII. Hydrocharideæ, 205.
CXIX. Scitamineæ.
CXX. Orchideæ, 159, 205, 206.
CXXI. Burmanniaceæ.
CXXII. Irideæ, 97, 104, 113, 130, 174, 206.
CXXIII. Amaryllideæ, 97, 114, 131, 172, 178, 206.
CXXIV. Taccaceæ.
CXXV. Dioscorideæ.
CXXVI. Roxburghiaceæ.
CXXVII. Liliaceæ, 104, 111, 122, 125, 129, 135, 145, 153, 154, 158, 172, 177.
CXXVIII. Pontederaceæ.
CXXIX. Philydraceæ.
CXXX. Xyrideæ, 207.

ORDER
CXXXI. Commellinaceæ.
CXXXII. Juncaceæ, 147, 153, 169, 207.
CXXXIII. Palmæ, 105, 107, 112, 119, 134.
CXXXIV. Pandanaceæ, 170.
CXXXV. Aroideæ, 99, 106, 157.
CXXXVI. Typhaceæ, 207.
CXXXVII. Lemnaceæ.
CXXXVIII. Naiadeæ, 207.
CXXXIX. Alismaceæ.
CXL. Eriocauleæ.
CXLI. Centrolepideæ, 207.
CXLII. Restiaceæ, 207, 208.
CXLIII. Cyperaceæ.
CXLIV. Gramineæ, 130, 132, 151, 157, 170, 180, 208, 209.

Class III.—Acotyledons.

ORDER
CXLV. Lycopodiaceæ, 209.
CXLVI. Marsileaceæ (Rhizospermæ).

ORDER
CXLVII. Filices, 111, 116, 118, 124, 133, 137, 177, 209.

BOTANICAL INDEX.

A.

Abnormal, 16.
Abortive, 18.
Achene, 54.
Achlamydeous, 46.
Acorn, 51, 53.
Acotyledons, 7, 20, 56.
Acrogenous, 20, 59.
Acrogens, 57.
Adhesion, 44.
Adventitious, 15, 16.
Aerial, 15, 16, 17.
Æstivation, 44.
Albumen, 2, 6.
Albuminous, 3, 6.
Algæ, 59.
Alternate, 26.
Amentum, 42.
Andræcium, 39.
Annuals, 12.
Annular fibres, 11.
Anthers, 42.
Apetalous, 42.
Apiculate, 31, 32.
Apocarpous, 50.
Ascent, 13.
Assimilation, 25.
Axial, 15, 16.
Axis, 23.

B.

Bacca, 53.
Bark, 22, 23.
Bast, 9, 23.
Berry, 53.
Bidentate, 32.
Biennials, 12.
Bifid, 32.
Bisexual, 46.
Bracts, 34, 35.
Branches, 23.
Branchlets, 23.
Bud, 3, 4.
Bulb, 17.

C.

Calycifloral, 45.
Calyx, 39, 40, 49.
Capitules, 34, 46.
Capitulum, 34.
Capsule, 53.
Carpels, 39, 50, 51.
Caryopsis, 54.
Catkin, 42.
Cauline, 26.
Cells, 8.
Cellular, 8.
Cellular tissue, 9, 10, 12, 21.
Central rib, 29.
Centrifugal, 33.
Centripetal, 33.
Chalaza, 4.
Chlorophyll, 10, 22, 26.
Chromogen, 26.
Chromule, 26.
Circumcissile, 52.
Cirrhi, 18.
Classes, 66.
Cleft calyx, 40.
Climbing stem, 18.
Cluster, 35.
Cohesion, 44.

Collecting ferns, 58, 70, 74.
Collecting plants, 58, 70.
Colouring matter, 22, 26.
Composite, 34.
Compound, 27.
Compound leaf, 27, 28.
Compound umbel, 38.
Cone, 55.
Cordate, 30, 31.
Corm, 15, 17.
Corolla, 39, 41, 49.
Corollifloral, 45.
Corymb, 35.
Corymbose, 35.
Costa, 29.
Cotyledon, 3, 5, 6.
Creeping stem, 19.
Crenulate, 26.
Crown, 17, 23, 57.
Cruciform, 41.
Cryptogamia, 64.
Cryptogams, 20, 21, 57, 61.
Culm, 19.
Cuneate, 31, 32.
Cuneiform, 31, 32.
Cyme, 38.

D.

Decandria, 63.
Deciduous, 25, 42.
Definite inflorescence, 33.
Dehiscent, 50, 52.
Dentate, 26.
Dentate calyx, 41.
Descent, 13.
Diadelphia, 63.
Diandria, 62.
Diandrous, 39.
Dichlamydeous, 46.
Dichotomous cymes, 38.
Diclinous, 46.
Dicotyledon, 4, 7, 20, 61.

Didynamia, 63.
Digynous, 39.
Diœcia, 64.
Diœcious, 46.
Disepalous, 39.
Disk, 44, 49.
Dissection, 74.
Dodecandria, 63.
Dorsal suture, 5.
Double flowers, 39.
Drupe, 53.
Drying ferns, 71.
Drying plants, 72.
Ducts, 10, 11.
Duramen, 22.

E.

Elliptical, 30.
Embryo, 2, 6.
Endocarp, 51.
Endogen, 4, 14, 21, 22.
Endogenous, 20, 22.
Endopleura, 5.
Endosmose, 10.
Endosperm, 2.
Enneandria, 63.
Entire calyx, 41.
Entire leaf, 26.
Epicarp, 51.
Epidermis, 12, 23.
Epigynous, 43.
Epipetalous, 43.
Epiphytal, 58.
Erect branches, 23.
Erect stems, 18.
Evaporation, 25.
Evergreen, 25.
Exalbuminous, 2.
Examination of plants, 74, 76.
Exocarp, 51.
Exogen, 14, 21.

BOTANICAL INDEX.

Exogenous, 20, 21.
Exosmose, 10.

F.

Falcate, 32.
Family of plants, 66.
Fern drying, 71.
Ferns, 57, 74.
Fertilization, 46.
Fertilizing organs, 40.
Fibres, 9, 10.
Fibrous, 15, 17.
Filament, 42.
Fleshy, 19.
Floral whorls, 39.
Florets, 34.
Flowerless plants, 57.
Flower leaves, 25.
Flowers, 33.
Foliage leaves, 25.
Follicle, 53, 55.
Foramen, 4, 5.
Fronds, 58.
Fruit classification, 56.
Fruits, 1, 48, 49.
Fungi, 59.
Funiculus, 4, 5, 45, 55.
Fusiform, 15, 17.

G.

Gamopetalous (*monopetalous*), 41.
Gamosepalous (*monosepalous*), 42.
Genera, 66.
Genus, 66.
Germ, 3, 4.
Germen, 44.
Germination, 3, 5, 6.
Glabrous, 28.
Gland, 28.
Glandular hairs, 28.
Glans, 53.
Glumes, 42.

Gymnospermous, 2.
Gynandria, 64.
Gynandrous, 44.
Gynœcium, 39.

H.

Hastate, 30, 31.
Head, 34.
Heptandria, 62.
Herbaceous, 18.
Hermaphrodite, 48.
Hesperidium, 55.
Hexandria, 62.
Hilum, 4, 5.
Hirsute, 29.
Hollow stems, 19.
Horizontal, 23.
Hybrids, 48.
Hypogynous, 43.

I.

Icosandria, 63.
Incomplete inflorescence, 39.
Indefinite inflorescence, 33.
Indehiscent, 50, 53.
Inferior ovary, 43.
Inflorescence, 33.
Insertion, 43.
Interior, 42.
Internodes, 23.
Involucre, 34.
Inward growers, 14, 22.
Irritable, 28.

J.

Juices, 13.

L.

Lactiferous, 11.
Lacunæ, 10.
Lanceolate leaves, 31, 32.
Lateral branches, 23.

Laterally, 23.
Latex, 11.
Leaflets, 27.
Leaves, 25.
Legume, 5, 54.
Liber, 9, 23.
Lichens, 59, 64.
Lignine, 9, 11.
Limbs, 23.
Linear leaves, 31, 32.
Linnæan system of classification, 62.
Lobe root, 17.
Lomentum, 54.

M.

Membrane, 54.
Mesocarp, 51.
Metamorphosed, 12.
Micropyle, 4, 5, 48.
Midrib, 4, 29.
Monadelphia, 63.
Monandria, 62.
Monochlamydeous, 46.
Monoclinous, 46.
Monocotyledons, 4, 7, 13, 20, 22, 61.
Monœcia, 64.
Monœcious, 46.
Monopetalous, 41.
Monosepalous, 40, 42.
Mounting plants, 75.
Multidentate, 32.
Multifid, 32.
Multilocular, 50.

N.

Natural system of botany, 66, 68.
Nodes, 23.
Notched, 40.
Nucleus, 4.
Nut, 53.

O.

Oblong, 30, 31.
Octandria, 63.
Operculum, 40, 52.
Opposite leaves, 26.
Orbiculate, 30, 31.
Order, 66.
Organs, 1, 5, 25, 44.
Outside growers, 4, 22.
Oval, 30.
Ovary, 43, 44, 49.
Ovate, 30.
Ovule, 5, 45.

P.

Panicle, 34.
Papilionaceous corolla, 41.
Parasitical, 16, 59.
Parenchyma, 8, 9.
Partite calyx, 41.
Pedicel, 33, 34, 35.
Peduncle, 34.
Peltate leaves, 30, 31.
Peltate palmatifid leaves, 31.
Pendulous, 23.
Pendulous raceme, 35.
Pentandria, 62.
Pepo, 53.
Perennial, 12, 57.
Perfoliate, 30, 31.
Perianth, 45, 46.
Pericarp, 49, 52.
Perigynous, 43.
Perisperm, 2.
Persistent, 26, 48.
Persistent calyx, 55.
Petals, 25, 41.
Petiole, 29.
Phanerogams, 21.
Phyllode (*Phyllodium*), 27, 30, 31.
Pinnapartite, 29, 31.
Pinnate leaves, 29, 31.

Pinnatifid, 32.
Pistil, 39, 44, 49.
Pith, 22.
Placenta, 4, 5, 45, 55.
Plumule, 3, 4, 5, 6, 7.
Pod, 5, 54.
Pollen, 42, 47.
Polyadelphia, 63.
Polyandria, 63.
Polyandrous, 39.
Polygamia, 64.
Polygamous, 46.
Polyhedral, 8.
Polypetalous, 41.
Polysepalous, 39, 40.
Pome, 53.
Pores, 12, 52.
Porous, 52.
Preservation of plant specimens, 70.
Primary axis, 34.
Primary veins, 29.
Prosenchyma, 8, 9, 10.
Protoplasm, 8.
Putamen, 53.
Pyrenes, 53.

R.

Raceme, 35.
Races, 66, 67.
Radical, 26.
Radicle, 3, 4, 5, 6, 7.
Ramose, 26.
Raphè, 4.
Raphides, 10.
Reniform, 30, 31, 33.
Reproductive organs, 39.
Respiration, 25.
Reticulate, 29.
Retroserrate, 26.
Rhizome, 15, 17, 58.
Rhomboid, 30, 31.
Rings, 22.

Rootlet, 7.
Roots, 14, 15.
Rosaceous, 41.
Runners, 19.

S.

Sagittate, 30, 31.
Samara, 53.
Sap, 13.
Sarcocarp, 51.
Scabrous, 29.
Scalariform, 11.
Scales, 17, 55.
Scaly bulb, 15, 17.
Scape, 35.
Scapose raceme, 35.
Scar, 4.
Secondary veins, 29.
Secund, 38.
Seed leaf, 3.
Sensitive, 28.
Sepals, 40.
Serrate, 26.
Sessile, 26, 42.
Setose, 29.
Sheathed leaf, 26.
Shrub, 19.
Silicula, 54.
Siliqua, 54.
Simple fruits, 50.
Simple leaves, 27.
Single flowers, 33.
Sinuate, 30, 31.
Soboles, 15, 17.
Solid stems, 19.
Sori, 58.
Sorus, 58.
Spadix, 35.
Spathe, 35.
Spathulate, 31, 32.
Species, 66.
Spheres, 17.

Spike, 34.
Spikelet, 34.
Spines, 23.
Spiral fibres, 11.
Spongy, 19.
Sporangia, 58.
Spores, 8, 58.
Sports, 40.
Stamens, 39, 42, 49.
Stems, 18, 19, 20.
Stigma, 44.
Stipules, 26.
Stomata, 12, 27.
Stone, 2.
Strobilus, 55.
Style, 44.
Sub-class, 66.
Succulent, 19, 51.
Superior ovary, 43.
Suppression, 44.
Suture, 5, 52.
Syncarpous, 50, 51.
Syngenesia, 64.
Systematic Botany, 60.

T.

Taproot, 16, 17.
Tegmen, 2, 5.
Tendrils, 18.
Terminal leaf-bud, 23.
Ternate, 30, 31.
Testa, 2, 5.
Tetradynamia, 63.
Tetrandria, 62.
Tetrasepalous, 39.
Thalamifloral, 45.
Thorn, 23.
Thyrse, 38.
Tissue, 21, 22.
Toothed calyx, 40.
Torus, 54.
Trees, 19.

Triandria, 62.
Triandrous, 39.
Trifid, 32.
Trigynous, 39.
Trilobed, 30, 31.
Trisepalous, 39.
Trunk, 19.
Tuberous, 15, 17.
Tubular corolla, 41.
Tunicate bulb, 15, 17.
Twigs, 11, 23.
Twining stems, 19.

U.

Umbel, 35, 38.
Umbilicus, 4.
Underground stems, 17.
Undulate, 30, 31.
Unidentate, 32.
Unilocular, 50.
Unisexual, 42, 46.

V.

Valve, 5, 45.
Valvular, 52.
Varieties, 47, 66, 67.
Vascular bundles, 10, 22.
Vasculares, 10.
Veins, 8.
Venation, 4, 27.
Ventral suture, 5, 53.
Vernation, 27.
Vessel, 11.
Viscous, 29.

W.

Whorled, 26.
Whorls, 23.
Winged seed, 53.
Woody, 8, 19.
Woody stem, 18.
Woody tissue, 9.

EXTRACTS FROM PRESS NOTICES

OF THE

FIRST BOOK OF AUSTRALIAN BOTANY

(First Edition, 1878),

BY

W. R. GUILFOYLE, F.L.S., C.M.R.B.S. Lond.

―――o―――

' A little rudimentary work on the botany of Australia has been prepared by Mr. W. R. Guilfoyle, the Director of the Melbourne Botanic Gardens. . . . The design of the writer is to direct the eye of the beginner to the principal parts of plants, and to explain the manner of growth. . . . The present publication will enable the reader to overhaul trees, shrubs, and plants with considerable effect.' . . . —*Melbourne Argus*, 5th August 1878.

' A book on the botany of Australia, such an one as which, while avoiding, on the one hand, the massiveness, not to say cumbrousness, of the many-tomed works on the subject . . . and, on the other, having a character entirely distinct from the meagre and eminently unsatisfactory articles on the subject appearing in some school-books . . . such a book, we are glad to say, we have now before us. . . . In conclusion, it is not a word too much to say that the work is a valuable addition to the literature of botany, and that it is one of the very best that can be placed in the hands of students.'—*Town and Country Journal*, Sydney, 24th August 1878.

'*Australian Botany*, designed specially for the use of Schools, by W. R. Guilfoyle, F.L.S., C.M.R.B.S. London, and Director of the Melbourne Botanic Gardens, is the unpretending title of a really useful and valuable primer on botany, as connected more especially with the Australian flora. . . . The book is really admirable so far as it goes, but can only be regarded as initiatory, and, it is to be hoped, will be followed by others.' . . .—*Castlemaine Representative*, 10th Augt. 1878.

. . . ' The first book which has reached us is profusely illustrated, and is arranged in a very clear and interesting manner. . . . The work cannot fail to be of great value to teachers and pupils.' . . . —*Ballarat Star*, 26th August 1878.

. . . ' We have especial pleasure in recommending this work, which is sure to become a text-book for the use of schools.'—*Warrnambool Guardian and Examiner*, 14th August 1878.

... 'It is a highly creditable production, written in a popular style for easy reading, and will, no doubt, be appreciated by public and private school instructors.'—*Geelong Advertiser*, 10th August 1878.

... 'It must be highly encouraging to Mr. Guilfoyle to receive from Mr. Ellery, Professors Irving, Pearson, Halford, Strong, and Andrew, Mr. Morris of the Church of England Grammar School, and Mr. Venables of the Education Department, opinions highly favourable of the merits of the book.' ...—*Australasian*, Melbourne, 21st September 1878.

... 'On the whole, it is a work well calculated to smooth the way for the first steps in this most delightful science.'—*The Queenslander*, Brisbane, 7th September 1878.

Also numerous other press notices and highly flattering letters from several literary and scientific gentlemen.

A FEW EXTRACTS FROM NUMEROUS NOTICES IN THE PRESS

OF

THE ABC OF BOTANY

(First Edition).[1]

———o———

'Mr. Guilfoyle's *A B C of Botany* is just such a book as was wanted for the purposes of elementary teaching in the science to which it relates. He traces the progress of a plant from its germination until it has accomplished the purpose of its existence by fructification, and relates to the processes involved. Mr. Guilfoyle has aimed at simplicity and intelligibility in his modest little manual for the use of schools.'—*Melbourne Argus*, 7th February 1880.

'Mr. Guilfoyle, F.L.S., Director of the Melbourne Botanic Gardens, has forwarded to us a very useful little work entitled *The A B C of Botany*. ... After looking through the *A B C* we can safely say that Mr. Guilfoyle has admirably succeeded in the pleasant task he undertook.'—*Melbourne Daily Telegraph*, 31st January 1880.

... 'It is not only an A B C easy of comprehension and devoid of crack-jaw terms, but it is an alpha and omega of the rudiments of botany, which, mastered, enables those wishing to do so to comprehend

[1] Samuel Mullen, 29 and 31 Collins Street, Melbourne.

all the important facts about a charming study.'—*Melbourne Herald*, 10th February 1880.

... 'Mr. Guilfoyle is to be congratulated on the completion of the most valuable first book of botany which has come under our notice.'—*Castlemaine Representative*, 10th February 1880.

... 'It is entitled *The A B C of Australian Botany*, and unlike many—we might say most—so-called elementary works, is really what it professes to be, and is so simply written that the most uninformed upon the subject can understand it.'—*Horsham Times*, 11th June 1880.

'In this unpretentious little work the Director of the Melbourne Botanical Gardens has embodied some elementary lessons of the science of botany. To those teachers who cannot find attraction in the more elaborate works of Balfour, Hooker, and Baron von Mueller, the book will be of service.'—*Australasian Schoolmaster and Literary Review*, 17th March 1880.

... 'The little brochure now before us is entitled *The A B C of Botany*, and is intended as a simpler guide to the science than the First Book. It is, in fact, a child's handbook, with which he—or the maturer student who has neglected to make himself acquainted with the fascinating mysteries of the plant world—can, without assistance, learn the rudiments of botany as effectually as if Mr. Guilfoyle himself was his personal instructor.'—*Melbourne Advice Note*, 8th June 1880.

... 'Mr. Guilfoyle, Director of the Melbourne Botanic Gardens, has written not only one of the best elementary works on the subject, but also one of considerable use as a work of reference.'—*Sydney Telegraph*, 7th February 1880.

... 'As an instruction book for the school pupil, and even as a manual for the maturer student, the work leaves little to be desired. While following a thoroughly scientific method, the author successfully disentangles intricacies, explains nomenclatures, and metamorphoses the definitions of philosophers into language that may be understood by the least scientific of minds.'—*S. A. Advertiser*, 17th February 1880.

'Mr. Guilfoyle is the author of a larger work—*A First Book of Australian Botany*—to which the little book under notice may be considered as an introduction. The title of the book is an indication of its nature and object, which is simply to enable the young student to master the elements of that most interesting science—botany. ... The publication of books of this class in the colonies is a gratifying proof of the existence of a demand for healthy and useful literature.'—*The Colonies and India*, London, 21st August 1880.

... 'It is a small elementary book of one hundred pages, fully illustrated with drawings from Australian plants, and aptly designed as a rudimentary botany, and a most excellent introduction to the *First Book of Australian Botany*; also a School Botany, by the same author.'—L. B. Case's *Botanical Index*, Indiana, U.S. America.

www.ingramcontent.com/pod-product-compliance
Lightning Source LLC
Chambersburg PA
CBHW021822230426
43669CB00008B/839